The Hybrid Age

The Hybrid Age

International Security in the Era of Hybrid Warfare

Brin Najžer

I.B. TAURIS

LONDON • NEW YORK • OXFORD • NEW DELHI • SYDNEY

I.B. TAURIS
Bloomsbury Publishing Plc
50 Bedford Square, London, WC1B 3DP, UK
1385 Broadway, New York, NY 10018, USA
29 Earlsfort Terrace, Dublin 2, Ireland

BLOOMSBURY, I.B. TAURIS and the I.B. Tauris logo are trademarks of
Bloomsbury Publishing Plc

First published in Great Britain 2020
This paperback edition published in 2022

Cover design by Adriana Brioso
Cover background © Dzyuba/iStock

A catalogue record for this book is available from the British Library.

A catalog record for this book is available from the Library of Congress.

ISBN: HB: 978-0-7556-0251-3
PB: 978-0-7556-3653-2
ePDF: 978-0-7556-0253-7
eBook: 978-0-7556-0252-0

Typeset by Deanta Global Publishing Services, Chennai, India

To find out more about our authors and books visit www.bloomsbury.com
and sign up for our newsletters.

Contents

Figures

About the author

Brin Najžer holds a PhD in international relations from the University of Aberdeen. His research interests focus on grand strategy, military history, strategic studies, European security and hybrid warfare.

Preface

The idea for this book came from examining the contemporary research into hybrid warfare but also from looking at how this phenomenon is being perceived in the general public. It is adapted from a PhD thesis, the idea for which emerged during my graduate and postgraduate studies while looking at the confusion and reactions to events which occurred in 2014 between Russia and Ukraine. Suddenly this new and terrifying phenomenon called hybrid warfare appeared in the media, and in the vocabulary of politicians and academics. Quickly, questions arose as to whether this was some new all-powerful tool of international politics which was threatening the Western way of life, or simply a tactic designed to scare the public through media propaganda. In doing the initial research it immediately became clear that there are more fundamental problems with the understanding of hybrid warfare. Not only is there no accepted definition of what it is, but it has also been misused, underused and overused, often by the same sources and often simultaneously.

As hybrid warfare is a relatively new phenomenon, the quantity and diversity of sources about it is relatively limited. This is particularly the case with sources dealing with the phenomenon from a strategic perspective. Most authors focus on specific elements in occurrences of hybrid warfare, but there is almost nothing on the strategic impact of it. It can persuasively be argued that it is precisely this lack of strategic understanding and elucidation that lies at the root of the panic surrounding hybrid warfare whenever and wherever it appears. This became the driving force behind the research: to really give a strategic overview and to clarify the phenomenon of hybrid warfare in a concise and strategic manner which the research field is clearly lacking.

The decision to adapt the PhD thesis into a book is a continuation of this effort. I wish to demystify hybrid warfare and also give it an overarching strategic umbrella which can be understood by the career academic dealing with abstract definitional issues; the political decision maker, who has to decide how best to counter-hybrid warfare threatening their constituents; the news reporter who is covering a hybrid conflict zone; and the individual soldier or officer who has to deal with the threat on the ground. While the scope of the monograph is academic, I hope that its historical and logical narrative, and its clearly articulated points, will serve to improve the understanding of this new hybrid age for a wide variety of readers.

Brin Najžer

Ljubljana, June 2019

Introduction

For as long as there has been history, there has been war. In fact, it is reasonable to look at human history as a history of conflict and coercion. If one follows that premise, the next logical step is to acknowledge that humankind has always sought out innovative and new ways of waging war and establishing new forms of warfare. While there have been many periods of both intense conflict and peace, the evolution of war continued throughout. Set against a background of global strategic instability, this process of innovation has over the last two decades produced a new and complex phenomenon called hybrid warfare. Distinct from other forms of modern warfare in several key aspects, it presents a unique challenge that appears to baffle policymakers and security experts, while giving the actors that employ it a new way of achieving their goals in the face of long-standing Western conventional, doctrinal and strategic superiority.

When it first appeared in the mid-2000s, hybrid warfare was generally considered just another in a long line of terms used to explain modern conflict. Nevertheless, it slowly gained traction and has now become not only a staple of national security discussions but also a household phrase in state capitals and general political discourse. In a term-rich environment, hybrid warfare has definitely made a mark for itself, particularly after 2014 and the Russian intervention in Ukraine. However, is it really such a great step forward or does it simply represent a necessary adaptation to the times and to the global strategic balance? The novelty of the term and the seeming impossibility of states to create solutions to face it, and deal with actors that employ it, suggest that it is a complex and important development that needs further study in order to define it accurately, and explore the ways in which it has been applied, with a view of assessing whether and how hybrid warfare will change the future of conflict. Unfortunately, the same term-saturated environment from which it has arisen also means that it has been regularly misinterpreted. As with any new phenomenon, there is much debate around its various iterations, from hybrid strategy and hybrid warfare to hybrid threats and hybrid actors.

One of the goals of this book is to give some much-needed order and structure to hybrid warfare. The approach will be twofold. First, the book will create a rigorous definition and build a framework for further debate about and scrutiny of the phenomenon. Second, it will apply that theoretical framework to a series of practical examples in order to establish the validity of the approach. The goal is to establish, and present, a unified theory of hybrid warfare which can then be applied to any case study. A unified theory of hybrid warfare will be able to identify the causes and reasons for its emergence as well as the key markers leading to future occurrences of hybrid warfare. By moving beyond the established orthodox way of thinking about hybrid warfare, this research will contribute to the field by proposing a theory, definition, framework and practical policy guidelines on the conduct and impact of hybrid warfare.

Every phenomenon occurs within a specific context or set of circumstances. There are numerous ways of examining the phenomenon of hybrid warfare, and this analysis will look at it from a theoretical perspective based on the discipline of international relations (IR). There are a number of major and minor paradigms that aim to explain the international system and the way the actors within and outside it relate to one another. Unlike many other books dealing with modern warfare, the present volume will remain firmly rooted in the realist paradigm. However, it is important to acknowledge that when dealing with European, or more widely, Western, IR approaches, it has become increasingly tenuous to limit the research to only one paradigm. The trend towards more liberal or postmodern thinking in IR has its roots in the Western world, and it is therefore important for the understanding of the reactions and positions of individual actors. Although warfare-related phenomena are rooted in realist thinking, the reactions to it, or the events leading up to it, may be a result of alternative approaches, even if the end result is a realist one. It is therefore crucial, especially when dealing with a new phenomenon, to keep in mind that different actors view new developments from different perspectives that might even be contradictory to one another.

Clearly, this work fits within the security sub-field of IR. However, with the proliferation of security studies and the associated broadening of the meaning of 'security', there is a danger of over-defining the scope of security, particularly in the liberal democratic Western world, where the focus has shifted quite significantly away from traditional security concerns, roughly coinciding with the emergence of hybrid warfare. As the following chapters will show, this shift affected the study of hybrid warfare because the securitization aspects of the phenomenon have been given extraordinary attention. However, such an approach fails to adequately sum up the essence and meaning of hybrid warfare, and a narrower and more focused examination is required. Therefore, while in broad terms the present work fits within the security sub-field of IR, it primarily emanates from the specialized field of strategic studies. Strategic studies are usually considered a military-centric, realist specialization of security studies which is part of the reason why strategic analysis of new phenomena had fallen into disuse in the securitization-focused Western world.[1] This book seeks to cut through the securitization perception of hybrid warfare and examine the phenomenon in a more focused and rigorous, strategic way. However, that does not preclude the examination from acknowledging the differing and often contradictory theories and paradigms surrounding hybrid warfare, as they represent a significant portion of the debate suffusing the topic. Rather, one of the goals is to reintroduce strategic thinking on the issue since the real-life consequences of failing to do so could be significant.

Every new phenomenon faces the problem of a lack of a universally accepted interpretation, but trends and patterns can still be established. This strategic analysis will seek to incorporate the full spectrum of hybrid warfare, from the technical and tactical military aspects to the influence of different cultures on the waging of war. The perception of events is a crucial component of any conflict and perhaps to a greater degree in hybrid conflicts, due to the ambiguity inherent in the hybrid approach and the need to keep tight control over possible escalation. This applies to both public and professional perception and the presentation of various actions associated with hybrid warfare. Popularization of hybrid warfare, mostly as a form of modern information-technology-based propaganda or cyber activity, is problematic in itself because it obscures its true character. That is not to say that propaganda is a particular and unique component of hybrid warfare. It is a vital part of any form of conflict; however, in the modern era perhaps too much emphasis is given to this aspect even though there are other, much more crucial and fundamental issues when dealing with hybrid warfare.

Cultural differences are also important as they play an increasingly significant role in domestic and international politics. The core notions of what constitutes a state or what reasons a state might have to wage any form of war differ greatly depending on the interests, geographical position, structure of the population and historical circumstances, to name only the most obvious factors. Socio-economic and geopolitical goals constantly overlap and compete in conflicts and should therefore be carefully considered when measuring the impact of a new concept on such goals. While sometimes referred to as a new type of power politics, hybrid warfare is typically used by actors who do not wish to engage in classic overt forms of power politics, but still wish to achieve the goals associated with it. It is designed to give an international actor the flexibility of an unconventional approach, and the potential for attaining goals normally associated with conventional war.

The main thrust of this book will focus on the question: *What is hybrid warfare and how does it work?* Its primary purpose is to establish a unified theory of hybrid warfare, which not only outlines but also places the term in its context, and provides the tools which enable an observer to identify and react to a future instance of hybrid warfare. This practical application of the theory is in keeping with the strategic nature of the book as it links the historical background, contemporary context and a theoretical framework in order to provide a glimpse of possible future conflicts. Hybrid warfare is a new phenomenon and not just a new name or a popularly created moniker. As a form of international coercion, it is politically attractive and operationally useful because it is efficient, cost effective and enables actors to achieve goals that they would not be able to achieve using other means. It is primarily employed by actors who wish to challenge the international system's balance of power and influence. Additionally, a hybrid approach can be used to challenge the hegemons of the international system in areas of intense strategic competition.

With such a wide scope, hybrid warfare can be seen as a tool of revisionist powers; that is, powers that seek to challenge the dominant world order in one form or another. The differences in perception, which correspond to political aims in war, are a reflection of each actor's particular set of circumstances. Therefore, if hybrid warfare is a tool of revisionist powers, which world order are they seeking to change? There is no simple answer to this question as terms like 'Western' or 'liberal democratic' are ambiguous by themselves. However, in the context of hybrid warfare such ambiguity is good as it demonstrates the fluidity on both sides of the conflict. As a reference point for this examination, the international order will be understood as encompassing the practical application of a certain set of concepts, on just arrangements and the distribution of power, with sufficient influence to affect the global balance of power.[2] Since the prevailing concepts that have this kind of global reach largely emanate from the Western, liberal democratic tradition, it is reasonable to present the contemporary international order as Western in nature. As a consequence, it is beneficial to emphasize the importance of the Western world to the perceived or actual detriment of the rest of the globe. Different regional and civilizational ambiguities and interpretations only strengthen this view and give credence to presenting hybrid warfare as the tool of actors which, because of their own concepts of just arrangements and the distribution of power, seek to revise the international order. Global order is not a static notion, but rather a process. The current hegemons of the system seek to strengthen or maintain it, while other powers seek to challenge it. While global confrontation over the nature of the system is doubtful in the long run, hybrid warfare is a useful instrument to assess the limits of the system and test the hegemons' resolve in maintaining it.

In order to explore the phenomenon of hybrid warfare in greater detail, several supplementary points will be discussed. These will focus on certain elements or aspects of hybrid warfare such as what precisely is new about it, what are its key components, how did it develop and how and where does it fit into an existing security landscape. Since the concept is far reaching and broad, the examination will focus on a strategic overview. Geopolitical, socio-economical and security implications will form part of the research, as will historical background. The other five key concepts that will be examined are: the components of hybrid warfare and their practical implementation, the differences between hybrid warfare and other 'new wars', the notion that hybrid warfare is an anti-Western or anti-hegemonic political instrument, the effectiveness of hybrid warfare and the relevance of hybrid warfare in the maritime domain.

Even a brief review of the relevant literature demonstrates that there is a distinct lack of a coherent, widely accepted definition of hybrid warfare. Even among the most eminent organizations, either governmental ones such as the UK Ministry of Defence or the US Department of Defense or non-governmental groups such as the International Institute for Strategic Studies, Royal United Services Institute and the Center for Strategic and International Studies, there is no clear agreement or any articulation of a definition. On the other hand, some organizations, such as NATO, the EU and the OSCE, have crafted definitions that are so all-encompassing that they lack any practical value. A good example of the latter is the Munich Security Conference (MSC) in 2015 which attempted to create a pan-European hybrid warfare definition. While it contributed to the body of knowledge, the definition of hybrid warfare, as a combination of multiple conventional and unconventional tools of warfare,[3] is too imprecise to be of any use. It is also a good representation of a problematic type of definition, listing features of hybrid warfare without providing an actual definition. A new form of warfare can be difficult to encompass within a single definition, but the guiding principle should surely be precise and concise. A definition that attempts to incorporate all aspects of modern war is not defining hybrid warfare just warfare itself. Even academic think tanks and military colleges are struggling with the definition of hybrid warfare. The problem of defining a phenomenon that is so vast is mostly political rather than military in nature, but nevertheless when it comes to the threat of military action or hybrid warfare, an analysis of this threat and the means to fight it are of immense importance. The vastness of the term 'hybrid' means that it incorporates more than simple kinetic coercion and outright conflict. Diplomatic, political and economic factors come into play as well, although it should be made clear that this is an aspect of any large endeavour by an international actor and is not unique to hybrid warfare. This point illustrates another key problem with defining the concept. How vast narrow should the parameters be to encapsulate the main features without distorting its practical value?

The literature on hybrid warfare is relatively recent and more debate is generated by think tanks, academics and policymakers on almost a daily basis. The body of the literature is therefore still growing and as such presents an additional challenge for the study of the term 'hybrid'. Much of the existing work is based on relatively few primary sources beginning with studies of the conflict in Chechnya[4] and the 2006 Lebanon War.[5] While providing a good starting point, these conflicts do not accurately illustrate the full spectrum of hybrid warfare, merely its nascent stage. As with any emerging concept, even the actors that employ it do not normally understand the full potential of, or implications resulting from, its use. The more recent conflict in Ukraine and the increased activities in the South China Sea give a better sense of how hybrid warfare works and its potential.

Placed between the 'boxes' of conventional and unconventional war and possessing the characteristics of both gives actors that use hybrid warfare the ability to combine or disperse their units as required in order to confuse the opponent and gain tactical and strategic superiority. The peak of such use was demonstrated by Russia in the 2014 invasion of Crimea and the subsequent conflict in the Donbas region of Ukraine. In a sense, most of the debate around hybrid warfare is a clear indication of its success. The fact that states cannot agree on a definition and whether it poses a great threat could be said to represent the culmination of hybrid warfare. A concept that was previously only used by non-state groups has now been employed by a major power and with considerable success. This has created new levels of hybrid threat and could encourage other states from pursuing it.

The state that is most likely to employ a hybrid approach in the near future is unquestionably China. The long-running disputes over islands in the South China Sea gives China a perfect arena for employing some hybrid strategy of its own. Indeed, it is already starting to happen. In its first use hybrid warfare was mainly perceived as a land-based type of conflict waged by non-state actors. Later, it evolved into land- and air-based conflict waged by state-like actors and states, and now it has potentially become a full-spectrum conflict comprising land, sea, air and other components (cyber and space). While certainly not a universal winning strategy, it does appear to exploit the advent of more readily available mass communication devices and the consequent increased social interactions. The strategic and tactical implications of such advances become much more evident through the use of hybrid strategy giving an actor more freedom of movement and deniability than ever before, while providing them with unparalleled abilities to shape their forces in a tactically optimum and more cost-efficient way.

Structure

Structurally the book will consist of the Introduction, seven core chapters and the Conclusion. The core chapters are grouped into two related blocks. The first block of four chapters will set up the definitional and contextual basis of the concept and provide the information needed for a more in-depth empirical analysis later in the book. It will also provide a theoretical and methodological basis for examination. The second block, consisting of three chapters, deals with the practical aspects of hybrid warfare through an analysis of three separate case studies.

Chapter 1 will set out the broad theoretical basis for the exposition. The primary focus of the chapter is to establish the theoretical concepts which underpin the major themes of this research. As those themes are primarily related to strategy and war, the theoretical framework is based on realism. Other major paradigms of IR, such as liberalism and constructivism, will be discussed where appropriate, but only to a limited degree, to explain some of the contemporary and historical context surrounding hybrid warfare, but not the phenomenon itself.

Chapter 2 will put forward a definition of hybrid warfare. It will look at the origin and the meaning of the term 'hybrid' and create a definition that will subsequently form the basis of research and comparison in later chapters. It will also deal with the dual nature of hybrid warfare, exploring why the concept is limited and should not be expanded endlessly as some scholars and organizations have attempted to do. A strict definition that sets the limits for hybrid war is key to understanding the phenomenon. A clear definition is vital not only to differentiate hybrid warfare from other modern forms of warfare but also to create a successful and effective strategy that is capable of addressing the new threat. Every form of warfare has its defining characteristics, its strengths and weaknesses, and it is designed to address a specific challenge of the age while keeping with the principle of the unchanging nature of war.

The other important aspect of the definitional enterprise is to make clear the myriad of terms associated with hybrid warfare. Terms like hybrid threats, hybrid operations and many more are defined very widely in the literature; however, while some consistency exists, there are also many instances of these terms overlapping or contradicting one another. Building a vocabulary of hybrid warfare is important as one single term can obviously not explain everything adequately; on the other hand, too many terms can create even more confusion if they are not clearly defined and limited.

Chapter 3 will place hybrid warfare into a wider framework based on an expanded interpretation of Clausewitzian thought, termed the 'quinity', in order to account for its success and the apparent inability of the international order to deal with it. There are two reasons for such an approach. First, the book is based on the classic Clausewitzian philosophical understanding that the nature of war is unchanging, and that every new form or concept will adhere to the same basic principles.[6] Second, while Clausewitzian principles still apply to large-scale conflicts, modern circumstances require an expansion of the frame of reference when dealing with conflicts that are less overt. While its individual components are not fundamentally new, hybrid warfare differs radically from other forms in terms of its impact and scope. Since the end of the Cold War era it has become increasingly rare for states to engage in trinitarian conflict; that is, conflict based solely on the Clausewitzian trinity. Various factors, such as the increased importance of international organizations, norms and values, combined with an overall decrease in capabilities of the major powers of the international system, mean that trinitarian war is no longer considered as an accepted form of conflict. The traditional trinity, consisting of the government, the military and the people of a polity at war,[7] has been deemed unacceptable to, and by, the leading powers of the liberal democratic international order, primarily states and organizations which can be described as Western or status quo powers.

Building on this shift towards a higher threshold for war, this book will introduce the concept of the 'quinity', by adding external legitimacy, and the need for allies or coalitions to the original Clausewitzian trinity. It is within this quinitarian framework that states must operate when fighting limited wars in the twenty-first century. On the other hand, actors engaging in hybrid warfare obfuscate these higher principles in order to engage in conflict which skirts below the threshold set forth by the quinitarian framework. This expanded approach not only allows for the study of the principles of hybrid war but also helps to explain why so many states have a problem in dealing with it. In a world where military intervention is seen increasingly as something that no one state should attempt on its own, the need for allies and external legitimacy is paramount. Hybrid warfare is designed to exploit these characteristics of the international order, by staying clear of easily identifiable state-on-state conflict of the original Clausewitzian trinity, as that would likely fulfil the additional requirements set forth in the quinity, leading to a large-scale conventional response.

Once the basis of the concept has been established and then placed into a useful framework, Chapter 4 will examine why hybrid warfare seems to be so effective through a doctrinal lens. The chapter will combine an overview of defence planning in leading or important states over the last two decades with the theoretical principles established in the preceding chapters. The goal of the chapter is to identify strategic policy and doctrinal 'weak spots' that have enabled the emergence and successful application of hybrid warfare. How an actor can exploit these weaknesses through a hybrid approach will be examined in the case study chapters. By combining the theoretical and policy spheres, this chapter represents the last part of the theoretical contribution and begins the process of examining the theory in practice.

The doctrinal overview will look at five states: the United States, the United Kingdom, Russia, Israel and Japan. The choice of actors is based on the premise that those selected represent the most influential or powerful actors in the international system (in the cases of the United States, the United Kingdom and Japan), or states which have experienced hybrid warfare first hand (Russia and Israel). Russia is particularly important as it is presently the only actor that has experience with hybrid warfare from both sides, as a target and as a user. The inclusion of Japan illustrates the global reach of the phenomenon and serves as an introduction to the maritime domain of hybrid warfare. The chapter will conclude by presenting the completed, unified theory of hybrid warfare.

Chapter 5 begins the second block of chapters, which will move the concept of hybrid warfare from the realms of theory and theoretical frameworks to practical examples. The first, in a series of three case studies, will examine the 2006 Lebanon War. As one of the most widely studied examples of hybrid warfare it represents a very useful starting point. It is also interesting because it illustrates how a non-state actor, in this case Hezbollah, can employ hybrid warfare to relatively great effect against a state; even a regionally powerful one like Israel. The 2006 Lebanon War is often considered the first hybrid conflict and it has served as the basis for the first widely known research and definition of the phenomenon conducted by Frank Hoffman. This research will argue that though earlier examples of hybridity can be found, the 2006 war still serves as a useful case study. The reason for its continued utility is the nature of Hezbollah, particularly its ability to act as a very state-like actor within the hybrid context. The chapter will examine, in great detail, the political and military structures which enable Hezbollah to operate in such a manner through an analysis of the lead up to and the conduct of the 2006 war. The status of Israel and the Israel Defence Forces (IDF) will also be examined, with particular focus on Israel's self-examined inability to counter Hezbollah's offensive successfully.

A key point within Chapter 5 is to establish what a state-like actor is and how they act. Over the last two decades a significant part of the debate on international security has focused on the role of non-state actors. This is due primarily to the rise of terrorism in a post-Cold War environment. The same period also coincides with the evolution of hybrid warfare, but this is not directly related to the issue of terrorism. The two phenomena are synchronous but not concurrent, the only link between them being that some non-state actors can engage in both. However, a major point of divergence is that hybrid warfare requires a much more specific type of non-state actor, one capable of at least limited conventional warfare. Part of the problem of establishing hybrid warfare as a phenomenon separate from other 'new' types of conflict lies in the fact that it was, for a significant time, subsumed within the overall debate on the role of non-state actors. The scope of hybrid warfare is much broader, and this chapter will specify precisely which types of non-state actors can wage hybrid warfare in order to delineate and place hybrid warfare in its own separate niche.

Chapter 6 will look at perhaps the most significant example of hybrid warfare, the Russian intervention in Ukraine in 2014. It was this crisis that thrust hybrid warfare into widespread use and reignited the interest and research into the phenomenon. If before 2014 the interest in hybrid warfare had declined somewhat, the crisis in Ukraine permanently established it as a feature of IR. The Russian seizure of Crimea in February 2014, and the subsequent conflict in Eastern Ukraine, caused massive consternation, and almost panic, in the decision-making circles of great and small powers, particularly in the Western world. The majority of recent research on hybrid warfare revolves around Russia and unfortunately ignores previous examples, treating it as the first example of the phenomenon. One of the aims of this chapter is to establish the historical and strategic circumstances which led to the crisis in order to arrive at a measured conclusion while cutting through the unhelpful excitement and anxiety which, to a degree, still surrounds the debate on the crisis.

The key question posed by Chapter 6 will be whether Russian actions in Ukraine can be said to represent the archetype of hybrid warfare. Russia has a long history of hybrid conflict, stretching back to the Chechen wars in the 1990s. The chapter will establish the historical and strategic timeline of Russian hybrid warfare experience, beginning with the Chechen wars, through the colour revolutions in Ukraine and Georgia, the 2008 Russo-Georgian War and culminating in the 2014 intervention in Ukraine. During this time, Russia transformed itself politically and militarily, and went from being a target of hybrid warfare – used by Chechens – to being the world's pre-eminent user of hybrid warfare in its own right. However, Russian success in Ukraine has been based on several preconditions which are not easily reproduced elsewhere. The impact of Russian hybrid warfare can therefore be said to be geographically limited but strategically almost universal.

The final case study in Chapter 7 will explore the advent of Chinese hybrid warfare. It is the most future-focused case study. The Southeast and East Asian regions are set to become two of the most important arenas of strategic competition in the future. This chapter will examine the often-overlooked maritime aspect of hybrid warfare through a lens of Chinese actions and activities in the South China Sea. The debate on hybrid warfare has hitherto been limited to land, and to a lesser degree, air warfare. However, as the definition put forward by this book argues, it is a full domain-spectrum concept and no examination of hybrid warfare can be complete without including the maritime domain. After all, it is precisely this broad appeal and potential that makes it stand out from other forms of conflict or coercion, and which makes it so appealing to some international actors. Additionally, by including China as one of the hybrid actors under examination, this research will demonstrate the global scope of hybrid warfare as well as its flexibility, making it a useful tool for a geographically, culturally and politically diverse group of actors.

Introducing the maritime domain requires a brief examination of the different rules and environments in which it takes place. Such a fundamentally different starting point requires different capabilities and operational principles, which China seems to be mastering rapidly. Artificial island building in the South China Sea is one of the most visible and contested issues in IR related to hybrid warfare. China's premier hybrid warfare fighting force, the maritime militia, is already producing significant results, while the complex legal environment means that maritime hybrid warfare has the potential for finer control over escalation, and therefore the ability to produce greater results than any other form of hybrid warfare. While all modern warfare is subject to varying degrees of legal influence, this is especially pronounced at sea. China's use and misuse of the legal frameworks will be examined both on its own and in relation to the island building and the maritime militia. A key feature, which connects all of these activities, and is particularly pronounced in the maritime domain, is the level of kineticism of action. The chapter will conclude by examining the features of non-kinetic maritime hybrid warfare and its possible implications for the future.

After establishing a theoretical framework and applying that to the case studies, the concluding chapter will summarize the key points, present the findings and definitively answer the research questions set out in the Introduction. Additionally, the Conclusion will also sum up the key points surrounding the debate on hybrid warfare and will establish the meaning of the term and its practical applications and consequences. In summing up, it is necessary to acknowledge the limitations of predictions, since it is very difficult for a single piece of research to encompass completely such a vast term. However, as stated earlier, the goal is not to present a final word on the concept, but contribute to, and hopefully inform, the ongoing debate in a constructive and substantive way – the next step forward.

Throughout the work, the author will attempt to keep in sight the strategic horizon of hybrid warfare. Actors who have used hybrid warfare in the past have done so due to its potential to achieve goals that could normally only be achieved through conventional war. Strategically, this translates to actors achieving goals which the status quo international system does not approve, as they strike at the foundations of its internal balance of power. Hybrid warfare is more than just a useful expedient; it is a way of addressing an imbalance (actual or perceived) in the international system without upsetting it entirely. To date, targets of hybrid warfare have primarily been on the margins of the major arenas of strategic competition. In a Western-led, liberal democratic international order, the future tool of choice for those wishing to challenge this status quo might well be hybrid.

1

Theory of hybrid warfare

The academic discipline of IR is incredibly diverse and far reaching. From relatively humble beginnings in the aftermath of the First World War, it has expanded to become one of the flagships of social sciences. Interestingly, it is a relatively recent academic discipline partly due to the fact that, before the First World War, everything that is now subsumed under the term 'international relations' was taken to be completely self-evident. Relations between states were entrenched in hundreds of years of traditions and history with relatively little or no impetus for change. War was regarded as the domain of soldiers and international politics was the purview of diplomats. Neither group could be challenged on their expertise in their field. Furthermore, there was a lack of intellectual interest and scholarly debate about what the soldiers and diplomats were doing.[1]

The destruction brought upon society and the disappearance of distinctions between civilian and military society caused a rethink; the self-evident truths were suddenly open to interpretation. From this extreme shift in history developed the two key schools of thought within IR, liberalism and realism. The fact that it was a *war* that caused this series of developments is important, as IR, as a discipline, is largely devoted to answering the question of why states go to war with each other,[2] or, to put it another way, why the international system is based on conflict and coercion. When a new kind of war-related phenomenon emerges, as in the case with hybrid warfare, it is within the field of IR that answers must primarily be sought in order to gain a better understanding. However, in such a wide field, there are a number of approaches available.

For the purposes of this research the approach of choice will be strategic. Strategic studies, a sub-field of security studies, is an important and finely focused speciality of IR, dedicated specifically to answering the questions regarding the role of coercion, in particular military power. While its focus might be sharp, the framework is not, since an understanding of the field requires a multidisciplinary approach, containing history, politics, economics, psychology and geography, to name a few, in addition to military knowledge.[3]

This chapter will provide a theoretical framework in which the concept of hybrid warfare will be examined and developed. It will tackle the contentious issue of the causes of wars and the concept of the use of force. Both of these will be examined more closely, to understand the meaning of coercion in international politics. Following these base observations, the concept of hybrid warfare will be examined through a realist lens in order to place it into a theoretical framework on which the book is anchored. This is a crucial first step in creating a solid and comprehensible definition of the phenomenon which will then be used to further develop the book.

The causes of war and the pursuit of security

While an attempt to answer the question 'Why states go to war?' could be a book in itself, for the purposes of this research, a brief overview will be sufficient. A useful starting point is Thucydides's work *The History of the Peloponnesian War* in which he established three base reasons for war: prestige (honour), fear and self-interest.[4] While Thucydides talks specifically about the causes of the Peloponnesian War between Athens and Sparta, his thoughts on the matter have retained their relevance throughout history. Even in the present day, scholars are referring to the 'Thucydides's Trap' that can lead to conflict between an emerging and a hegemonic power. While it may sound implausible to modern observers that a state would go to war over prestige, it is far from impossible, particularly when combined with fear. Deep resentment over past humiliations, perceived unfair treatment or simply conviction that the international system is 'rigged' to support the established great powers at the expense of others are all rallying cries that can be heard on the streets (and in government buildings) in the Middle East, Asia and Africa. The formally announced grievances might be more finessed, but, as Thucydides points out, that does not hide the real reason behind them.[5] An emerging power will, almost always,[6] attempt to challenge the hegemon of the day for dominance and the hegemon will likely resort to war once other options run out, or become too costly. Both are acting out of a combination of prestige (the emerging power wishes to gain more of it while the hegemon feels the need to defend it) and fear (the emerging power fears being attacked and destroyed or reduced in status by the hegemon while the hegemon fears that its power will not suffice to maintain its position) and are fuelled by self-interest (both desire the political, economic and social benefits that come with hegemony).

As the hegemon of the day is currently the United States, it is unsurprising that other aspiring great power challengers are competing with it; most notably China,[7] but also Russia. This notion is of course not limited only to the global hegemon, but can take place in a regional setting as well. Good examples of this viewpoint are Israel, which is arguably the sub-regional hegemon of the Middle East, and NATO in Europe, challenged by Russia. Since the hegemons of the day tend to be technologically and militarily very strong, the challenges might come in a different form from open war, with hybrid warfare being the most recent and preferred type of challenge.

In modern times, particularly in the West, wars are seen as something abnormal, and the historical record of wars as the norm for the conduct of foreign policy is perceived as amoral or even criminal. And yet, war, as an instrument of state policy, persists in ever more refined forms both within, but particularly outside, the Western world. Building on the legacy of Thucydides, Michael Howard offers a valuable insight into the causes of war. War should not be regarded as pathological and abnormal, but, at its core, simply as a form of conflict among a particular social grouping, that is, sovereign states. So without states 'one would have no wars, as Rousseau rightly pointed out – but, as Hobbes equally rightly pointed out, we would probably have no peace either'.[8] Wars occur through a perception of fear, with Howard echoing Thucydides, but are initiated by a set of conscious, rational decisions or, as Howard put it:

> Men have fought during the past two hundred years neither because they are aggressive nor because they are acquisitive animals, but because they are reasoning ones: because they discern, or believe that they can discern, dangers before they become immediate, the possibility of threats before they are made.[9]

Wars are therefore not caused because the human race is inherently bellicose or because they crave the possessions of others; war can be so risky that it is only resorted to for rational reasons, no matter how convoluted or disreputable. Nor is this calculation limited to one side in a conflict as it requires at least two states to wage war with 'conscious and reasoned decisions based on the calculation, made by *both* parties [emphasis in the original], that they can achieve more by going to war than by remaining at peace'.[10]

Of course, the international system is now different in some ways from what it was in 1984 when Michael Howard published *The Causes of Wars*, and even more so from it was in the time of Thucydides.[11] However, as the former so succinctly put it, the revulsion to war that seems to characterize society is only useful if it is universal. If it is not, and the post-Cold War world offers many examples to support such an assumption, then 'societies which continue to see armed force as an acceptable means for attaining their political end are likely to establish dominance over those which do not'.[12] The advent of hybrid warfare connects both sides of this argument. As it aims to avoid open war, hybrid warfare can be said to be a form of conflict which suits an international order which does not wish its members to engage in large-scale war but nevertheless gives states the means to achieve their aims through a distinctive brand of coercion.

Building on the core assumption that the international system is anarchic, questions arise about how states, as the most important actors, seek to secure the ultimate prize they seek: security. The answer is twofold; states primarily use the prospect of coercion or the actual use of coercion to attain their goals, and they do so through the application of strategy. The two terms are inextricably linked and form the basis of interstate relations and statecraft.

First, some definitions are in order. The *Oxford English Dictionary* (*OED*) defines 'coercion' as 'constraint, restraint, compulsion; the application of force to control the action of a voluntary agent'.[13] A more functional definition by Art characterized the relationship between international politics and coercion as 'the necessary, but not the sufficient precondition for its effective functioning'.[14] As it quickly becomes evident, the key component of coercion is force, which is usually described in terms of military power or capabilities. How integral such use of force is to the study of IR is best summed up by Waltz's statement: 'In politics force is said to be the ultima ratio. In international politics force serves, not only as the ultima ratio, but indeed as the first and the constant one.'[15] However, coercion has a more general meaning, which is not limited solely to the use of military force. States have many power assets, including their population, geography, governance, values, wealth and leadership.[16] In a similar line, Rob de Wijk defines 'coercion' as 'the deliberate and targeted use – or threat to use – of power instruments to manipulate and influence the politico-strategic choices of an actor, or player, defined as an entity that plays an identifiable role in international relations'.[17] How effective states are in utilizing their assets depends on the effectiveness of their strategy.

The word 'strategy' is often used in a variety of settings, most of which are, unfortunately, misuses, particularly in the world of management and economics, but increasingly also in politics and IR. Most definitions of strategy will describe it as a method of connecting ways, means and ends. Colin Gray's definition is a good example, with strategy defined as 'the attempted achievement of desired political ends, through the choice of suitable strategic ways, employing largely the military means then available or accessible'.[18] Alternatively, Gray offers a narrower definition, based on the use of force in which strategy is 'the use that is made by force and the threat of force for the ends of policy'.[19] Connecting the ways and means with ends can sometimes be very simple and, although it could qualify as a strategy, as Lawrence Freedman points out: 'When the ends are easily reached, when inanimate objects rather than people are involved, and when very little is at stake, this barely counts as strategy'.[20] Strategy is not merely a synonym for a plan; it comes into play when there is actual potential for conflict. Human affairs are notoriously unpredictable and often lead to frustration due to the number of different, even opposing, views and interests. A plan is based on the predictability of events that lead to an expected conclusion, while a strategy must assume that opponents will do everything they can to prevent that from happening. It must therefore be much more flexible and imaginative.[21] Plans may be instruments of strategy, but they are not strategy.

In principle then, building on the logic of the chapter, in order to achieve security in an anarchical system, a state will identify a list of national interests that it must pursue and employ, primarily, coercive and non-coercive means against other states and actors in order to do so. Cooperation between states should be kept to a minimum, as other states cannot be trusted to act in one states' individual interest, but all states exist in a position of strategic interdependence where none has complete control over its own fate. The relative gains of one state, however, outweigh the absolute gains of all. States use the best combination of their power assets in order to gain an advantage which is achieved through the proper use of a correct strategy. In a largely hegemonic system, the tools they use must be adapted, for fear of the hegemon overreacting. In such an environment, hybrid warfare has emerged and flourished.

Realist theory and hybrid warfare

As an examination of the concept of hybrid warfare deals primarily with the political use of coercion, its natural habitat lies within the realist domain. Power relations and politics, coupled with coercive, primarily military, force among states or state-like actors, are the foundations of realist thinking. It makes logical sense then, that realist theories are best suited to explain not only the emergence of hybrid warfare but also its uses, implications and future impact. With that in mind, it is also important to note that the responses to hybrid warfare from individual states are not always based on realist thinking. In Europe and the wider Western world particularly, policymakers often try to avoid realist approaches, which are seen as unethical or amoral by their domestic constituencies, and they portray the opponent as the clear aggressor in the eyes of world public opinion. In such an environment, liberal and constructivist tenets have gained more traction within the realm of foreign and defence policy. Nevertheless, the approach to hybrid warfare, for the purposes of this volume, will be strategic, and will consequentially rely heavily on the realist school.

Towards a theory of hybrid warfare

While it is impossible to create an absolute theory of war, or any specific kind of war, it can be useful to create a set of theoretical characteristics that can signal a certain form of conflict. The theory of hybrid warfare described later is an attempt to create a prescriptive model of conditions and circumstances that can lead to hybrid warfare. Its purpose is to alert theoreticians and practitioners to the possibility of hybrid warfare occurring, rather than create absolute predictions. As such, it forms the theoretical basis for further examination of the concept itself and the preconditions necessary for its implementation. The practical implications of this theory will be explored further in the following chapters, and the conclusion will sum up both the theoretical and practical parts into one unified theory of hybrid warfare.

There are two levels of characteristics that influence an occurrence of hybrid warfare, systemic and individual. Systemic conditions are present at all times and stem from the nature of the international system itself and the actors within it. Individual characteristics are more conflict specific and arise from the motivations and interests of the individual actors involved. Both kinds are present simultaneously and can combine and overlap, depending on the circumstances.

Systemic characteristics are based on the nature of the international system, specifically its anarchy. The chief actors within that system are states, which, to a large extent, are self-interested and suspicious of the intentions of others. States pursue relative short-term goals whenever possible, although short term in this sense can be a time frame of several years if not more, depending on the issue. Cooperation within the system is minimal and the system itself can be hegemonic or non-hegemonic.

As states find it so difficult to trust one another on important issues, conflict and competition arise, but because the routine use of brute force is increasingly seen as costly and possibly escalatory, states initially seek to pursue other options.

Individual characteristics come from the actors, primarily states, themselves. Every state seeks to secure its own individual goals, based on national interests, which can be very diverse from state to state, even in a narrow geographical area. The ultimate national goal is security, which is perceived as a relative gain; not the absence of conflict but the management of it. If systemic conditions are conducive to the paramountcy of one state, powerful states tend towards becoming the hegemon, while in non-hegemonic systems (regional groupings of similarly powerful states) the tendency is to pursue a balance of power. While states have specific motives for their actions, the basic reason is identical – the pursuit of security. States use coercion, actual or prospective, to achieve their goals through an application of a strategic approach.

Coercion ties together the systemic and individual characteristic; it is the clearest way of achieving goals within the system as it is and, while the circumstances for individual states can change dramatically (and must be accounted for), the characteristics of the system remain unchanged. An important aspect of this theoretical basis is that it can also be used by less powerful states. As hybrid warfare is a low-level conflict to which actors resort when outright war is undesirable, it can be used by a less powerful state, or state-like actor, to challenge a more powerful one, or between two lesser powers. Each state's perception of its own power will influence the choice of tools, but hybrid warfare offers a very useful alternative that is both innovative enough to achieve the element of surprise and contains enough of the familiar concept of coercion through military force that it can be applied with relative ease.

The definition of hybrid warfare

This chapter aims to study the current state of research on the hybrid warfare phenomenon, and create a definitional framework for further examining it. By providing clear definitions the chapter will serve as a basis for subsequent, more in-depth thinking and exploration. Defining what a phenomenon is, constitutes the first step towards understanding it. It also gives an actor the ability to prepare in advance for what is a known threat. The structure of the chapter will consist of three parts. The first part will look more broadly at the origins of both parts of the term 'hybrid warfare' in order to come to a clear understanding of what it means not only in a technical, political or strategic but also in a linguistical sense. The second part of the chapter will then give a definition of hybrid warfare and deliver an in-depth explanation of its various components and traits. After an analysis of the existing definitions, an argument will be made as to why this definition is the most useful and clear. Finally, the last part of this chapter will define the various terms associated with hybrid warfare in order to create a core vocabulary with which to furnish the remainder of this book. By clearly defining the various terms and phrases associated with the phenomenon of hybrid warfare, the examination aims to further the knowledge and understanding of this topic and provide a clear and coherent common vocabulary that can then be used to further the debate about and research of the topic, and avoid redundancies, discrepancies and inconsistencies.

Language is a key, and an often overlooked, part of the process of naming new phenomena. Before embarking on a wider debate about the precise definition of the term 'hybrid warfare', it is perhaps best to make a brief foray into the field of etymology. It is evident that 'hybrid warfare' itself consists of two separate terms: 'hybrid' and 'warfare'. In order to better understand what the term stands for and how to define it, the best place to start is to look at both words separately to identify the key concepts in order to correctly apply them to the phenomenon itself.

What does 'hybrid' mean?

One of the main problems with the various definitions of this phenomenon is that the creators of those definitions have used the term 'hybrid' incorrectly. Etymologically, hybrid comes from the Latin word *hibrida*, meaning the offspring of a tame sow and a wild boar.[1] The *OED* defines 'hybrid' as 'the offspring of two animals or plants of different species, or (less strictly) varieties; a half-breed, cross-breed, or mongrel'.[2] The adjective of hybrid is defined as 'produced by the inter-breeding of two different species or varieties of animals or plants; mongrel, cross-bred, half-bred'.[3] The key feature of these definitions is that hybrid is a product resulting from a merger of two distinct antecedents, no more, no less. This is a very important point to note when creating a definition of hybrid warfare; by its very name it is limited to only two constituent parts. The two constituent parts of hybrid warfare are *conventional* and *unconventional* warfare. If an analogy is made back to its Latin roots, the tame sow could be said to stand for the conventional part while the wild boar represents the unconventional part, with their offspring being a hybrid.

Both 'conventional' and 'unconventional' are broad enough terms in and of themselves, enabling actors to incorporate a large number of tools and possibilities in them without resorting to adding more. Hybrid warfare is a deliberately opaque merger of the two and as such presents enough difficulties in definition and identification. A typical example of a problematic definition is that which was set forward during the 2015 MSC. Although the definition itself is not overly problematic, the wording and the accompanying graphics are. The Conference defined 'hybrid warfare as a combination of multiple conventional and unconventional tools of warfare'.[4] This creates an unnecessary ambiguity as to the number of constituent parts of this new phenomenon. The chart that accompanies this definition shows that these tools are: diplomacy, information warfare and propaganda, support for local unrest, irregular forces, Special Forces, regular military forces, economic warfare and cyberattacks.[5] When combined, these tools represent more or less the term 'warfare' in its entirety. It also fails to identify which tools belong in which category. Some, like regular military forces clearly fall into the conventional category, but the use of Special Forces and cyberattacks is less easily categorized.

In order for the constituent parts of hybrid warfare to make sense there needs to be a vertical differentiation between the various levels of the term itself (see Figure 1). Simply throwing everything together at once is an exercise in futility. On a vertical scale there are three levels to the definition of hybrid. The first

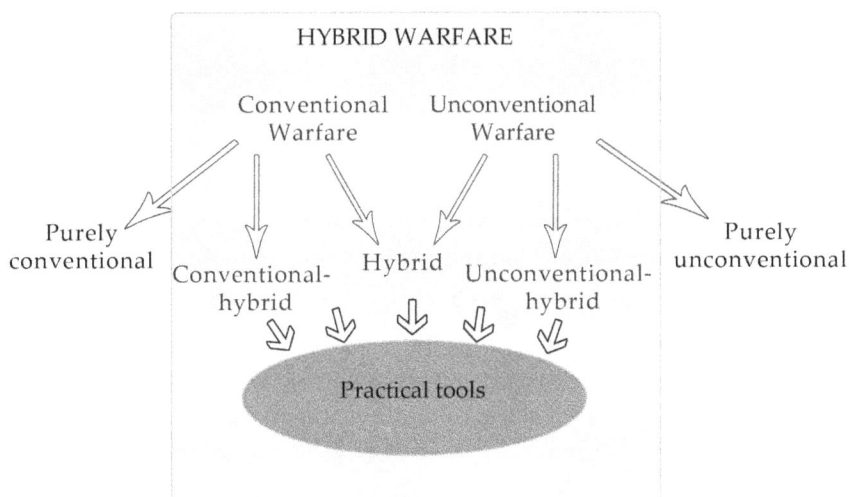

Figure 1 Levels of hybrid warfare.

level is the clear split between conventional and unconventional. The further branching of both terms on the second level illustrates the tools and concepts that fall into each category as well as those that span the gap and are not as easily categorized. It is precisely this 'out of the box' part that gives hybrid warfare its potency and raises the most problems with defining it and engaging actors that employ it. The third level shows the practical steps derived from one or a combination of several of the higher branches.

Throughout this work the definition of hybrid used will be the one from the *OED*, since it provides the clearest definition supported by etymological roots that enables a deeper insight into the concept as a whole. Despite the fact that the *OED* is not always representative of the most common usage of any given term; it is nevertheless still an excellent and highly reputable source when definitions are considered.

What is 'warfare'?

Of the two terms that constitute hybrid warfare, the latter is without a doubt the more difficult one to define adequately and to place into a coherent structure. An important point to note is that the term 'warfare' is often used interchangeably with the term 'war'. While this is normally unproblematic, it does become an issue when a clear, coherent and concise definition is required. The nuanced difference between the terms becomes more important when one is a component of a different term which could, if substituted, lead to a whole new meaning of the term. Interestingly, much of the literature treats both 'war' and 'warfare' as clearly understood and self-evident terms, although they can mean very different things. The US Department of Defense (DOD) glossary of terms, for example, does not include a definition of either warfare or war, although it is filled with definitions of various kinds of both.[6] Even so, there are a number of definitions available, which are much more disparate than those for hybrid.

The *OED* defines 'warfare' as 'a going to war; the action of carrying on, or engaging in, war; the act or state of conflict; military life or service'.[7] However, this explanation is only partially helpful, as the term 'war' requires further expansion in order for the definition of warfare to be of use. The legal definitions of what constitutes a war are numerous and problematic for a number of reasons. The most (in)famous of the criteria for war is the number of battle-related deaths which must occur per calendar year before a conflict can be termed a war. These estimations range from 25 for 'armed conflict' to 1000 for 'war'.[8] While such arbitrarily precise definitions might be useful for scholars of international law, this book will focus on more practical, political definitions of war. A good starting point is once again the *OED*, which defines war as

> hostile contention by means of armed forces, carried on between nations, states, or rulers, or between parties in the same nation or state; the employment of armed forces against a foreign power, or against an opposing party in the state.[9]

As with most dictionary definitions, it attempts to encompass the widest possible spectrum of the term and as such fails to address the more technical aspects of it. Carl von Clausewitz offers a simpler option by defining war as 'an act of force to compel our enemy to do our will'.[10] In a more modern sense, a simpler and more strategic definition states that war is 'a contest between states, or groups within states (civil war), carried on by degrees of coercion, usually military force, in an effort to achieve objectives'.[11] This definition points out that the use of military force is not the only way to conduct a war, a point that is further reinforced by the definition put forward by Colin Gray. 'War is a relationship between belligerents, not necessarily states. Warfare is the conduct of war, primarily, though not exclusively, by military means.'[12]

Separating war and warfare might seem like a pointless epistemological exercise, but the fact that there are numerous other coercive ways of waging war than simply by military force is a crucial distinction. Over the decades the coercive power of non-military actions such as political or economic sanctions has been well documented. Whether coercive actions committed by militias or terrorist groups fall under the military means clause has fuelled many scholarly debates, and it is therefore much more sensible to include it under 'other' means or waging war. These distinctions become even more important when defining hybrid warfare, due to its merging of conventional and unconventional warfare, as well as other aspects of the hybrid terminology.

For the purposes of this book, the following definitions of war and warfare, combined and distilled from various aforementioned sources, will be used in order to facilitate understanding.

War is a hostile contest between states or other belligerents, carried on by degrees of coercion in order to achieve political objectives.

Warfare is the conduct or act of engaging in war, primarily, though not exclusively by the use of military force.

Hybrid warfare

Having established the individual terminology of the components, the definition of hybrid warfare will be presented. As of the time of writing, there is no widely agreed upon definition of hybrid warfare; therefore, this part of the chapter will begin by looking at some of the major theorists in this field. An additional hurdle confronting the definition of hybrid warfare is the lack of a clear vocabulary describing the phenomenon. Some definitions refer to it as 'hybrid warfare', others use the term 'hybrid war' and there is a large segment of the debate that uses the term 'hybrid threat'. When talking about the epistemological basis of a term, it is, of course, almost unnecessary to point out that the term 'threat' has a very different meaning than either war or warfare. Most definitions that use the term 'hybrid threat' are actually definitions of hybrid warfare, and the most important ones will be included in the debate while others will be included later in this chapter with the expanded vocabulary of other 'hybrids'. The list is not exhaustive, but it does represent the opinions and views of the key actors, scholars and institutions.

Origin

The precise origin of the term is difficult to pinpoint, but most sources agree that the term in its current iteration emanates from a paper written by William J. Nemeth in 2002. In it, Nemeth postulates that hybrid warfare will be the dominant form of future wars and offers the Chechen insurgency in the First and

Second Chechen Wars as the case study. The paper itself does not contain a clear definition of what hybrid warfare is, although one can be surmised. Nemeth sees hybrid warfare as a form of warfare practised by hybrid societies; that is societies that have devolved away from a modern state system.[13] He characterizes it as follows: '[Hybrid warfare], the contemporary form of guerrilla warfare, is a continuation of pre-state warfare that has become more effective because it employs both modern technology and modern mobilization methods.'[14] The main argument of his thesis is that warfare is a reflection of the society that wages it; therefore, a hybrid society will engage in hybrid warfare. This kind of warfare is based on guerrilla tactics and employs personal and family ties among combatants to ensure safety and cooperation while also being capable of using advanced technologies at the same time. Such warfare is considered total from the perspective of the guerrillas and therefore sanctions the use of any and all tactics at its disposal. The inherent strengths of such a system are often neglected by Western militaries.[15] Hybrid military forces, which, according to Nemeth, include Fourth Generation Warfare (4GW), New Warfare and terrorism, wage warfare that is based on ideas and therefore have an advantage over Western forces fighting 'advanced technology' warfare.[16]

While Nemeth's paper provides an interesting insight into what are considered the beginnings of hybrid warfare, his definition and the subsequent research is rooted in the nature of the society waging the war, coupled with tactical recommendations, and not only ignores the view of the opposing forces but focuses almost exclusively on non-state actors. Chechens might have operated largely as guerrilla groups in the First Chechen War, but by the time of the Second, they were a nominally independent state. A progression towards an independent, if still clan-based, state seems to represent progress opposite of that, which Nemeth argues, identifies a hybrid society. An important part of this work, however, is the advice that hybrid forms of warfare will be the dominant form of warfare faced by Western states in the twenty-first century and that a doctrinal shift is required.

Building on Nemeth's work and events during the 2006 Second Israel-Lebanon War, Frank G. Hoffman gives the most well-known definition of hybrid warfare. According to Hoffman:

> Hybrid Wars incorporate a range of different modes of warfare, including conventional capabilities, irregular tactics and formations, terrorist acts including indiscriminate violence and coercion, and criminal disorder.[17]

This definition is much more comprehensive than Nemeth's and represents new lessons learnt from Hezbollah as well as those from the continuation of the conflict in Chechnya. It also drew upon the doctrinal and theoretical shift exhibited by US analysts in the light of the conflicts in Afghanistan and Iraq. If the criticism of Nemeth's definition is based largely upon his reliance on non-state actors, Hoffman introduces his definition by saying: 'Hybrid Wars can be conducted by both states and a variety of non-state actors.'[18] An interesting observation is that neither author actually gives a clear-cut definition of hybrid warfare. Hoffman's definition refers to wars, although the actual wording describes various ways of fighting a war and is therefore a definition of warfare.

Contemporary uses

Following the 2006 Lebanon War, there was something of a lull in the hybrid warfare debate with the more classic insurgencies in Afghanistan and Iraq pushing hybrid warfare to the sidelines. Within the US defence community there was a debate over whether the 2008 Russo-Georgian War was a hybrid conflict, with the US Air Force designating it as such although other institutions did not.[19] Hybrid warfare was of course not forgotten, but the terminology had shifted towards referring to it as the 'hybrid threat'. While there is still no official DOD definition of hybrid warfare, unofficial definitions can be found in military concepts throughout the US armed forces. As such the US Joint Forces Command defines hybrid warfare as 'conflict executed by either state and/or non-state threats that employs multiple modes of warfare to include conventional capabilities, irregular tactics and criminal disorder.'[20]

In 2010, a NATO Military Working Group came up with a definition of what constitutes a hybrid threat, a definition that was officially adopted by NATO. A hybrid threat is defined as 'one posed by any current or potential adversary, including state, non-state and terrorists, with the ability, whether demonstrated or likely, to simultaneously employ conventional and non conventional means adaptively, in pursuit of their objectives.'[21] The UK likewise focuses on hybrid threats, although in a different configuration. The Joint Defence Doctrine talks about hybrid threats as those that 'occur where states or non-state actors choose to exploit all modes of war simultaneously using advanced conventional weapons, irregular tactics, terrorism and disruptive criminality to destabilize an existing order.'[22]

The situation changed dramatically in 2014 however; first, in February/ March 2014 with the Russian seizure of Crimea from Ukraine and, secondly, in June 2014, when the Islamic State in Iraq and Syria (ISIS) conducted a successful operation to seize the Iraqi city of Mosul. Up until that point ISIS was viewed as a very dangerous terrorist organization but was deemed to lack the conventional capabilities to threaten the territorial integrity of both Syria and Iraq.[23] Its actions left many security analysts baffled and brought about the revival of hybrid warfare analysis as states, scholars and institutions struggled to explain what had happened. The Russian use of hybrid warfare was the first time an internationally recognized state had resorted to using it, and it did so to great effect. The spread of the conflict to Eastern Ukraine only reinforced the idea that Russia had indeed mastered the art of hybrid warfare, while in the Middle East, ISIS built on the successful capture of Mosul and the collapse of Iraqi forces to push on and capture Tikrit and reach the outskirts of Baghdad. Although the two cases are somewhat different, they share many similarities, particularly the fact that military and civilian scholars were baffled as to how to respond to them. For Europe, the Russian actions in 2014 were a particularly abrupt wakeup call and led to a renewed debate about the future of European security and the new threats it faced. As stated earlier, a good example is the 2015 MSC Report.

In April 2017, after the signing of the memorandum of understanding between NATO and the EU, a special European Centre of Excellence for Countering Hybrid Threats (Hybrid CoE) was established in Finland. While not a body of either NATO or the EU, the participating countries are all members of either, or both, organizations. The Hybrid CoE defines hybrid threats as 'methods and activities that are targeted towards vulnerabilities of the opponent'.[24] It then goes on to list some of these vulnerabilities and concludes that should the 'user' of hybrid threats find it difficult to achieve its aims, the result will be hybrid warfare where 'the role of military and violence will increase significantly'.[25] While establishing a centre for the study of hybrid phenomena is a step in the right direction, the definition, offered by the institution, is simply too vague. Additionally, a list of possible vulnerabilities, which includes, among others, historical memory, legislation, technology and geo-strategic factors, can be of practical use only when combined with a working and precise definition of hybrid warfare.

The definition

The trend with the definitions examined previously appears to be twofold. Some, like Nemeth's and Hoffman's, are very technical and tactical, while others, proposed by various institutions, tend to be very broad and even vague. The latter in particular appear to favour a long list of possible components of hybrid warfare without combining them into an actual definition. If one were to compile a list of all possible components of any kind of warfare, the list would become utterly impractical in very short order. Therefore, a new, more precise, definition is required in order to examine the phenomenon of hybrid warfare in greater detail and explore its nuances. Building on the works listed earlier, this book offers an alternative definition, which incorporates recent developments and views, and attempts to balance the technical minutiae and the broad policy implications. The goal is not to create a final comprehensive definition, since any concept continues to evolve, and the definition must be able to do so likewise. Therefore, instead of being comprehensive, the following definition strives to be concise and strict but welcoming amendments. In short, the proposed definition aims to be strategic. This definition will form the basis of further research and debate that is to follow in the subsequent chapters.

Hybrid warfare is a distinct form of low-level conflict spanning the spectrum of capabilities. It is a deliberately opaque merger of conventional and unconventional warfare and conducted under a single central authority and direction of a state and/or state-like actor. The aim of hybrid warfare is to achieve political objectives that would not be achievable, or would incur too high a cost, through the use of either form individually. The blend of conventional and unconventional enables the actor to exploit an opponent's strategic or doctrinal weakness while maintaining deniability and strategic surprise.

As there are a number of terms included in this definition, they require closer scrutiny. The idea of hybrid warfare is based on the premise that it is a form of warfare that enables an actor to achieve its political aims without having to resort to large-scale conventional war. Much has been said about the decline of large interstate Clausewitzian style conventional wars in recent decades and the trend does seem to confirm these observations. If such conflict has fallen out of fashion, as it were, it is only natural to assume that others would emerge to fill the gap. Historically, such conflicts were termed as 'low-intensity conflicts' (LIC). The US Army defines LIC as 'a political-military confrontation between contending states or groups below conventional war and above the routine, peaceful competition among states'.[26] Such conflicts are often seen as protracted and usually coupled with the connotations of insurgency or revolutionary warfare. The term 'low-intensity conflict' in its purest and simplest form, without the sobriquets of protraction or insurgency, is a useful way of describing a low level of conflict in the context of hybrid warfare. This is not to say that hybrid wars cannot include elements of insurgency or be protracted, but it is not a defining characteristic.

The reason why this definition does not refer to hybrid warfare as a low-intensity type of warfare is not because of its intensity but its relative escalation. Hybrid warfare is a form of low-level conflict because it aims to remain under the threshold of a large-scale conventional war, but with the understanding that a smaller-scale conventional conflict is an integral part of the hybrid concept. It is a form of limited war, because it is a tool of those actors which seek to address some imbalance in the global or regional distribution of power, but at the same time it is not suitable for outright confrontation; its goal is to avoid total war. It is important to note that the terms 'limited' and 'total' war are not absolute, but rather dependant on the perspective of different actors. The Russian intervention in Ukraine was a limited war for Russia but must have seemed like total war to the population in the Donbas. Similarly, China's activities in the South China Sea have been of a limited nature but could be perceived as the start of a total war by Indonesia or Vietnam, should those activities sufficiently threaten their core national interests.

When referring to the 'low level' of conflict, therefore, the term seeks to combine the limited nature of hybrid warfare, its opaqueness, unlimited capabilities and the necessity for controlled escalation to encapsulate the phenomenon better. The intensity with which an actor pursues a hybrid strategy is entirely dependent on circumstances and not relevant to whether a conflict is hybrid or not. As the above examples illustrate, Russian hybrid warfare has been of a greater intensity that China's. However, they both attempted to keep their activities to a lower *level* of conflict – a level that does not threaten the core national interests of the guardian powers of the international order – a point that will be further explained in the next chapter. Successful maintenance of this lower level is also important when judging the success or failure or hybrid war. Hybrid warfare can only be deemed successful if it manages to maintain this low level and stay below the threshold of large-scale conventional war. If an opponent reacts to it in a conventional large-scale attack, which imposes a higher cost than the gains attained, a hybrid strategy has failed. The ability to control and manage this escalation is the crucial aspect of hybrid warfare.

When defining a form of warfare, it is a good practice to make some mention of the capabilities the form in question can utilize. A full spectrum of capabilities means that an actor can employ any and all means at its disposal to conduct hybrid warfare so long as the other basic criteria are met. Many criticisms of hybrid warfare mention that all of its facets are already covered by other forms of war. For example, a prevailing view in the US DOD is that hybrid warfare falls under the doctrine of Full-Spectrum Operations (FSO) and therefore does not require a specific approach to counter it.[27] This, however, is an error. FSO, as defined by the US military, means that it encompasses all aspects of conflict (offensive, defensive, stability and civil support).[28] That is simply another way of saying, wage war. The nature of hybrid warfare means that it can employ regular conventional ground, sea and air forces as well as, at least theoretically, nuclear forces in addition to irregular formations or militia units. It also includes cyber and space warfare in either their conventional or unconventional iterations. The idea behind the phrase 'spanning the spectrum of capabilities' simply means that there is no limit to which capabilities an actor employs, in order for a conflict to be deemed hybrid, so long as the conventional conflict threshold is not breached (see Figure 2). In other terms, the concept of hybrid warfare cannot be practically limited by simply referring to a set of specific components, as most other definitions have attempted to do. There is no fixed set of components for hybrid warfare because it is context specific. Hybrid warfare is a method of combining as many, or as few, of the tools of coercion as is required, which makes it distinctive from other forms of warfare which are, by and large, limited by their choice of tools.

When referring to hybrid warfare, it is necessary to always keep in mind that the blending of conventional and unconventional is deliberate and not simply a tactical expediency. Nor is it a Mao-esque process of progression from unconventional guerrilla war to conventional conflict. Both parts are present simultaneously from the very beginning of the conflict and used by separate

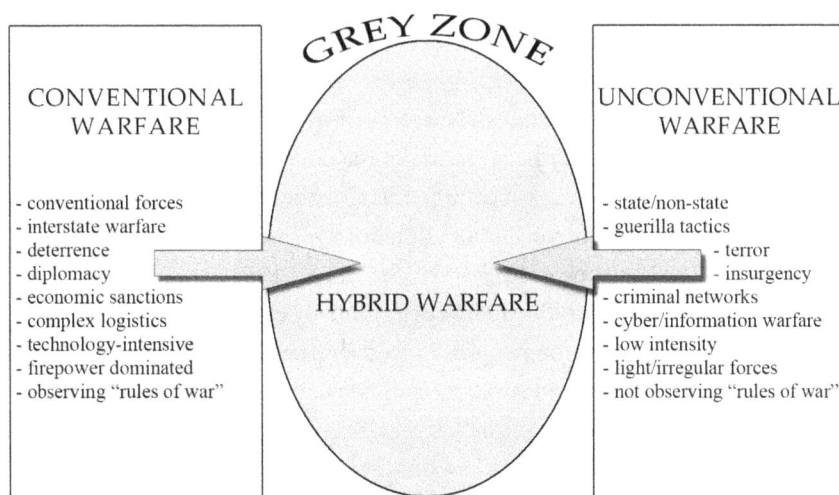

Figure 2 Hybrid warfare is a blend of conventional and unconventional warfare.

or same units in the same strategic theatre. The goal is to deprive the opponent of easily identifiable conventional or unconventional targets. A hybrid unit can operate as conventional units, wearing uniforms and possessing an integrated command structure, fighting with sophisticated weapons in the morning and then disperse and blend with the civilian population to fight as insurgents or militias in the afternoon. Rapid mobilization, using modern information technology, is the key factor. When dispersed in 'unconventional mode', hybrid units require only cell phone coverage or access to the internet in order to re-form. As an added feature, such communication can be disguised so that it is not easily traced to government institutions, although it loses much of the security inherent in high-level military communication. This is in stark contrast to conventional forces, which require large and complex logistical and support apparatuses. When hybrid units are re-formed they only need to be re-integrated into the pre-existing logistical support and are able to continue fighting. In historical terms, the hybrid model of mobilization is the most modern expression of Helmuth von Moltke's famous railway timetables.

Such a high level of coordination can only be achieved through a centralized decision-making process, which requires a certain amount of institutionalized bureaucracy and technical support. As the definition points out, the reason behind an actor reaching for hybrid warfare is the fact that it enables that actor to conduct simultaneously both conventional and unconventional operations using tools from both, although the two parts need not be equal. Hybrid warfare is highly adaptable and can, depending on the situation, contain a higher proportion of conventional than unconventional units or vice versa. However, due to the demands of conventional warfare the actor that employs hybrid warfare has to be a state or a non-state actor with some very state-like characteristics. Purely non-state actors (terrorist groups, insurgents or guerrillas) usually do not, due to their very nature, possess the structure or the doctrine required to wage even low-level conventional war. As such they are incapable of waging hybrid warfare and rely simply on the unconventional tactics and tools. Conventional war is usually viewed as that being waged between states. Hybrid warfare, however, adds a certain amount of fluidity to that definition. By engaging in some elements of conventional warfare combined with unconventional means, even a non-state actor can be said to engage in some form of conventional warfare. Despite this, not all unconventional warfare is hybrid warfare.

Centralized decision-making has another side that can be limiting to hybrid warfare. If the same actor engages in conventional warfare in a certain strategic theatre and an irregular force develops outside its control, or in a different strategic theatre, such a conflict is not hybrid, but rather two separate conflicts from the perspective of the opponent. One conflict is conventional, the other unconventional and the opponent can fight the two simultaneously with different tools without encountering the challenge of hybridity. This illustrates the importance of engaging deliberately in hybrid warfare, or risk being defeated twice.

A further point to note with regards to highly centralized decision-making is that it makes it very difficult for democratic states to actively engage in hybrid warfare. The political system and the corresponding structures require a high degree of openness and transparency which is anathema to the opaqueness which is crucial for the conduct of hybrid warfare. Democratic states normally exercise broad civilian oversight over military activities, and there is a public expectation that key strategic and doctrinal documents are publicly available. Neither of these factors is conducive to hybrid warfare and would likely create a legitimacy shortfall if a democratic state wished to engage in it. That is not to say that hybrid warfare can be conducted exclusively by authoritarian actors, but the very nature of it makes its active use by democracies practically improbable.

As Clausewitz wrote in 1832: 'No one starts a war – or rather, no one in his senses ought to do so – without first being clear in his mind what he intends to achieve by that war and how he intends to conduct it.'[29] This simple dictum illustrates well the idea of war being fought for political goals. This has been a part of many definitions of war, including the one used here, and it seems so obviously clear that no previous definition of hybrid warfare even mentioned it. The same rule indeed applies to hybrid war, but with a twist. Hybrid warfare enables an actor to achieve an objective that a purely conventional or unconventional approach would not, either because it faces overwhelming odds or because such actions would bring more harm than good. International condemnation, sanctions or military intervention are likely to result from an actor's solely conventional or unconventional actions, particularly if directed against the leading states, or against the interests of the leading states, in the international order, which enjoy a sizeable technological and doctrinal advantage over the rest. The same advantages can become a source of weakness when confronted with an approach that does not clearly follow the established ways of waging war, as accepted by the Western-led international order. The requirements for international legitimacy and allied support can hamper a Western response to a hybrid war, a feature that will be discussed in greater depth in the next chapter.

When the definition speaks of cost, the term is not limited solely to the financial cost of operations. It is used in its broadest, grand strategic meaning, encompassing, among others, financial, economic, political, diplomatic, military, prestige and strategic costs. Although most of these can, in some form or another, be expressed in numerical terms (a monetary value), some crucial costs cannot be so calculated. Any political decision carries a corresponding cost, even if the full 'price' is not immediately obvious. When dealing with matters of war and peace, the amount of 'blood and treasure' which an actor might spend can escalate quickly. However, the days of making 'war pay for war' are over and decisions to conduct war are rarely made for financial considerations, although financial considerations might affect the manner in which such decisions are carried out. For example, estimates of the financial cost to Russia following the annexation of Crimea range around $4 billion a year,[30] at least for the first few years, in addition to a similar amount spent on the new bridge, spanning the Kerch strait which connects Russia to its newest territory.[31] Additionally, these figures do not include the costs of the actual military operation, or the economic sanctions imposed on Russia. Nevertheless, Russia has been willing to accept those costs because of overriding prestige, security and, above all, strategic weaknesses which would have followed had it not annexed the Crimean peninsula. The determination of the 'value' of the goals is ultimately up to the actor which seeks to attain them.

Finally, an additional feature of hybrid warfare is that it gives the actor a certain amount of deniability and strategic surprise. While conventional forces carry insignia and are therefore attributable to a state, hybrid units are not bound to that rule. Even if they appear in uniform, and fight as conventional forces, they might not carry insignia. The unconventionality of hybrid forces gives the state or other actor the ability to deny involvement even in situations where it might be blatantly obvious who the actor is by simply stating, for example, that the units in question do not carry identification marks. In the world of international law, sometimes even absurdly weak deniability presents great problems for making the case for legally sanctioned interventions, which is one of the reasons for the development of hybrid warfare. The other main reason is the potential for strategic surprise. An opponent might be proficient in fighting conventional wars or have great experience dealing with insurgents, but a combination of the two brings about problems that are not easy to solve, due to the fact that solutions to those two approaches are often diametrically opposite to one another. A conventional response to an unconventional force will not be successful, nor will an unconventional response in the face of a large conventional army. The hybrid approach is therefore a way for an actor to avoid the dilemma of having to fight according to the Western art of war, in which it would be outclassed, by creating a new way to fight wars that is the antithesis of the Western tradition.

What makes hybrid different

When attempting to describe a new phenomenon like hybrid warfare it is useful to look at a broader field of trends and terms that already exists in order to place hybrid warfare in the correct category. The debate over how warfare of the future will look is perennial and several terms already exist. In order to examine what makes hybrid distinctive, the two most prominent terms closest to hybrid will be scrutinized: 4GW and compound wars.

Fourth Generation Warfare

Perhaps the most famous of the two is 4GW, proposed by William Lind in 1989 and expanded by Thomas X. Hammes in 2004. Both Nemeth and Hoffman refer to 4GW in their analysis of hybrid warfare. Nemeth uses the term 'hybrid military forces' for a group of concepts that contains 4GW, New Warfare, LIC and terrorism,[32] while Hoffman directly engages with the concept of 4GW and examines how it differs from his own proposed idea of hybrid warfare.[33] Hoffman then goes on to list the ways in which hybrid warfare theory has built upon the debate surrounding 4GW, and the parts he used to create his definition of hybrid warfare. The blurring nature of conflicts and the loss of monopoly of force by the state are the major contributions of 4GW to Hoffman's hybrid warfare. The 4GW concept has attracted a lot of controversy and has been rejected by a large number of scholars due to the selective use of historical examples and scholarly indiscipline.[34]

The central premise of 4GW is that since 1648 the world has gone through three generations of warfare (linear, firepower, manoeuvre) and has now reached the fourth. This fourth generation is a complex form of insurgency that thrives in the absence or collapse of the state and is therefore a return to the pre-state wars that occurred before the Peace of Westphalia embedded the primacy over the use of force with the state.[35] The hallmarks of 4GW are the use of terrorism, advanced technology and sophisticated psychological warfare. These are very similar to Nemeth's hybrid societies and their hybrid ways of conducting war. 4GW has seen a surge of interest following the wars in Iraq and Afghanistan, although its advocates failed to provide any useful insights beyond what was already known and some scholars have called for the complete abandonment of the term due to the fact that it obscures more than it reveals. The super-insurgency proposed by 4GW advocates has failed to develop, certainly in the way they suggested it would.[36]

It is perhaps too harsh to summarily dismiss the entire concept of 4GW. If nothing else it has contributed to the debate by providing another, if misguided, viewpoint on the future of warfare. However, its contributions are indeed very limited and provide little beyond what the established theories already deal with in regards to irregular war. By focusing solely on insurgency as the dominant form of future war, the theory of 4GW has been doomed from the start, as insurgencies never take place in a stateless vacuum.

Compound wars

The concept of compound wars was first put forward by Thomas Huber in 1996. In his work he described compound warfare as 'the simultaneous use of a regular or main force and an irregular or guerrilla force against an enemy'.[37] Huber also lists a number of historical examples as case studies for the concept of compound war, ranging from North American colonial wars of the seventeenth century, through the Napoleonic wars and the Anglo-Irish war, to the war in Vietnam and the Soviet invasion of Afghanistan. The key concept behind compound wars is the cooperation between conventional armies and irregular forces. This forces an opponent to both concentrate and spread out at the same time, in order to address the different threats and denies it a single focal point.[38] In this regard it serves as a precursor to hybrid warfare; however, there are a number of differences.

The concept of compound wars does not include non-state actors or more modern threats like cyber warfare, nor does it account for the flexibility of hybrid forces. Compound wars are interstate wars with elements of insurgency and irregular warfare. The cooperation between regular and irregular units in the examples used is still limited to the operational and tactical spheres. They might on paper follow the directions from a central authority, but they are not used as part of the same force or even as two parts of the same strategy. The irregular force merely provides help to the main conventional force and there is no fluidity among them. Irregular troops in compound wars do not fight as guerrillas in the morning and turn into regular units in the afternoon, nor vice versa. In the case of Vietnam, which most proponents of compound wars list as the best illustration, the North Vietnamese Army and the Viet Cong did coordinate to a degree and were directed by a central authority, but they fought in different theatres and did not fuse into a single force. The fact that the United States had trouble dealing with the type of war fought in Vietnam had little to do with hybridity.

This particular selection of historical examples is not limited to Huber, but has also appeared in a remarkably similar form in the book on hybrid warfare edited by Murray and Mansoor. They use Hoffman's definition of hybrid warfare and attempt to apply it to a number of historical examples. The collection of essays on the various historical cases of 'hybrid warfare' is useful, but the conclusions are largely limited and unhelpful. The fact that the authors do not make the distinction between hybrid and compound wars further blurs their contribution.[39] As it is written from a historical, rather than a strategic, perspective, such flaws are easily excusable. Hybrid warfare, in the modern sense, was not possible in the 1980s and early 1990s, and especially not in the times of the Roman Empire, Peninsular War or the US Civil War, mainly due to the limited level of communications technology then available but also because warfare was viewed somewhat differently in the past. Irregular units were not considered 'real' soldiers for much of military history, and in many cases are still not. Hybrid warfare capitalizes on this, largely Western, prejudice in order to present a non-uniform opponent and a multifaceted threat that Western militaries, focused on high-tech conventional war, have a problem combating.[40] Technological advances have transformed the art of war and raised the effectiveness of both conventional and unconventional combat forces.[41] While such advances are perhaps insufficient to have transformed the character of war by themselves, they have certainly contributed to the transformation process in a way that is sufficiently different from the historical examples mentioned above.

Complexity has always been a part of warfare and a combination of irregular and regular units fighting in the same campaign has been a staple of war since the dawn of civilisation. This aspect of hybrid is not new but the way the two parts interact is novel. The fusion, together with the opportunities and difficulties it presents, of conventional and unconventional is a new kind of warfare, but not a new form of war. The main reason for dismissing the historical examples as truly hybrid is the fact that a hybrid force, possessed of the ability to rapidly transform from one form to another, requires real-time communication and flexibility that were simply not available before the era of mass communication.

A hybrid vocabulary

As the main part of the definition has been examined, this is a good point to expand the hybrid vocabulary by explaining some other terms associated with the concept. When dealing with the various definitions this book has already encountered several difficulties in the fact that none of the definitions could even agree on what they were defining. Is hybrid warfare the same as hybrid war? Is a hybrid threat an element of either or a separate term? The definitions discussed earlier have been selected because they referred to, what in this book will be called, hybrid warfare. The following definitions of other 'hybrid' terms has been provided to clear up the muddled phraseology. In subsequent chapters these terms will be used as defined here, unless referenced otherwise.

> 'Hybrid threat' is a term that most definitions use when they try to define hybrid warfare. This is an unwise choice. The term 'threat' itself connotes something that has yet to happen. The *OED* defines it as 'a declaration of hostile determination or of loss, pain, punishment or damage to be inflicted in retribution for or conditionally upon some course; a menace'.[42] Therefore, it is only useful before any events take place. It is also a much narrower term that fails to encompass the full spectrum of what hybrid warfare means. By using threat instead of warfare, the definition is in danger of not providing enough information to the user.
>
> 'Hybrid strategy', like any other strategy, is 'a way of connecting power to objectives'.[43] In this case an actor employs hybrid strategy to connect the means at its disposal to the political goals it wishes to achieve, through the use of hybrid warfare. It is also a strategy for waging hybrid war. The opponent engages in a Counter-Hybrid Strategy (CHS).
>
> 'Counter-hybrid warfare' (CHW) is a term similar to Counter Insurgency (COIN) in both meaning and use. The actor that begins using hybrid warfare is engaging in it. The actor that seeks to counter-hybrid warfare therefore engages in CHW. Depending on the perspective, the roles can, of course, be reversed and manipulated, but this is the general guide.
>
> 'Hybrid defence' is a term that has gained increased traction in the last few years. Unlike CHW, which is an active, kinetic method of warfare designed to directly engage a hybrid actor once it had already launched its hybrid warfare campaign, hybrid defence is a method of deterring, preventing, and protecting from future hybrid warfare.

When a new term appears, purporting to define coercive behaviour that is controversial as well as dangerous, defining it is always an uphill struggle. This chapter had three goals to achieve: to clear up the confusion surrounding the definition of hybrid warfare, to place the term into its proper context and to clarify the terminology that surrounds the phenomenon. By looking at the constituent parts, from a linguistic perspective, this chapter demonstrated what precisely the term stands for and where its limits lie. This is an important first step in understanding the subject matter. Misuse of terms is always to be avoided and that tends to be easier when their meaning is clear and precise.

No phenomenon occurs in isolation or in a completely unrelated manner. The debate about hybrid warfare has not only spawned a body of work that includes new contributions but also shed some light on concepts that have been either lost or forgotten. Compound war was a largely obscure term, until it re-surfaced in connection with its modern derivative, hybrid war. A precursor in spirit if not entirely in application or meaning, it is now largely outdated and subsumed under the umbrella of hybrid. The connection to 4GW is also an interesting aspect of hybrid warfare. The rise of complex non-state actors and the blending of modalities are useful contributions, although the remaining body of work on 4GW is flawed. Both of these concepts are contested and the same can be said of hybrid warfare, although arguably less so. Both also fail to explain adequately all aspects of modern conflicts, and as a result, this book argues that the term 'hybrid' is much more suitable to describe modern conflicts which, despite the prophesized rise of non-state actors, still tends to be state-dominated.

Readers will have noticed that throughout this chapter, no mention was made of the term 'globalization'. The reason for this omission is simple; the term 'hybrid warfare' is complex enough to define without referring to a term that is so vague it can stand for almost anything. While it might sometimes seem easier simply to refer to globalization when talking about the modern world, that is not the case in reality. The decline of the state, and correspondingly of interstate war, is often ascribed to the process of globalization, although this connection is far from proven. It does form the wider context for the debate on hybrid warfare but it has limited practical use.

The myriad of terms surrounding hybrid are often misused or misapplied, particularly in the press, and the trend has begun to affect senior officials and policymakers. In terms of the hybrid debate, this is of course unproductive, and hopefully this book will aid in redirecting the term 'hybrid warfare' back to its origins. Another use of the wider vocabulary is to introduce terms that required clarification, such as hybrid strategy, counter-hybrid warfare and hybrid defence. This is a very simple, yet very important, part of the research that has so far been overlooked, because it was taken as self-evident. It is important, however, when dealing with a new term to take as little as possible as self-evident in order to avoid unnecessary confusion and to achieve precision.

The hybrid framework and the quinity

The concept of hybrid warfare is best understood when placed within a suitable framework. No phenomenon occurs in a vacuum. It is always subjected to various external influences, pressures and events. In the context of hybrid warfare, there are two crucial pillars of the framework: the rules-based, Western-led international order and the closely related, Clausewitzian understanding of the nature and character of war. This chapter will establish the basis of the two pillars and provide the theoretical framework for the understanding of hybrid warfare. The following chapter will then build on this concept and create a theory of hybrid warfare.

The issue of the rules-based, Western-led international order is paramount in understanding the phenomenon of hybrid warfare. Not only does the phenomenon itself occur in a specific framework, but so do the other elements of that framework. Arguably, the overarching framework which influences all others is the international order. This assumption is based on the argument that states are the principle actors in the international system. The states have, in turn, created several international organizations which enable them to project or fulfil their national interests better. Therefore, it logically follows that states, and their institutional groupings, are the highest legitimate and legal sources of authority in an otherwise anarchical system. Rather than attempt to explain the entirety of the international order, this examination will focus on those aspects which are important for the understanding of hybrid warfare.

When dealing with the nature and conduct of warfare, the core element of the framework surrounding any new concepts should either be based on, or be derived directly from, Carl von Clausewitz's seminal work *On War*. The structure and contents of the second part of this chapter will therefore rely very heavily on the same. First, the chapter will present the original trinity and some of the debate surrounding it, both historical and contemporary. Second, the chapter will expand the Clausewitzian framework to add two new parts to the trinity: additional legitimacy and allies. This expanded framework can therefore be called the 'quinity'. In this regard this book will propose a hybrid quinity, in order to better explain the complexities associated with hybrid warfare. The third and final part of the chapter will combine the two parts and deliver a verdict on the relationship between hybrid warfare and its strategic environment.

The international order

There have been, broadly speaking, three types of international orders since the Peace of Westphalia in 1648. The first is multipolar (the era of great powers), the second is bipolar (Cold War), and the last is unipolar (the disputed post-Cold War US 'unipolar moment'[1]). Arguably since the 1990s, but certainly since the turn of the century, the international order is once again moving towards multipolarity. While this is not surprising, it should be equally unsurprising that such a drift is accompanied by an increase in occurrences of war, as multipolar systems tend to be more stable, but also more war prone.[2] All of these systems stem from the fundamental assumption that the environment in which the actors operate (the system) is anarchic. The types of international orders mentioned earlier represent different attempts at survival in such an environment. Whether it is already multipolar or still in the process of becoming such, the contemporary international order is a product of the post-Second World War thinking. As such it is more liberal than the preceding multipolar international order, which can be described as largely realist, and based on the idea of preventing the re-establishment of the conditions within the international system which led to the two world wars.[3]

Underpinning this fundamental goal are the core principles of the international order. It has been envisaged as universal and liberal, in the sense that it is rule- and law-based (including protections for human rights) and respectful of sovereignty and the territorial integrity of states.[4] Their principles are often associated with Western liberal democracies, although they are not specific only to them. Considering that the system was established as an Anglo-American idea, this is not surprising. The other great power at the time, the Soviet Union, only partook in this process as a war measure and avoided participating in the organs of the system beyond its ability to prevent the whole of the system from being used against it. However, the international order as it was originally envisaged was not solely based on democratic norms and values. As the leading power of the era, the United States became the guarantor of the system. This means that the system was backed not only by what today would be termed 'soft power', that is the US economy, currency, alliance system and leadership,[5] but also by the US military and 'hard' power, which undoubtedly helped keep the Soviet Union within it.[6] As the international order has evolved over the decades, other leading Western powers (UK, France and Germany) have recovered and developed, and taken prominent, although still secondary, roles in the defence of the international order. Together with the United States they can be termed as the most influential 'guardian powers' of the system. After the end of the Cold War, the advent of US unipolar hegemony, together with the rise of the EU and its 'soft power' approach, led to the international order moving from its more traditionally liberal, but still hard power guaranteed, roots to a more liberal-expansionist model, which not only offers but also promotes and enforces democratic values and ideas actively. A good representative example of this approach is the US/NATO enlargement policy, of which more will be said in the next chapter.

Before moving on to analyse the shift in the international order further, the term 'guardian powers' needs to be clearly defined. In its broadest meaning, guardian powers refers to any actor (state or non-state) which has an active interest in the preservation of the international order, either on a global or on a regional scale. In a narrower meaning, the term refers to a relatively small group of leading states within the system which can be described as 'Western' in their political ideology (liberal, market economies) and governmental organization (democratic), and also possess the capabilities to perpetuate and sustain the system. Unless otherwise specified, the term will be used in its latter meaning throughout the book. As with any system, the international order provides adherents with certain benefits, which increase with the relative power of the actor within it. In this sense the guardian powers and other passive supporters of the system can be viewed as 'status-quo' powers. Other actors can also derive benefits, but will willingly work within the constraints of the system only for as long as these benefits outweigh the costs of breaking with the system. The challengers of the system can be viewed as 'revisionist' powers, in the sense that they wish to address either the internal systemic balance of power or certain aspects of the system; such as their position in it. The role of the guardian powers is to ensure compliance with the rules of the international order. They view it as a truly global order, which means that their enforcement is equally far reaching, applying even to states which are unsatisfied with the system, or their place within is, as well as those that openly challenge it.

This shift from a passive order, which was the result of Cold War tensions, to an aggressive promoter of Western liberal democratic ideology brought the international order into conflict with its own core premise: respect for state sovereignty. The Responsibility to Protect (R2P) doctrine represents the height of such thinking. However, it has been largely abandoned because of its failed application during the 2011 intervention in Libya, and the carte blanche it gave, or, more importantly, was perceived to have given, to the guardian states in their pursuit of the continuation and promotion of the international order.[7] Nevertheless, the process of globalization and the drift towards multipolarity have forced a new approach to protecting the system. While not representing a fundamental rethink, the trend of change is significant enough to call the contemporary international order 'World Order 2.0'.[8] This second iteration, Haass argues, stresses 'sovereign obligations', which are obligations that states have towards other states in the system, rather than to their populations. In essence, the system respects the domestic sovereignty of states, but their international sovereignty is respected only insofar as they follow the norms of the system.[9] These norms include UN treaties and declarations, respect for international law and the acceptance of liberal democratic values. Clearly, these are a reflection of the values and interest of the guardian powers, which use the system to promote their vision of international order.

However, the guardian powers are also bound by those same rules and norms, although they occasionally breach them themselves. The two most obvious examples are the creation of the proto-state of Kosovo in 1999 and the legally disputatious invasion of Iraq in 2003. While the invasion of Iraq can be said to represent a 'stretching' of the rules of the international order, the case of Kosovo is far more problematic. When the US-led coalition created the de facto independent polity, it broke all of the fundamental principles of its own international order; a fact that was ignored when Russia was accused of changing the borders in Europe in 2014 by those same states. Despite protests from other states, the guardian powers interpreted the rules to suit their interests, confirming Thucydides's adage that 'the strong do what they want and the weak do as they must'.[10] The considerable power disparity between the guardian powers, collectively, and any potential individual opponent, or grouping of opponents, means that apart from criticizing the (mis)use of the system, there is not much an opponent can do, at least not openly.

While the guardian powers can sometimes be arbitrary and contradictory in their adherence to the international order they have created, for the most part they tend to follow its guidelines. The most important principles that the international order has imposed on its members are the severe constraints it places on military interventions. While logical from the historical perspective, these stringent conditions are a double-edged blade. On the one hand, Western conventional military superiority is unmatched, therefore Western states wish to act, or wish to be seen to act, as responsible international actors. They are the ones that place constraints on the use of their own power, in accordance with the rules of the international order, in the hope that this will convince all other actors to follow suit. On the other hand, should any actor fail to adhere to these constraints, the guardian powers would have the reasons for intervening. The political and societal support required for such actions can only materialize if the vital interests of the state are threatened. These range from outright military threats, through access to resources or trade routes, to political subversion.[11] While that holds true for any state, for guardian powers, the continuation of the international order represents an additional vital national interest; therefore, they will be highly motivated to deal with any potential threat, so long as it can be clearly identified.

Before delving into the connections between the international order and hybrid warfare, some additional analysis is required. As the relationship between them revolves around the concepts of conflict and coercion, an examination of the nature and character of war will now be addressed.

The nature and character of war

On War has become one of the cornerstones of modern strategy, not just in the West but across the globe, and as such it is prudent to consider its implications very carefully, when dealing with new concepts. Ever since its publication, scholars and professionals have been arguing over the exact meaning and application of the ideas Clausewitz put forward. This is not helped by the fact that the work is somewhat unfinished and only the first part was fully edited by the author. In such an environment it is natural that, over the centuries, different interpretations have emerged. For most of this time traditional, interstate warfare was the dominant way of fighting wars, so much so that it was given the sobriquet of Clausewitzian or trinitarian war. After the end of the Cold War, however, a shift occurred, with many authors foregoing Clausewitz on the basis that future wars would not fall so neatly into the interstate 'box'. The most prominent of such thinkers were Martin van Creveld and John Keegan.[12] But has the major shift in the nature of war that these authors prophesized actually occurred? A clear answer to the question is not forthcoming, although an argument can be made that their theories had, at least in part, been disputed by the continuation of many interstate wars. Whether the very nature of war itself is subject to change is more problematic. Clausewitz based his work on the idea of an unchanging nature of war, but one that can have various different characters. In that regard, he postulated the existence of a 'paradoxical' trinity[13] which represents the essence of war.

Traditional trinity

The classical Clausewitzian 'trinity' is a theory expanded from quite a short paragraph in *On War*, although there are references to various elements of it throughout the text. The core principle behind the trinity is to reduce the concept of war to its core components and characteristics; a blind natural force, full of chance and probability, and subordinated to reason alone. The three parts are connected by Clausewitz to correspond with the people, the military and the government.[14] The link, however, is not universally accepted as the individual characteristics of one or another part of the trinity can be said to reside in another, depending on the circumstances. There is also some debate whether there were actually two, closely interconnected trinities created by Clausewitz. Colin Gray has advocated for the existence of two, 'unstable trinities'. The first or primary trinity is comprised of popular feeling, military performance and political direction, or passion, chance and reason, while the second trinity consists of the people, the army and its commander, and the government or policy.[15] Such duality is not unusual in many writers of the period, and Gray is not alone in picking up on this long-standing German intellectual tradition of duality. It stems from a philosophical legacy of the enlightenment and Kantian thought, to which Clausewitz, as his writings indicate, most assuredly subscribed. That is not to say that he embraced all aspects of Kantian philosophy, but he would have been aware of it and would have come across it during his schooling as well as his military career.[16] Every concept or phenomenon is considered to have objective and subjective natures or parts. Therefore, the first trinity, composed of violence, hatred and enmity, the free spirit and subordination, is the objective one; the one that all wars have in common. On the other hand, the subjective part encompasses more institutionalized actors, such as the people, the military and the government, along with the external circumstances that vary with every war. The two parts cannot be separated from one another, and they represent both the nature and character of war, respectively.[17] Duality of the trinity is in many ways fundamental for its understanding and examination, as it not only reflects the original time period in which Clausewitz wrote but also explains why

PEOPLE

INTERNAL
LEGITIMACY

GOVERNMENT   MILITARY

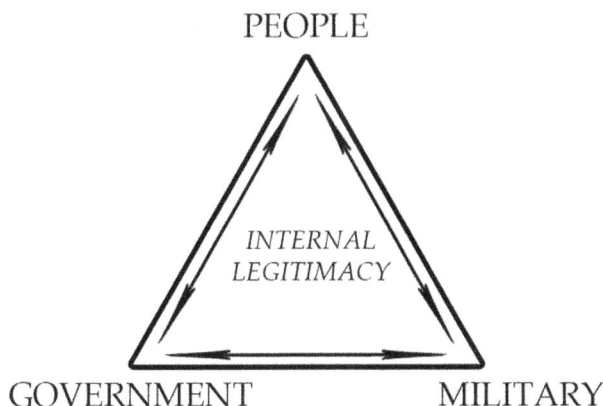

Figure 3 The traditional trinity.

the trinity has maintained its value to the present day. As each component of the trinity is examined in more detail it is very important to keep in mind that they are not discrete units, but rather a group of interconnected and interdependent entities (see Figure 3). They can come together in any number of different ways, depending on the time and surrounding circumstances, but will always strive to maintain balance; as Clausewitz phrased it: 'Our task therefore is to develop a theory that maintains the balance between these three tendencies, like an object suspended between three magnets.'[18]

As the fundamental part of any society it is only appropriate that the people take pride of place. In terms of the theory of war, the people represent the emotions and passions that inspire war. They embody primordial violence, hatred and enmity that go on to make up the blind natural force.[19] They are the passion of the trinity, so to speak, and its main source of legitimacy. Following on the duality principle, they are the most subjective component, but they rely on the other two not only for balance but also for the initial flair of force. If the government and the military wish to start a war, they must kindle the passions of the people, which requires those passions to exist already in the public consciousness,[20] which is not always an easy task. Some conflicts even defy this notion, providing that the conflict is short enough or the people are not interested enough in it, and the objectives are achieved quickly and relatively painlessly, like the Wars of Frederick the Great or the US-sponsored war in Bosnia.[21] Needless to say, there is an enormous element of risk with such an approach, for if the war continues longer than expected, the public will have more time and gain more interest in it, particularly if the longer duration is coupled with higher casualties. The support of the people is vital in any war, as the loss of this support and the corresponding legitimacy could spell disaster.

Existing in the realm of possibility and chance is the second part of the trinity – the military. It, more so than the other two, must deal with the unpredictable nature of war since it must face it not only on a grand strategic level, but in everyday tactical operations as well. Perhaps this is why Clausewitz gave the military the rather poetic environment where 'the creative spirit is free to roam'.[22] The military is required to come up with the various ways in which to fight a war, and it must do so effectively if it is to succeed in its task. The myriad of contingencies for which any military must prepare might not turn out to be relevant in the war they eventually fight.[23] A crucial component in this effort is the military commander. This might seem an old fashioned notion in the modern world, but individual commanders can still make or break a campaign, or even a war. Like the final part of the trinity, the government, the military is also highly dependent on public support, although it is less affected by it directly, since most societies see their military forces in a somewhat favourable light. This stems from the notion that the primary duty of a state is to protect its people, with the military as the main tool in the government's arsenal. This relationship perhaps best illustrates the interconnectedness of all the parts of the trinity.

The final part of the trinity is concerned with control and formulation of policy. The government must, according to Clausewitz, hold a monopoly over the creation of political aims. This is to prevent the military objectives from becoming overall goals, with the end result being that a state would fight a war, simply in order to fight a war. War must be subjugated to policy and fought for political goals; it is a political instrument. Clausewitz summed up this point most astutely with perhaps his most famous dictum, where war is 'merely the continuation of politics by other means'.[24] This rational outlook is the responsibility of leaders or governments and does not mean that war is the natural recourse to any and all disagreements among states, or that, once war commences, all other forms of interaction should cease; merely that war is one instrument among many and that it should not be viewed as something that must be avoided at all times.

An important point to note is that when Clausewitz referred to 'government' or 'state' and the political subjugation of war to it, he did not necessarily limit the concept of war to the interstate brand. As Rupert Smith points out, the concept of 'political' is often connected to the modern view of the state, when it is 'the activity and interaction of both the formal and informal political entity'.[25] There is certainly nothing in *On War* that would lead to the conclusion that it only applies to interstate wars, which is an interpretation that has been imposed through secondary references to Clausewitz, mostly by his critics. While the majority of his historical research has focused on interstate wars, his own military experience and thought does include references to guerrilla wars or insurrections.[26] The primacy of policy is not dependent on a particular state or system of government, so long as the centre of decision-making is legitimate in the eyes of the population and the military it controls.

Limiting the use of military force to all but the last resort is a popular, if misguided, modern approach to deal with conflicts, particularly in the Western world. It is one of the key constraints placed upon the use of force in the international order. The idea that the use of armed force should be the last resort is not only un-Clausewitzian, it is a conscious rejection of the ability of a state to use military force as a tool of securing anything short of its own survival. As the restrictions are so oppressive, only a clear and undeniable threat can trigger the mechanisms of the trinity, which would allow a state to react coercively. This, of course, creates ideal circumstances for the use of hybrid warfare. With the examination of the classical trinity now complete, it is time to expand the framework in order to deepen the understanding of the complexities surrounding hybrid warfare.

The quinity

Two centuries along the historical timeline, the world today is very different than it was at the time Clausewitz wrote *On War*. Many things have changed, but some have remained the same. The political nature of war is still unchanging, but the character of war would hardly be recognized by a nineteenth-century strategist. One of the newest characteristics of war is hybrid war, and in order to understand the concept better, it is necessary to examine how Clausewitz's ideas have been adjusted to the modern day. This is not to say that the original, classical trinity, no longer applies. It is still very much relevant, particularly to an actor employing hybrid warfare, as will be illustrated later in this chapter. Building on the definition of hybrid warfare, presented in the preceding chapter, it is clear that hybrid warfare is waged for political goals, that it requires the support of the people and is subject to the same realities of warfare as any other form. It is, by its nature, very Clausewitzian, which is to say, trinitarian in the classical sense. The need for an expanded framework comes from the fact that responding to hybrid warfare is much more difficult than waging it. Why hybrid warfare appears to be so successful and why some states have such a problem countering hybrid warfare are two important questions which will be covered in the next chapter. First, however, the framework of the international order must be connected to the character of hybrid warfare. As argued earlier, the contemporary international order has 'modernized' Clausewitz and modified his views to correspond with the concept of twenty-first-century warfare as understood and practiced by the guardian powers. Through the establishment of the international order, certain features of the classical trinity have been given extraordinary importance, to the point where they can be elevated to such a degree that they require distinctive recognition. There are two such elements, hence the 'trinity' has been transformed into a 'quinity' (see Figure 4).[27]

The original trinity of the people, the military and the government still applies to all sides in a hybrid conflict, particularly if the fundamental security or even existence of a state is threatened. However, hybrid warfare is not usually waged directly against powerful opponents, but rather against weaker, peripheral actors that are located on the borders of areas of strategic competition. Additionally, the character of hybrid warfare stresses opaqueness, deliberately designed to allow an actor to achieve its goals without running a very high risk of a large-scale conventional response. In the context of the international order, hybrid warfare aims to remain below the threshold of what the guardian powers would consider a clear threat. For example, Russian actions in Ukraine were aimed at a state which was not a member of either NATO or the EU, nor was it in any meaningful way an ally of any powerful states that Russia views as its competitors. If the Kremlin had seized a significant part of Poland or Estonia, that would very likely trigger a large-scale conventional response under Article 5,[28] therefore, a hybrid strategy

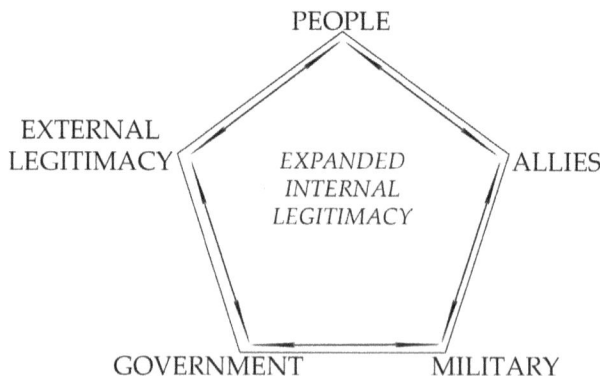

Figure 4 The quinity.

would not be appropriate. Hybrid warfare is designed to confuse and blunt the threat of a Western military intervention in an area that is clearly on the margins of its sphere of interest and which is not fully integrated into a defensive, military structure. In such a scenario, the only coercive recourse available, which would prevent the hybrid actor form achieving its goals, is a conventional military intervention, but the requirements for one are more complex than those for territorial defence or deterrence. Modern military interventions are conducted in a quinitarian, rather than a trinitarian framework, because of the constraints, political and legal, that the guardian powers have placed upon themselves and, by extension, on the system as a whole. For example, both the EU and NATO require a number of difficult conditions to be fulfilled before they would undertake an intervention, chief among them is an authorization or mandate from the United Nations Security Council (UNSC).

In the absence of a clear threat to vital interests and/or an outside mandate, the resolve of guardian powers is quickly eroded because the internal mechanisms of the trinity have been deemed insufficient. Furthermore, even if such authorization is given, there are only a handful of states that have the capabilities to carry out such an intervention. There is a clear need, indeed a requirement for additional legitimacy, which comes not only from the people 'inside' the trinity but also from the wider international system. The problem of sufficient capabilities, even among the guardian powers, requires willing allies, which also help with the issue of additional legitimacy. Both external legitimacy and the participation of allies are elements which can be found within the original trinity. However, they are considered additional assets rather than fundamental components. The decision-making of a trinitarian polity requires only internal cohesion in order to wage war. If the people support the decision to go to war and the military has the capabilities to wage it, with the government formulating the political goals, then that is all that is required. It is the framework of the quinity that has elevated additional external legitimacy and the need for allies into fully fledged prerequisites for the conduct of war.

Additional legitimacy

Legitimacy is central to the Clausewitzian trinity. The government derives its legitimacy from the people who are, in turn, protected by the government-controlled military. The military relies on the government for their legitimacy and provides protection in return. They are also the vehicle for the government's provision of protection to the people by which the government maintains its legitimacy with the people, and in turn legitimizes its own existence. This is the 'internal' legitimacy of the trinity and it suffices in a traditional sense, if the security of the state is in question; however, when faced with an external military intervention, additional legitimacy is required. This additional 'external' legitimacy, which allows the actor to respond to any kind of threat outside its own borders, must come from the outside. The sources of the external legitimacy, however, are limited to international organizations (UN, EU, OSCE, NATO, etc.) or to the wider international community as a whole (allies, friendly states or other international actors).

Before delving deeper into the concept of legitimacy, it would be beneficial to describe what the term stands for. It is a term that is widely used yet, often as not, lacks a definition. The *OED* defines legitimacy as 'conformity to the law, to rules, or to some recognized principle; lawfulness'.[29] The concept is therefore both related to, but to a degree disconnected from, the law, depending on the circumstance. At this point, it is important to note that legitimacy and legality do not have the same meaning. An action may be legal but perceived to be illegitimate or vice versa, as becomes clear if the definition of legitimacy is compared to that of legality. Turning again to the *OED*, which states that legality is 'the quality or state of being legal or in conformity with the law; lawfulness'.[30] It is interesting to note that the same *OED* entry mentions that in earlier use, the term 'legality' was synonymous with legitimacy. Precisely when the two concepts diverged is not important for this line of research, so long as the distinctions between them are taken into consideration. As with many things in IR, the particulars of any given example are often reduced to a judgement call and the distinction between legality (in international law) and legitimacy surely falls under this heading. What this means is that the two terms can often be conflated or separated, depending on the viewpoint from which one approaches them. For the purposes of the discussion in this chapter, they will be deemed to be complimentary to one another as the focus is not on the finer legal points of international law but the basic concept of the perceived legitimacy of action in the international arena.

The 2003 European Security Strategy (ESS) makes it very clear that any use of armed forces by the EU would, in principle, require a mandate from the UNSC by stating that 'the United Nations Security Council has the primary responsibility for the maintenance of international peace and security'.[31] To some degree, the EU is, in effect, trying to avoid having to make a decision on its own. In light of this, it can be surmised that the EU believes that its own legitimacy is not sufficient to allow it to intervene outside its borders. This is of course a self-imposed restraint, but it nevertheless means that the EU is at the very best slow to respond to hybrid warfare or, at worst, completely incapable of action. If one of the permanent members of the UNSC engages in hybrid warfare, as was the case with Russia in 2014, such a mandate would not be given leading to an EU handicapped by its very own rules. The legitimacy, given to the EU by the people living in it, is not enough when the EU itself is not threatened, because the public support is simply not there, nor, in the case of Russia, is there a political will to carry it out. The political character of the EU, particularly its democratic deficit, makes legitimacy in issues of war and peace deeply problematic. Interestingly, this requirement for UNSC mandate is not specifically mentioned in the 2016 EU Global Security Strategy (EUGS). However, the EUGS does commit the EU to supporting a 'strong UN as the bedrock of the multilateral rules-based order'.[32] Presumably then, any external military intervention would still require a UN mandate.

In the case of NATO, the need for UNSC authorization has never been officially articulated. However, in practice it has become a necessity. The alliance was prepared to fight a limited war in Yugoslavia in 1999 without a UNSC mandate, although it was at least partially legitimized (three months after the war started) with Resolution 1244, which established a de facto independent state of Kosovo,[33] but since then, with the experience of Iraq and Afghanistan looming large on many a member state's mind, NATO has been reluctant to repeat the scenario. When, in 2011, NATO was contemplating intervention in Libya, the requirements for legal approval were considered paramount, and the alliance only intervened once the UNSC Resolution 1973 was passed. During the parliamentary debate on Libya, the UK prime minister David Cameron presented, in no uncertain terms, which requirements must be met in order for NATO to intervene: a demonstrable need, regional support and clear legal basis.[34] These conditions were fulfilled, for example, for the 1991 Gulf War and for Libya in 2011, but have been absent in the case of Syria, leading to a lack of any meaningful coercive Western response. The reluctance of the UNSC to pass a similar resolution in part stems from NATO seriously stretching the meaning and wording of the resolution on Libya but also because of the deeper involvement of Russia.[35]

While these examples do not directly concern instances of hybrid warfare, they serve to demonstrate a clear trend. The internal legitimacy of the classical trinity is simply not considered enough. In a modern, globalized world, international legitimacy with at least tacit approval is the accepted norm, which is a double-edged sword. When it is given, it creates a very powerful mandate for intervention, but should it be withheld, the state, wishing to counter-hybrid warfare outside its own borders, finds itself constrained, regardless of the massive technological and doctrinal superiority. Another point to consider is that this kind of thinking creates a psychological 'comfort zone' for many states, peoples and other actors, who publicly clamour for action but are privately not willing to commit to it.

The same rules apply to individual states, which might wish to undertake a military intervention against an opponent employing hybrid warfare. Any state that might decide to intervene unilaterally could receive global condemnation and could potentially face economic and diplomatic sanctions. This fact can be exploited by a hybrid actor when deciding on the aims it wishes to achieve. When Hezbollah launched the 2006 war against Israel it could be fairly sure that Israel would respond in some way. When Israel responded with a large-scale conventional attack it weakened Hezbollah but it also damaged Israel's international standing, as the attack was perceived once again as the actions of an overly aggressive and bellicose state, devastating a weaker opponent.[36] A military victory was never realistically within Hezbollah's grasp, but a humiliated Israel would allow them to score at least a moral and public relations victory. The situation was, of course, a lot more complex than that, and a more in-depth examination of the 2006 Lebanon War will follow in a subsequent chapter.

Allies

Clausewitz does include possible allies as a factor in a war, but they are not central to a state's decision to wage it. In fact, he sees the alliance as something of a business deal, where the allies calculate their relative gain against a potential loss of a certain number of troops.[37] This is perhaps the most obvious point of departure for modern warfare, as opposed to early nineteenth-century warfare. Clausewitz lived and wrote his treatise at a time when national conscript armies were becoming prevalent, and every polity or state aimed to be self-sufficient in terms of manpower and war-waging resources. It was also a period of heightened nationalism and corresponding suspicions. The reliability of allies had to be taken with a certain degree of scepticism, as evidenced by his use of the phrase: 'One country may support another's cause, but will never take it so seriously as it takes its own.'[38] This is a very realist view of alliances but reflects a great deal of historical wisdom as many states have learnt to their dismay. The *OED* definition of alliance also follows roughly the same trajectory, with a healthy dose of realism. It defines an 'alliance', in a political sense, as the state or fact of being united for a common purpose or for mutual benefit, esp. of nations or states; confederation, partnership'.[39] Taking this into account, it becomes very clear that when the term 'alliance' refers to the military kind, the problems tend to multiply.

The number of large, multi-state, genuine military alliances in the world today is difficult to judge, as they can be either ad hoc groupings of states, brought together to face a common enemy or threat, or more institutionalized ones existing in peacetime. The only unquestionable example of the latter is NATO, with the Collective Security Treaty Organisation (CSTO), the Shanghai Cooperation Organisation (SCO) and the EU's Common Security and Defence Policy (CSDP), as groups, developing, in future, some kind of a military alliance structure. Ad hoc alliances tend to be much more numerous and, by their very nature, shorter in duration. Examples of such alliances are the 'coalition of the willing' during the 2003 Iraq war or the current Global Coalition to counter the Islamic State of Iraq and the Levant (ISIL), created in December 2014.[40] Smaller alliances in a more traditional sense, such as those between only two states (Anglo-Portuguese alliance, US-Japan alliance, etc.) are, of course, more numerous. While these are theoretically less susceptible to the problems associated with large alliances, they are not immune from them.

Even with today's professional armies, the cost of war is monumental, mainly due to the technology-intensive way the West fights its wars. Ironically, the number of states, which possess the capabilities for successful unilateral military intervention, has dwindled in the last two decades. By examining the defence spending of most Western states in this period as a percentage of their GDP,[41] it becomes clear that there has been an overall marked decline, leading to a diminution of capabilities. This makes it paramount to utilize the aid of allies. At this point, the quinity is at its most distant from the classical concepts of the trinity, as the reliance on allies has greatly increased in modern times. The role of allies in the expanded Clausewitzian framework is twofold, providing additional legitimacy and, most importantly, filling the gaps in capabilities. Some allies can contribute both, others can help with only one of the two options but in both cases their participation is reliant on their willingness to do so. Additionally, there are two kinds of allies any given state can turn to, long-standing, sometimes treaty-enforced allies, and ad hoc coalition allies. The combination of allies a state chooses, or is capable of rallying to its cause, depends on the circumstances of each individual case.

Even the United States, the world's greatest military power, must carefully consider any prospect of intervention alone. It might not need any help in terms of capabilities, but, always conscious of its standing in the world, it strives to build up ad hoc coalitions if its formal allies and partners prove unwilling to support it. While its security documents stress the possibility of unilateral action, it is usually only in the context of preservation of core national interests. In practice, this means that while it maintains the possibility of unilateral action, the probability of that happening is relatively low and dependant on the definitions of core and, more importantly, non-core national interest which are subject to the interpretation of the government of the day. Unfortunately for this kind of security strategy, hybrid warfare, if executed correctly, would not allow or at the very least make it very difficult for, the United States to claim that its national security is threatened enough to justify a unilateral intervention. A further analysis of the US national security posture will follow in the next chapter.

In terms of the types of allies, any state would be justified in assuming that its long-standing friends, who may be formal allies in other regions, would support it in its endeavours, but that might not always be the case. If the case for intervention was judged to lack the required proof, or the friendly states were unwilling to risk their forces for any number of different reasons, even long-standing supporters might become reluctant bystanders. Alliances like NATO would fare better in a classic trinitarian war, but when having to decide on 'out of area' operations, external to the alliance contract, it has proven itself to be very indecisive and slow to react. Ad hoc allies could be an alternative, but their support might stem from selfish reasons, that could be counterproductive or they might be unable to contribute in any meaningful way with the problem of capabilities. In some cases their international standing might be poor enough that even their endorsement might not provide enough external legitimacy.

Quinitarian and hybrid warfare

In order to summarize the arguments presented here, it might be useful to consider them from two perspectives: that of the 'target' of hybrid warfare and that of the 'user' of hybrid warfare. As stated earlier, there can be little doubt that a target state, facing an opponent using hybrid warfare against its interests, would be inclined to resort to a conventional trinitarian war to counter it. As the threat against it is relatively clear, it would, in principle, not need allies or external legitimacy in order to resist; whether it would be successful without these factors is a different matter. However, it must do so cautiously for two important reasons. First, as the case of Israel illustrates, an overly aggressive response, while operationally successful, might play into the opponents' hands. Secondly, it must also be aware that an attack from a hybrid opponent might be difficult to present clearly as an aggressive move to the international order. While the circumstances might seem clear to the target state, the international order operates on quinitarian lines and therefore requires additional proof. From the perspective of the 'user', the actor using hybrid warfare is fighting a trinitarian conflict, albeit a lower-level one. However, it must be acutely aware that its goals can only be achieved if the friends and allies of the target, as well as the guardian powers, do not react in a trinitarian way, as that could spell disaster. On the other hand, providing that the actor can successfully maintain control over the escalation of hybrid warfare, it can count on the quinitarian international order to constrain and proscribe even the target from defending itself in a trinitarian way.

For the states which are not directly involved as either users or targets of hybrid warfare, the situation is even less clear. In the absence of a direct threat, the only framework in which they can operate is quinitarian, because they face an internal legitimacy shortfall. The opaque nature of hybrid warfare means that it gives the actor that employs it a certain amount of deniability, which makes a case for intervention very difficult. The requirements for additional legitimacy could, in the absence of a clear threat, lead to no response at all, or one that would impose a price that the hybrid actor was more than willing to pay in order to achieve the set political goals. Russia seems more than willing to endure the economic sanctions imposed on it as a result of its actions in Ukraine, and Hezbollah is still a significant force in both Lebanese and Syrian politics, despite the damage inflicted on it by Israel in 2006. On the other hand, NATO and the EU face serious internal problems and disagreements on how best to proceed, and neither seem likely to assist Ukraine militarily or intervene militarily in Syria in any kind of decisive capacity, apart from the continuing air and missile strikes and Special Forces operations.[42]

An additional consideration particularly for the guardian powers is the democratic political system. Democracy is seen as the most desirable political system not only for the great powers of the international order but also for the order itself. This desire is a further reflection of the history and influence of the guardian powers in regards to the establishment of the current international order. However, with the increased erosion of the principle of sovereignty, the nature of the domestic political system of the states within the international order became an important issue. The reason why the quinitarian system evolved along the lines it has is because of the perceived need to democratize the practice of IR both by increasing the number of democratic states within the system and by modifying the nature of the system itself. While this liberal goal might sound appealing, democracy can be a significant obstacle to timely decision-making. In foreign policy, rapid action is often a necessity, and this is particularly the case when facing hybrid warfare. The two significant hallmarks of domestic democratic politics are the increase of the number of stakeholders in the decision-making process, and a desire to seek a wider consensus on issues. Both points are supposed to increase the legitimacy of the decision-making process as well as the final decision. However, in the realm of international politics, such policies can lead to slower decision-making or, in the extreme case, to a paralysation of the decision-making process on either national or supranational levels.

In a conventional military sense, the advantage in any war is normally with the defender and by employing hybrid warfare an actor places itself in a position of tactical offensive, but strategic defence. This is not a new invention, as the primacy of the defence has been a feature of the art of war since at least the development of gunpowder. In terms of hybrid warfare, it has so far proven to be somewhat successful. By applying the offensive strength of hybrid warfare against a weaker opponent, while simultaneously taking up a strong strategic defensive position vis-à-vis the broader international order, the actor has the opportunity not only to achieve its goals but to do so at a relatively low price. This makes hybrid warfare not only militarily useful but economically practical, a point that will be developed further in the next chapter.

In summary, to grasp the full implications of the phenomenon of hybrid warfare, the traditional concept of the trinity is no longer sufficient. The international order, through its guardian powers, has developed a framework which has given increased salience to the features of legitimacy and alliance. Therefore, every actor within the system has to operate with two parallel frameworks, internal and external. The original trinity is internal to an individual actor, be it state or non-state. However, the external framework, the quinity, supersedes the internal one through its adoption and application as part of the international order itself. The additional legitimacy can only be granted through the mechanisms and bodies of the system, such as UNSC mandates or widespread popular support. It is also much more likely to be given, if it delivers legitimacy to an action that supports the continuation of the international order and can be shown to be in response to a credible and undeniable threat. The problem of additional legitimacy can be mitigated with allies, old or new, which automatically bring some additional legitimacy with them. However, their chief value lies in their ability to support or complement the coercive capabilities of a target actor, or a guardian power acting on behalf of that actor.

At its core, hybrid warfare is purely trinitarian. In essence, it represents a type of coercion that has been prominent and accepted in the international system from its creation. However, because it must now be conducted in a quinitarian environment, it must endeavour to be opaque. The actor that employs it is doing so in a Clausewitzian manner towards the target, requiring nothing but the internal legitimacy fundamental to the trinity. Simultaneously, it is taking advantage of the quinitarian restrictions which affect the rest of the world, potentially also including the target of hybrid warfare. Based on the earlier analysis, it can be argued that hybrid warfare represents the most efficient way of challenging the international order and its guardians without having to completely destroy the system itself. Since the guardian powers will only conduct a military intervention if the quinitarian requirements are met, the hybrid opponent can pursue their own goals with relatively little risk, providing that the conflict does not escalate to the point where it would become a profound challenge to the vital interests of the system and its guardians.

4

Hybrid warfare strategy

The previous chapter placed the concept of hybrid warfare in a wider theoretical framework in order to understand its principle ideas. This chapter will build on that foundation in order to examine what makes a hybrid strategy so effective and why conventional military structures find it so difficult to identify and deal with it. In short, it will establish the basic principles of hybrid warfare strategy and extrapolate a unified theory of hybrid warfare. Structurally, the chapter is intended to bridge the gap between the theoretical approaches of the preceding chapters and the case study chapters which will follow. Its purpose is to operationalize the theoretical framework by combining it with a review of the defence policies of the leading great powers within the international order. The states and organizations that will be examined more closely have primarily been selected because they have faced, are facing or in the near future could face, opponents utilizing hybrid warfare. Other considerations for selection include their role as guardian powers in the international order (both globally and regionally) and a desire to expand the concept of hybrid warfare somewhat outside its Euro-centric origins.

This chapter will examine policymaking and defence planning in order to answer two crucial questions: Why do conventional military structures find it so difficult to deal with hybrid warfare, and, which are the identifying characteristics of hybrid warfare? An overview of defence planning will identify 'weak spots' which a hybrid strategy aims to exploit. These 'weak spots' can be either political or doctrinal or related to capabilities. The chapter will begin with the United States and the United Kingdom before broadening its purview to include NATO. After that the focus will shift away from the North Atlantic area to the Middle East and Israel, followed by Russia and Japan. Collectively, these actors represent the bulk of military and political power either globally or in their respective regions. In order to arrive at an informed conclusion, the chapter will look at how these states define, or whether they define, hybrid warfare and how this definition affects their policymaking. Defence spending is another vital component of this examination, coupled with a review of existing doctrines; using both as tools in order to discover whether the policy declarations or definitions have translated into practical security policies and actions and, if so, whether anything has been learnt from the experience. The last part of the chapter will bring all the elements together, both from this and the preceding chapter, in order to formulate a theory of hybrid warfare.

The definition of hybrid warfare, proposed in the second chapter, reveals two distinct parts. The first deals with the recognizable characteristics, which make hybrid warfare what it is. The second part focuses on the reasons for an actor resorting to hybrid warfare. The characteristic blend of conventional and unconventional warfare enables the actor to exploit an opponent's strategic or doctrinal weakness while maintaining deniability and strategic surprise. It is precisely to this part of the definition that the current chapter will turn, examining precisely the weaknesses that hybrid warfare targets.

Security strategy and defence planning

When examining different security strategies and defence plans, official documents are the usual primary sources. For the individual states, this means national security strategies and other similar documents, as well as statements from leading political and military figures and prominent citizens. In the case of NATO, strategic concepts and the views of individual officials and member states fulfil the needs, respectively. There is little value in examining outdated documents, as the concept of hybrid warfare is relatively recent. The time frame for this examination, therefore, will loosely correspond to the time frame in which hybrid warfare is deemed to have developed: from the beginning of the 1990s to the present day. Emphasis will be given to more recent works, while earlier documents will be used to provide a context for them.

At this point, it is necessary to make an important point. Formulation of security strategies (either military or grand strategies) and defence planning in general is rightly considered to be, hopefully educated, guesswork.[1] These documents are future-oriented and, as is the nature of strategy, there are simply too many unknowns for them to be considered objectively reliable. However, they provide a guide towards new concepts and emerging threats. They also provide official insight into the thinking about new phenomena and the methods of tackling them. Therefore, while they can never be considered completely reliable or above criticism, they are nevertheless useful tools for an examination of trends and threads in defence planning. The term 'defence planning' itself can be contentious; however, for the purposes of this book, Gray's definition will be used, which defines defence planning as 'preparations for the defence of a polity in the future (near-, medium- and far-term)'.[2] Although brief, this definition provides the best and most coherent understanding of the term.

United States

As with all global or regional security matters, special attention should always be given to the United States, since its breadth of capabilities, doctrinal depth and military strength make it an important actor. But even a superpower is not without its weak spots and identifying those is crucial in order to build a counter-hybrid strategy – a task that will be examined in the final chapter of this book.

The primary document, outlining US national security goals is the National Security Strategy (NSS). Generally published every few years (although by law it should be presented each year) by the sitting president, it presents the US view of the world and identifies current and upcoming threats, followed by a review of national goals and aims. Additional information will be extracted from the Quadrennial Defense Review (QDR) published every four years from 1997 to 2014, and the 1993 Bottom-Up Review that preceded the QDR. As a document that presents the official US military doctrine and defence policy and planning, it is crucial to the examination of past operational and strategic planning and offers a useful insight into the debate surrounding funding and capabilities of the US armed forces. The latest, 2018 QDR, has been renamed the National Defense Strategy (NDS) and is now a classified document. Therefore, the non-classified summary of the NDS will be used.

After the Second World War, the United States debated what role it should play in the largely war-torn and increasingly ideologically charged world. With the Truman Doctrine of 1947, the United States essentially became a global superpower.[3] Since much of the global trade, production and finance relied almost exclusively on the industrial potential of the United States, this was a role that the country could fill quite easily. Nevertheless, one huge challenge remained. What was to be done with the expansionist and imperial appetites of the Soviet Union? In the now famous NSC 68 Directive, Truman set the course for US policy that would last for the next four decades. Containment became the grand strategy of the day and along with it came various other policy priorities that were necessary in order for the policy of containment to be successful. Among the most important policies set forward in NSC 68 are the increase in military funding and capabilities, increasing US military presence in vital areas around the world and actively preventing the spread of communism, primarily in Europe but also across the rest of the world.[4] Not only were these policies to prove crucial to the conduct of the Cold War, but they also continue, to a varying degree, to underpin US strategy to the present day. Containment might have officially ended with President Clinton's policy of 'Engagement and Enlargement', but it still holds relevance.

Perhaps the most enduring legacy from the 1940s has been the 'two wars' doctrine, the principle of which is that the United States should at any time be able simultaneously to conduct two large-scale wars in two different parts of the world. The historical roots of this doctrine emanate from the US experience in the Second World War. Being a continental power, the United States had to fight essentially expeditionary wars across both the Atlantic and Pacific oceans simultaneously, against two determined and quite different opponents (Germany and Japan, respectively). The policy of containment was not explicitly focused around the two wars strategy, but it did gear the United States towards fighting a direct war against the Soviet Union or communist China, or both, while at the same time retaining the capability to intervene in another part of the world in order to deny the opposing block the possibility of distracting the United States with a conflict in one area in order to make gains in another.[5] The 'two wars' doctrine has remained the core guiding principle in US defence till the present day and therefore is an important factor to consider when examining the US position regarding modern hybrid threats.

With the fall of the Berlin Wall in 1989 a sense prevailed in US defence thinking that new policies were required, but no clear answers could be quickly given as to what those might be.[6] There was a clear shift towards a more UN-centric internationalism with emphasis on cooperation and peacekeeping, largely as a result of the 1990–1 Gulf War caused a perceptual shift towards regional security threats. The 'unipolar moment' had come but few were ready and willing to exploit it.[7] As the significance of the events of the early 1990s sank in, it is understandable that some degree of reflection was in order. As such, some Cold War policies continued, albeit in a slightly modified form. The perceived new security environment and resulting significant reductions in defence budgets under President Clinton, dropping from 4.3 per cent of GDP in 1993 to 2.9 per cent in 2001,[8] meant that the two wars policy had to be revised, but not abandoned. Under President Clinton, a new term, 'Major Regional Conflicts' (MRC), emerged, which also reflected the shift from a global Soviet threat to regional threats posed by regional powers.[9] What precisely constitutes an MRC was not made clear and has therefore been open to interpretation, but they can be thought of as essentially smaller-scale interventions. It is a move away from the massive Second World War, Korean War and the Vietnam War interventions and closer to Gulf War-sized conflicts or peacekeeping missions. Examples of such conflicts can be Somalia, Haiti, Bosnia, Iraq (both 1991 and 2003), Afghanistan and the partial interventions in Libya and Syria.

The early 2000s saw a shift towards a more proactive stance in US thinking, embodied in the principles of preventative and pre-emptive self-defence as presented in George W. Bush's 2002 NSS.[10] This period also marked the beginning of the Global War on Terror (GWOT) which led to the US invasions of Afghanistan (2001) and Iraq (2003). The accompanying 2001 QDR was mostly written before the terrorist attacks on 9/11 but was still influenced by it.[11] It acknowledged the trend towards conflicts with non-state or failed state actors and called for a new form of deterrence that was required in order to deal with these threats. Perhaps the most innovative aspect of it was the so-called capabilities-based approach to defence. No longer would the United States plan against specific threats from specific actors, but rather it would focus on how an adversary would fight, regardless of its identity and location.[12] While in principle such a step was in keeping with the times and the rise of transnational terrorism, it creates a very broad strategic dilemma. The ways in which an opponent could challenge the United States or its allies are numerous; therefore, rather than slimming down the decision-making and defence planning, it tasked the US armed forces with having to prepare for any and all eventualities. The US Army's Full-Spectrum Operations doctrine is one aspect of this policy and is, as mentioned before, too broad to be of much use in dealing with future challenges.[13]

The first major US national security document to mention hybrid threats was the 2010 QDR.[14] While not providing a definition, it is nevertheless significant that the premier military force in the world has recognized the blurring of the lines between modes of warfare. While it is similar to other preceding QDRs in many regards, it is important for the development of the two wars doctrine in two ways. It provided a brief definition of what an MRC actually is,[15] and it proposed the notion that in the future preparing for such conflicts might not be enough. Simultaneous MRCs in Afghanistan and Iraq were the first examples of such operations since the introduction of the policy. The conflicts stretched US military capabilities to and beyond their limits, raising questions over the efficacy of the MRC policy and whether a different approach could be adopted, particularly one which de-emphasize purely military victories in conflicts which were not wholly conventional.[16] Coupled with the earlier nod to hybrid operations as the possible future template, this can be seen as a big step towards re-orientating the US defence planning towards different types of conflicts while recognizing that maintaining capabilities to fight two MRCs in different areas of the world is fundamental to the US global ambitions.

The 2014 QDR and the 2015 NSS are much more managerial in their tone, focusing more on fiscal restraints and budgetary issues. A further decrease in defence spending in the United States, down from 4.7 per cent of GDP in 2010 to 3.3 per cent in 2015,[17] reflected a perceived post-conflict return to peacetime operations (officially the wars in Afghanistan and Iraq ended in 2014[18] and 2011,[19] respectively). Such constraint was reflected in the constriction of the two wars doctrine. The 2014 QDR discusses more of a 'one and a half' MRCs.[20] Additionally, while maintaining the possibility of 'hybrid contingencies', the 2014 QDR once again focused more on conventional threats, most likely as a result of the 'pivot to Asia' policy. While the document acknowledged that the US armed forces would no longer be large enough for prolonged stability operations, it aims to preserve expertise gained in the decade of counterinsurgency and stability operations in the Middle East. Unfortunately, drastically downsizing forces is usually not the best way to preserve such knowledge as the post-Vietnam War era demonstrates.

The 2015 NSS was even more ambiguous regarding military action. It still emphasized US global leadership,[21] while offering very little in terms of concrete options. It strongly emphasized deterrence, largely due to budgetary restrictions, although various documents, including past NSSs, as discussed earlier, have pointed out that new threats from non-state actors or regional powers might be difficult to deter. Hybrid warfare, in particular, which was not mentioned at all, is designed to get around the rules of deterrence. The document offered no solution to his problem, barring some very broad policy goals.[22] While grandiose sentiment is pertinent due to the nature of the document, it represented a backward step in a world in which many actors are quickly catching up to the United States in terms of capabilities. Of course, US forces should be capable of dealing with as many potential threats as can be reasonably foreseen and should, to an extent, be full-spectrum forces. However, such forces can only be effective if they are of a reasonable size.

The latest pair of policy documents, the 2017 NSS and the 2018 NDS, is significantly better in terms of clearly recognizing this emerging US weak spot, which is also a clear sign of the drift towards a more multipolar world. The 2017 NSS does not categorically state that the United States will unilaterally pursue its goals and is somewhat more open to the notion of engagement through international institutions. However, it also makes clear that this might not apply in situations where US core national interests are threatened.[23] In a much more realistic appraisal of the contemporary world, it singles out China and Russia as strategic threats and lists them as the top priorities in the new 'competitive world'.[24] North Korea and Iran are also specifically mentioned as threats, particularly in their pursuit of a nuclear programme. Interestingly, the 2017 NSS points out that the attempted engagement and inclusion of competitors (including the four aforementioned states) in the institutions of the international system has, to a large degree, failed to persuade them to become responsible members of the international order.[25]

The 2018 NDS represents the latest incarnation of the QDR. Unfortunately, as it has now become a classified document only the summary is available for analysis. In keeping with the tradition that the defence policy documents are much more practically oriented than the NSS, the executive summary of the 2018 NDS is even more so. It clearly identifies that the US position vis-à-vis the rest of the world has weakened in relative terms, but it claims that the United States is now pursuing actively policies which aim to bring an end to the period of 'strategy atrophy'.[26] The document points out that the security environment is much more violent and complex, with many actors wishing to challenge the rules-based international order.[27] Of particular importance is the call for the formation of the Joint Force which would be capable to match newly re-emerged strategic competition, rapid dispersion of technologies and 'new concepts of warfare and competition that span the entire spectrum of conflict'.[28] While not specifically mentioning hybrid warfare, it would seem to include hybrid as one of the new concepts of war to which it is referring. This assumption is based on the part of the 'strategic analysis' segment of the 2018 NDS, which includes the paragraph describing that

> both revisionist powers and rogue regimes are *competing across all dimensions of power*. They have increased efforts *short of armed conflict* by expanding coercion to new fronts, violating principles of sovereignty, exploding ambiguity, and *deliberately blurring the lines between civil and military goals*. (emphasis added)[29]

Much like its complementary NSS, the 2018 NDS also makes references to Russia and China but goes further and refers to them as 'revisionist powers' which are 'undermining the international order from within the system by exploiting its benefits while simultaneously undercutting its principles and "rules of the road".[30] This categorization clearly fits within the quinitarian understanding of the international order proposed in the previous chapter. The 'two wars' doctrine also appears to have been slightly modified. The document envisions the US Joint Force as capable of defeating aggression by a major power while simultaneously deterring opportunistic aggression elsewhere. It also adds a third task, that of disrupting imminent terrorist and weapons of mass destruction (WMD) threats.[31] The latter addition is interesting because, during peacetime, the US forces are tasked with degrading such threats. Its inclusion in the wartime posture section of priorities suggests that the United States is willing to be a troubleshooter and aggressively act against terrorist threats or WMD use, possibly in addition to fighting one major war and one or more minor conflicts. This section is presumably aimed at Iran and North Korea, and designed to signal that, no matter what other contingencies may occupy its forces, the United States will aim to have the capabilities to strike rapidly against such threats.

United Kingdom

The UK's strategic position both inside and outside Europe gives it a unique perspective on security matters. Coupled with a long and distinguished military record, its views and policies carry a lot of weight. The long-acclaimed expertise in counterinsurgency operations that the UK has built up is also an interesting starting point for an examination of how it deals with hybrid warfare. For a state that has grasped the principles of COIN better, perhaps, than any other, it becomes vital to apply that knowledge to a mode of war that shares some elements with insurgency.

UK defence planning is centred on the NSS. Up till now, only three such documents have been published (2008, 2010 and 2015), reflecting a more US-style approach to high security policy documents. Before that the key UK defence documents were Defence White Papers, published at irregular intervals. As there is no statutory requirement for the creation and publication of these documents, they appear on an as-needed basis. Some of them[32] are merely budgetary corrections or individual policy proclamations, rather than full-scale strategic documents. While some information from them will be used as part of the argument presented here, these documents will not form the backbone of the research.

The early 1990s saw the UK following in broadly a similar path to the US documents, examined earlier. The three major strategic priorities were a strategic nuclear deterrent, effective defence of the UK and the defence of Europe.[33] In addition to the radical restructuring, as a result of budgetary and personnel cuts, it was also the start of a transformation towards capability-based rather than a threats-based policy.[34] Overall, the proposed reforms aimed at creating smaller, more flexible, professional forces.[35] In this respect the UK seems to have been a few years ahead of the United States, and was faster to exploit the 'peace dividend' following the end of the Cold War.

The first major fully post-Cold War review was the 1998 Strategic Defence Review (SDR). It was a document designed in an uncertain security environment, though not stemming from the Cold War but rather from regional, multi-centric threats. The report outlined that the three core interests of the UK are in European security relations, safety of international trade and the maintenance of international stability.[36] In order to sustain these interests the SDR moved towards amphibious expeditionary forces and greater interoperability between services. While asymmetrical and terrorist threats are mentioned, they are largely related to Northern Ireland.[37] In other theatres terrorism does not receive much attention, nor is there any mention of hybrid warfare or insurgencies. The SDR was essentially focused on conventional, state-centric threats (including terrorism and state collapse).[38] Military strategy was still based on experience from the 1982 Falklands War, the 1990 Gulf War and the 1992–5 Bosnian War. The *2004 Defence White Paper* further developed that point by steering the armed forces towards counterterrorism and peacekeeping operations, while maintaining (at some notice) the capability to conduct a *Telic*[39]-sized operation. Such operations would need the cooperation and support of the United States or other partners, such as NATO, the EU, or ad hoc coalitions (but usually under US leadership).[40]

The first UK NSS was published in 2008. It largely continued the policies set out before, with terrorism as the number one threat, followed by WMD proliferation and organized crime. Interestingly, the more traditional threats such as global instability and conflict and state-led threats are relegated to lower ranks although the document points out in several places that such threats must not be forgotten.[41] In terms of capabilities, there is, again, a clear move towards more multilateral action through international organizations (UN, EU, NATO) although unlike the *2004 White Paper*, it still maintained that the UK should retain sufficient capabilities for unilateral action.[42] Despite experiences in Afghanistan and Iraq, there was no mention of asymmetrical threats, insurgency and counterinsurgency, or hybrid warfare.

The 2010 NSS and the accompanying Strategic Defence and Security Review (SDSR) were more evolutionary documents. The shift towards multilateralism of previous papers is retained, but there is a return to more traditional power-oriented thinking. While terrorism remained the top threat, the second place was assigned to cyberattacks, a reaction to modern computer-based warfare. International military crises followed with accidents or natural hazards placed at the end.[43] The strategic context had also been expanded, with the risk of destabilizing insurgencies and transnational terrorist groups identified as the most prominent causes of destabilization and consequentially conflict.[44] In order to address these issues, the UK Armed Forces were to be reorganized again, mostly on similar lines as before, stressing the expeditionary character of future conflicts as well as their regional scale.[45]

The most recent document under examination is the 2015 NSS and SDSR. It is also the first UK national security document to discuss hybrid warfare. The document itself sets rather ambitious terms in the foreword, relaying the UK's commitment to a number of set goals, such as the 2 per cent GDP spending on defence required by NATO.[46] Although this does not represent a relative rise from 2014, in real terms it is actually an increase. In fact, even though the UK defence budget has been shrinking as the wars in Afghanistan and Iraq have wound down (down from 2.5 per cent GDP in 2008 to 2 per cent in 2014), this also coincided with the rebalancing of the global and national economies following the 2008 financial crisis. If one compares the numerical values between 2008 and 2015, £3.76 billion and £3.64 billion, respectively, this represents a much smaller decrease than the 0.5 per cent of GDP would suggest.[47]

The three core national security objectives broadly identified are: protecting British citizens, projecting global influence and promoting prosperity.[48] Contextually, the challenges these objectives must face are very similar to the 2010 list, but with the resurgence of state-based threats coming in at number two on the list as a result of Russian actions in Ukraine in 2014. The crisis also caused, for the first time, the appearance of the term 'hybrid tactics' in UK defence documents.[49] Uniquely in Western policy documents, the UK also created the first military unit specializing in counter-hybrid warfare, the 77 Brigade.[50] While the document mentions hybrid, it does not provide any clear definition of the term, merely a list of some of its possible components.[51]

Israel

Israel is included in this list because it represents one of the first actors that encountered hybrid warfare. Although a more detailed examination of the 2006 Second Lebanon War will follow in the next chapter, at this point the current parameters will be examined. Its experience of dealing with non-state actors is undeniable as is its ability to keep the unfriendly surrounding states at bay, but the question arises: Can Israel successfully combine the two in the face of the hybrid threat?

Documents pertaining to Israel's security policy and defence planning are confidential. Until the publication of the 'IDF Doctrine' in 2015, no official security strategy had ever been published; in fact the State of Israel does not seem to have had a formal, written national security doctrine since its first prime minister David Ben-Gurion.[52] This presents a number of challenges to the analysis of Israeli defence planning, so the focus here will be on documents and articles published by other organizations, primarily the Institute for National Security Studies (INSS) and the Washington Institute, as well as selected media outlets. For the only available primary source, the 2015 IDF Doctrine, we will be relying on the only readily available English translation published by the Journal of Palestinian Studies, a publication of the Institute for Palestinian Studies (IPS).[53] As a state that has faced hybrid warfare in the 2006 Lebanon War, Israel's inclusion in this chapter is crucial to the examination of the concept, the scarcity of primary documents notwithstanding.

Prior to the 2006 Lebanon War, the IDF were developing a new military doctrine (the process began as far back as 1995[54]), which was signed into effect by the Chief of the General Staff mere months before hostilities erupted.[55] This doctrine was based around the concept of Systemic Operational Design (SOD), stemming from work initiated by the Operational Theory Research Institute (OTRI), and it incorporated principles of Effects-Based Operations (EBO), building on the US doctrine at the time. However, while EBO was included in US military doctrine,[56] SOD was not and has fallen under severe scrutiny and criticism, partly because of the performance of the IDF.[57] SOD was a Foucaultian post-structuralist-based approach, coupled with systems theory and philosophy. It emphasized the re-framing of the concept of warfare in an epistemological and holistic way based on the principles of the General System Theory and its proponents claimed it rendered classical military theory irrelevant.[58] SOD has been presented as a philosophical, as opposed to a scientific or technical, concept which helps its user to understand the non-linear nature of conflict which creates an indestructible system. Such systems, according to SOD can only be upset or interrupted which means that the traditional 'linear' view of warfare is ineffective against them. In practice, this meant that SOD sought to introduce a completely new vocabulary and a more philosophical way of operational and strategic planning.[59] As such it seemed to have been of little use to battlefield commanders and political leaders during the 2006 conflict, although its chief architect claims that it was not the concept itself to blame, but the attitude and approach of the majority of IDF's field commanders.[60] The concept appears over-complicated and philosophical, driven by etymological and psychological theories rather than no-nonsense pragmatism, which would indicate that it might not be the best foundation on which to build a military doctrine. Partly as a result of this, the conduct and performance of the IDF in the 2006 War was severely criticized.[61] Unfortunately, there is no official copy of the document(s), so it is almost impossible to discover what the actual IDF version of SOD was like. Shimon Naveh, one of the chief designers and head of OTRI from 1995 to its dissolution in 2006, pointed out that while SOD theory was the basis of the defence doctrine, it was never fully integrated into it.[62]

Some years later, in 2015, the Chief of General Staff LTG Gadi Eisenkot released the first public document relating to national security planning and military doctrine. Variously called the Eisenkot Document or the Gideon doctrine – Gideon being the name of the classified five-year plan for IDF long-term strategic and budgetary planning, but officially titled as 'IDF Strategy' – it represents a significant departure from previous Israeli security policy, provides more clarity and insight, and aids external examination of IDF doctrine. Unlike other policy documents discussed earlier, the IDF Strategy is very straightforward. It is also not a typical 'Western' NSS. The key identified threats are hostile or failing states, sub-state organization and terrorist groups. Hostile states are further divided into distant (Iran) and near (Lebanon), while failing states or states in the process of breaking down refer to Syria. Sub-state organizations (linked to a particular identified state) are Hezbollah and Hamas, while other groups are listed as terrorist groups unaffiliated with a particular state or community (including ISIS).[63] The goals, listed in the document, are very broad and exactly what any such document would refer to, the secure, prosperous and resilient State of Israel, which has good international standing as exists in peace.[64] The strategy is relatively well deserving of its name, as it attempts to connect the goals with the available means in the light of the listed threats, which is the fundamental basis of any strategy.

While the majority of the document is similar in structure and wording to the US NSS and the QDR, there are several aspects that are unique to Israel's geo-strategic and political situation. There is an accepted assumption that Israel should unilaterally use military force whenever the situation demands it. This is evident throughout the document. In terms of military strategy, while deterrence and a reliance on defensive security strategy are heralded as the primary pillars of Israel's security, the document recognizes that defence alone cannot defeat or successfully deter all threats and that offensive military strategy is just as important.[65] Offensive actions take priority in the kind of future conflict that the document predicts, with a greater reliance on manoeuvre as opposed to firepower (reflecting lessons from the 2006 Lebanon War) and greater emphasis on surprise operations (using Special Forces). All of this is underlined by the continuing need for a qualitative and technological edge as well as critical mass of the required capabilities.[66] When dealing with countries that do not share a border with Israel, widely assumed to refer primarily to Iran, Israel should maintain the capabilities and reserve the right to carry out pre-emptive strikes.[67]

Interestingly, there is a strong emphasis on the preservation and improvement of Israel's international standing and the importance of legitimacy. When referring to offensive military action,[68] planning of operations[69] or dealing with Western countries,[70] there is an imperative that the legitimacy of such actions must be taken into account from beginning to end. There is a whole section of the strategy dedicated to achieving and preserving legitimacy. This reflects Israel's experience with the reaction of the international community to its actions in the conflicts with Hamas and Hezbollah, as well as the observation that its opponents might take advantage of such a situation. Article 34 illustrates this clearly when it states: 'The enemy is also active in nonmilitary-kinetic dimensions, and in the past has managed to offset IDF gains in these fields. There are defensive and offensive aspects to this campaign. It seeks to generate legitimacy for Israel (including freedom of action for the IDF), while simultaneously delegitimizing the enemy (and thus restricting its actions).'[71]

While the document does not mention hybrid warfare per se, it is written with the experience of the 2006 Lebanon War in mind and, therefore, does attempt to address some difficulties associated with hybrid warfare. First, while the state threat is still present, it has been given a reduced importance, with the IDF focusing on state-sponsored or non-state actors. Cyber warfare has a strong presence throughout the document and is an important part of both defensive and offensive strategies, including the media aspect of it. The most important observation, however, is that Israel's opponents have moved from state-based Arab nationalist movements with regular armies to a combination of regular, guerrilla and terrorist operations, and a supplementary 'soft' campaign.[72] Such a mixture of capabilities is consistent with the definition of hybrid warfare put forward by this book, a point that will be examined in more depth in the final part of this chapter.

Russia

Russia is in a unique position as an international actor, having been both the target (Chechnya) and a practitioner of hybrid warfare (Ukraine). As such it is *the* crucial actor to examine in order to identify both sides of the hybrid warfare concept. Being both a European and an Asian power, it is also a useful point of comparison between Western and Eastern approaches to warfare.

The Russian Federation has published four (1997, 2000, 2009, 2015) national security strategies since the dissolution of the Soviet Union in 1991. Particular emphasis will be given to those of 1997 and 2000, since they coincide with the First and Second Chechen Wars, conflicts that have some hallmarks of hybrid warfare. Comparing how Russia viewed security threats before and after the conflict in its national defence publications will be of great use.

The 1997 Russian National Security Blueprint was the first strategy document to be published after the tumultuous period following the end of the Cold War. It begins by outlining the transition towards a multipolar world order which, it claims, will be a lengthy process. It then immediately adopts a counter-unipolar moment rhetoric by warning against attempts to make changes to the international order on the basis of one-sided policies. Part of this process is the perceived threat of NATO expansion into Eastern Europe.[73] When compared to the US NSS of roughly the same period, it becomes evident that they are almost diametrically opposed to one another. While both recognize the change in the geopolitical situation, the perceptions of what it means are radically different.

Threatening the pace of important reforms, as well as Russian security in general, is a somewhat long list of threats, chief among which are economic and social. Even in terms of the numbers of words, socio-economic threats outweigh the more traditional defence and IR threats by about two to one, indicating the importance of the perilous economic situation in which Russia found itself and the corresponding societal pressures. Inter-ethnic relations and social polarization, as well as an unfavourable demographic structure, are seen as the primary worries, next to the economic ails. Internationally, Russia wants to maintain its influence, particularly in the near abroad (Eastern Europe, Near East, Transcaucasus and Central Asia). The list of defence threats is relatively standard for the time, recognizing the diminished threat of interstate violence and focusing on WMD proliferation and low-level conflicts near its borders, without mentioning any region in particular. There is no mention of Chechnya and only a brief mention of terrorism as an emerging threat, which is unusual considering that the First Chechen War predates the document.[74]

The 2000 National Security Concept of the Russian Federation is more focused on classic strategic matters. The narrative of the changing multipolar world is abandoned, replaced by a worry about the US-dominated international system, 'designed for unilateral solutions (primarily by the use of military force)'.[75] This position is somewhat ironic, since Russia unilaterally intervened in Chechnya during the course of the First and Second Chechen Wars in 1994–6 and 1999–2000 respectively, although the latter was more of an internal intervention since the breakaway Chechen Republic was not internationally recognized and operations therefore took place inside Russia. The Security Concept was written and published while operations were still under way in Chechnya and can therefore be considered something of a war document. The circumstances and timing of its creation are broadly similar to the later 2002 Bush NSS. The Second Chechen War was triggered by a number of terrorist attacks in Russia, and as a consequence the Security Concept lists terrorism as a major threat, although socio-economic threats are still given more attention.[76] National interests remain largely the same but there is a peppering of references to terrorism and its dangers. There is also a continuation of commitments to the near abroad as well as worries about NATO. This policy reflects not only NATO enlargement but also actions in Yugoslavia and Kosovo. Russia sees this as a dangerous attempt at destabilizing the international system as a whole and a return of state-based threats. Additionally, there is a general trend throughout the document of downplaying the importance of international organizations.[77]

While both the 1997 Blueprint and the 2000 Concept are mostly short- to medium-term documents, the 2009 NSS has a more long-term outlook. Officially titled 'Russia's National Security Strategy to 2020', it attempts to establish a long-term basis for policy decision-making based on the idea that the uncertain times have passed, and such commitments can now be undertaken. However, in terms of goals and national issues, not much is new. Terrorism once again receives less attention and no new specific threats are mentioned. Even so, there are two interesting developments that can be observed: the use of energy resources as a strategic bargaining chip and a tendency to elevate nationalism to a strategic element. Energy issues are identified as both a strength and a threat to Russian security.[78] This indicates sound reasoning given the rising demand at the time and certainly provided Russia with some long-term guidance in terms of focusing on energy, as well as the importance of the Arctic, which to a lesser or greater extent was ignored by other major powers. Competition over sources of energy was identified as a possible threat to Russia.[79] The economic sections of the strategy are still vast and economic growth is deemed important not only because of beneficial financial effects but also in terms of prestige.[80] Although it does not categorically list trade in oil and gas as potential diplomatic leverage, the importance of energy identified in the strategy coupled with large Russian reserves did make such a policy a viable one.

While the importance of national culture and philosophy has been included in all previous strategic documents, as noted earlier, the 2009 Strategy builds on that by elaborating that 'authentically Russian ideals and spirituality are being born, alongside a dignified attitude to historical memory'.[81] When considered alongside the importance of energy, it is clearly a sign that Russia sees itself as a global power in a multipolar world with distinctive and important cultural contributions; a posture that is further reinforced with military power. Militarily, the 2009 Strategy is more evolutionary than revolutionary. All the principles of national defence are identical to previous ones. The only difference is a major restructuring of the regional deployment and recruitment organization of the armed forces. The strategy also requires the increase in numbers of higher readiness and active duty divisions that are available for rapid response to crisis.[82] This reflects the improved status of the Russian economy as well as experience from the 2008 Georgian War. The strategy also lists the 'departure from international agreements pertaining to arms limitation and reduction'[83] as a threat; a response to the 2002 decision by US president George Bush to withdraw from the 1972 Anti-Ballistic Missile (ABM) Treaty.

The latest policy document, *The Russian Federation's National Security Strategy*, was approved on 31 December 2015 and published in early 2016. In the time between 2009 and 2015 three important changes have taken place: the Ukrainian crisis, the seizure of Crimea and the resulting economic sanctions, and the immigration flow crisis in Europe. All of these receive some mention in the document, but otherwise it is more or less identical to the previous one, the only significant difference being a more aggressive wording and general approach to dealing with the actions of NATO and the United States.[84] Chief among the developments was the 2014 Ukrainian crisis, which not only destabilized a neighbouring country but also prompted a Russian military intervention to seize the Crimean peninsula. As a result of this, the United States and the EU enacted a series of economic sanctions against Russia and began supporting the allegedly pro-European government in Kiev. At the same time, Europe experienced an enormous influx of immigrants from the Middle East as a result of the escalating conflicts in the region.

Identifying the US/EU actions before, during and after the start of the 2014 Ukrainian crisis as a major threat to Russian security has led the Russian

Federation to adopt a much less friendly attitude towards the Eastern European near abroad in the strategy. As Russia sees these states (Belarus, Ukraine and Moldova) as firmly within its sphere of influence it attempted to create a more integrated regional block, similar to the EU. However, perceived Western interference was the chief culprit when those plans did not come to full fruition.[85] Such rhetoric is not uncommon in Russian security documents, but the Russian reasoning for an increased military posture becomes clearer when added to the, not completely unfounded, allegation that the West has practised overthrowing domestically legitimate political regimes and provoked intrastate instability.[86]

Another interesting development is the beginning of a closer relationship 'of all-embracing partnership and strategic cooperation'[87] with China. This is likely as a result of US/EU sanctions and a degree of isolationism towards Russia. The strategy is oriented quite significantly towards economic and political relations with Central and Far Eastern states, while Europe and the Middle East are mentioned more often in the threat sections. Militarily, there is a commitment to ongoing reforms and a general increase in readiness, but not clear articulation of targets or capabilities. There are no mentions of hybrid warfare or insurgencies and only passing general references to terrorism. The focus of the document is clearly on state-based threats.

All Russian national security strategies are very general documents, and even the supplementary military doctrine publications do not offer much clarification. Most high-level policies are still classified and only approved for limited publication, so precise defence planning is often difficult to ascertain from primary sources. The real-world application of these policies, particularly as they pertain to hybrid warfare, will be examined in depth in a subsequent chapter.

Japan

The inclusion of Japan on this list is a decision made in anticipation of the future. As a subsequent chapter will examine the possibility of hybrid warfare in the South China Sea, the position of Japan is very important. Its armed forces are not a wholly Western military organization, a trait it shares with Israel, but it is often seen as part of the geopolitical Western world. How it deals with hybrid warfare could illustrate the advantages and disadvantages of a different cultural and philosophical approach to war and the strategic environment. It also represents the state in East Asia with the most organized and publicly accessible defence planning publications. The issue of Chinese defence planning will be covered in the South China Sea case study chapter.

Until recently, Japan did not have a formal national security policy since Article 9 of the Japanese constitution, the so-called Peace Constitution, renounces Japan's right to fight wars and prohibits it from maintaining military forces.[88] When combined with the US-Japanese alliance, such a peaceful disposition made sense for almost sixty years. In more recent times, however, the relative decline of US power in Asia, coupled with an assertive China, has caused Japan to begin reconsidering its national security policies. In 2013, Prime Minister Shinzo Abe created the National Security Council (NSC), which replaced the earlier Security Council. While such councils have always existed in Japan, they were largely consultative. The new NSC is much more centralized and policy oriented. Alongside the new NSC, the Government of Japan also published the first (and so far, the only) Japanese NSS in 2013.

Japan's 2013 NSS is clearly based on the US model both in structure and tone. It begins with a broad list of basic national values and ideals and reiterates Japan's peaceful orientation.[89] As an island state, maritime security takes an important place in the document, as do free trade and the protection of shipping lanes, much more so than any other strategy examined here. The strategy identifies six global challenges or risks: shifts in the balance of power, WMD proliferation, threats of terrorism, risks to global commons, threats to human security and the risks of global economy.[90] This examination will focus on the threats emanating from the shift in the balance of power in East Asia and the risks to the global commons. The reason for this limitation is twofold, they represent the most significant threats to Japan and they are topics which other national security documents have not addressed in much detail, unlike the rest which are more or less standard on all lists of threats.

The shift in the balance of power in East Asia is primarily driven by the rise of China. The strategy focuses on Japan's relationship with China based on its geographical proximity as well as economic and geopolitical competition. The United States is seen as a major regional power, and an overall global superpower; however, the document acknowledges that regional challengers are beginning to confront it.[91] Since a large proportion of Japanese deterrence and military security depends on the strength of the US-Japanese alliance, such regional decline is not taken lightly. In fact, strengthening the alliance is seen as a national security priority.[92]

Tied into addressing the regional imbalance is the Japanese concern over the global commons, including the sea, outer space and cyberspace. As Japan is highly dependent on sea routes both for importing energy and natural resources and exporting products, Chinese provocative actions receive high priority. The

Japanese view is based on such policies as the "'Open and Stable Seas" [that] constitute the basis for peace and prosperity of the international community as a whole', which is clearly designed with China in mind as is the warning that 'there is a growing risk of incidents at sea, and of possible escalation into unexpected situations'.[93]

While the Strategy does not mention hybrid warfare, it does refer to the occurrence of 'grey-zone' situations in the region. It defines 'grey-zone' situations as 'situations that are neither pure peacetime nor contingencies over territorial sovereignty and interests'.[94] The clear implication of these situations is that they fall under the threshold of conventional war and that they are difficult to characterize as the normal competitions between states. This would make them examples of a hybrid conflict, but not yet hybrid warfare, although the paragraph concludes with a warning that 'there is a risk that these "grey-zone" situations could further develop into grave situations'.[95] Unfortunately, the idea is not expanded further but it does offer a valuable insight into the development of hybrid threats in the region, particularly concerning China.

The biggest threat from China is seen to be territorial expansion, particularly to islands in the East and South China Seas and on the borders of Japanese waters. In a significant break from historical examples when dealing with such threats, Japan has committed to a policy of proactive engagement, management and development of remote islands.[96] Since the Japanese perspective on security is still largely based on peaceful international norms, it is easy to understand how a rising, more assertive, China, seeking to change the status quo throughout the region[97] and acting aggressively towards Japan in particular,[98] could shock Japan into such a large revision of its defence policies.

Common themes and issues

Before delivering concise answers to the questions posed at the beginning of the chapter, it would be useful to establish some common themes, present in all the reviewed documents. There are four themes: primacy of conventional threats, brief mentions of terrorism, attempts to achieve more with less and the increasing inclusion of non-security-related issues.

Throughout the documents it is clear that states still see other states as the primary opponents in the international arena, although the number of references to non-state actors and their importance rises over time. Nevertheless, not a single state or organization reviewed here characterizes non-state actors as existential threats. While this is most likely a historical reaction to the destructive power of interstate wars, it is also a reflection of the conventional mindset that is prevalent in defence planning. Even the 2002 US NSS, famous for encapsulating the GWOT principles was based on the idea of a pre-emptive and preventative strike with conventional capabilities against a terrorists-harbouring state. This over-reliance on firepower, primarily air- and sea-based, has been addressed to a certain degree in the latest documents that emphasize full-spectrum, effect-based operations which would, probably, include ground manoeuvre as well. Israel's policies, arguably the most non-state actor-oriented, are conventional as well, particularly in the pre-2006 era and, based on experiences from the Yom Kippur War of 1973, emphasizing firepower above all else. To Israel's credit, the latest military doctrine is much more in tune with the times, although it remains to be seen if its implementation will follow suit.

Terrorism has become a catchphrase in national security documents that is mostly listed as a threat which supposedly covers all other non-conventional possibilities. Even so, most documents offer no useful definition of what terrorism is or how exactly is it to be tackled. Additionally, this vagueness is sometimes seen as a positive trend in defence planning, a fundamentally flawed logic which has, to a degree, also affected the debate surrounding hybrid warfare. By paying lip service to terrorism, states are simultaneously presenting it as an overarching threat, while offering counterterrorism as a panacea to all issues in contemporary international security. It might be calming to the population that the government is aware of the problem, but when compared to other policies it is alarmingly underdeveloped. Even the UK, which has extensive experience in both domestic and foreign terrorism, seems to have slipped away from unconventional thinking and returned to the conventional 'box'. Although, in fairness, the establishment of a hybrid warfare unit is a good sign, even though its mission is primarily psychological, essentially being a social-media-oriented public relations department. Russia is the surprising case in this category since it faces a very dangerous mix of, often both together, nationalist and religious extremists in the Caucasus. And yet terrorism is but a mere footnote compared to the pages and pages of national security documents devoted to economic development and social issues. Arguably, Russian actions in this matter are much more focused than the policy documents, at least the published and readily available ones, would suggest.

It seems a staple of everyday news media that they report on the constriction of defence budgets or the shrinking of the armed forces, particularly in the North Atlantic area. While the trend is beginning to reverse slightly, the mantra of 'doing more with less' still holds strong. In the light of Western technological advantage, it makes a certain degree of sense. If one modern destroyer can target up to, for example, 200 aircrafts, as is the case with the UK Type 45,[99] you probably do not need twenty of them since no air force in the world maintains 4,000 frontline strike aircrafts. But when you consider that the UK only has six such vessels and not all of them can be deployed at once, adequate delivery of security becomes problematic. The United States is in a similar position, as are most NATO states, and the reductions in Army figures are even greater. During the late 1990s most European NATO states could not deploy significant numbers of troops outside their own borders[100] and, as the 2011 campaign over Libya showed, the situation has hardly improved.[101] There is a certain point where quality can no longer substitute for quantity, a lesson history has shown on a number of occasions, and whether the West is approaching that point or is already past it is hard to gauge. This trend is not present outside the North Atlantic area. Both Russia and Japan are increasing their military potential, not only qualitatively but also quantitatively and so is China, arguably the most important challenger to the global balance of power.

One additional important aspect of this policy is that purely conventional forces and capabilities are often replaced by multi-use ones. While that makes financial sense, the lack of specialization could in the long term cause the loss of valuable knowledge and experience. An argument could be made that, in order to face a hybrid opponent, multi-use capabilities and forces are much more useful, but that is not actually the case. The argument could be valid if multi-use capabilities incorporate a counter-hybrid component, but the multi-use forces are usually configured for multiple *conventional* uses. For example, they are converted from armoured units into mechanized infantry units that can be more readily deployed overseas in an amphibious operation. Such forces potentially lack even the conventional deterrence effect that might persuade a hybrid opponent that its control over escalation has failed. Hybrid warfare is a mixture of conventional and unconventional modes of war so single-purpose, counter-hybrid warfare units would have to be capable of both conventional and unconventional operations, akin to the forces they are facing. As such forces are highly unlikely to be created in the Western world, the only alternative are full-spectrum interoperable capabilities which would enable actors to counter at least some conventional and unconventional advantages of hybrid warfare. However, the key problem with such forces is not their creation, but the lack of resolve to employ them.

The last common theme, which has been increasing over time, is the inclusion of other, non-security-related topics to fill out the documents.

While a valid argument can be made that economic, social and environmental factors contribute to the overall national security, they do not pose the same existential threat as military threats or geopolitical competition. They certainly do not do so in the same, relatively short timeframe. In some cases, Russia for example, it is understandable that a significant amount of the strategic doctrine is devoted to economic and energy security, especially in difficult times after major political upheaval, but it could easily be argued that it is deeply negligent to focus so much time and effort on socio-economic issues when some core security questions remain unanswered. It is not the purpose of this book to expand significantly on this debate except insofar as it is important to the development of thinking on hybrid warfare. This is not to say that such debates are unwelcome or unhelpful, since most of the documents mentioned before are grand political statements and normally they should include all policy aspects. However, those debates should take place in other fora and should not significantly affect strategic thinking. Hybrid warfare, as a new strategic phenomenon that has potentially life-threatening consequences and which can, in the long term, have a great effect on those very socio-economic policies should, reason would dictate, take some priority.

A unified theory of hybrid warfare

At the outset of this chapter, there were two questions that needed answers: Why do conventional military forces find it difficult to deal with hybrid warfare and, which are the weak spots that hybrid warfare targets? After reviewing the major policy aspects of strategic planning by strategically significant national actors over the last two and a half decades these questions can now be answered. The common themes observed previously go some way in answering the first question and they also highlight some of the potential weak spots that hybrid warfare seeks to exploit. To formulate the best answer, a different theoretical framework has to be adopted, one that combines the two questions into a concise unit. This framework will be extrapolated from the proposed definition of hybrid warfare, the environment in which it occurs, examined in the preceding chapter, and based on conclusions drawn from the aforementioned examination. By combining the theoretical principles and frameworks, this book will present a unified theory of hybrid warfare. A unified theory seeks to combine all the elements of a given phenomenon, as well as possible future additions, into a coherent whole. Its purpose is to identify the key features that enable the creation, use and detection of future incidents of hybrid warfare. A unified theory of hybrid warfare therefore explains what hybrid warfare is, how it works and in what kind of circumstances it occurs. Additionally, it can serve as a theoretical guide which international actors can use to scan the horizons and identify instances of hybrid warfare earlier.

The unified theory of hybrid warfare revolves around the notion of exploitation of weak spots. It is therefore necessary to establish what a weak spot is. In the broadest sense, weak spots are deficiencies, weaknesses, faults or misconceptions emerging from, or present in, a state's defence or national security policy. They can be part of the policymaking process, parts or the entirety of a single, or multiple, doctrine or policy or they can be a combination of both. Specific weak spots, some of which will be expanded in the case study chapters, include zero tolerance to friendly casualties when vital interests are not at stake, the necessity to abide by the rules and norms of the international order (including the rules of war), the desire to keep coalitions together, the overemphasis on technological solutions and intensive media coverage.[102] To some degree these are difficult to avoid, as no human endeavour can ever be perfect or predict every single possibility. However, the theory under construction here does not refer to those, but rather to the identifiable and (relatively) predictable ones. It is the essence of the practice of strategy that it must accept a degree of uncertainty, but it is equally important to try and devise the best possible strategy, based on known facts and possibilities, rather than to ignore them and either come up with a seriously flawed strategy or none at all.

Critical to the understanding of the unified theory is the notion, distilled from the above examination, that contemporary defence and national security doctrines are based on a clear delineation between the conventional 'box' and the unconventional 'box'. The trend has been underway ever since the end of the Second World War and, the occasional foray into counterinsurgency notwithstanding, still continues. State military establishments, particularly in the West, are confident of their expertise and superiority in the conventional box and, in most cases, can also claim expertise in the unconventional box. Particularly the UK, with its long history of dealing with insurgencies and its remarkable ability to preserve that knowledge, can claim pride of place in this regard; the United States could also stake a similar claim for a period of successful COIN operations in Iraq and Afghanistan, but it has not been as successful in preserving or applying those lessons to the same degree.

Israel has historically proven to be very proficient in conventional state-based wars, evidenced best by its continued existence and stability, and can claim a number of successes in dealing with non-state actors such as Hamas and Hezbollah. However, things became more complicated when the latter group assumed a hybrid posture in 2006, which was followed by a deep crisis in the IDF because its response was deemed inadequate. While Israeli defence planners attempted the merging of the conventional and unconventional boxes before the conflict, that process was never completed and showed little promise.

Russia, by its virtue of not being a classic Western liberal democratic state, has more room to manoeuvre in its approaches to dealing with either conventional or unconventional threats. Its policies have proven to be remarkably successful in quelling rebellious terrorists in Chechnya as well as squashing Georgian hopes of NATO membership and greater prominence in the Caucasus. As its deterrence and defence policy is largely based on strategic and tactical nuclear forces, its conventional forces can be more adaptable, which could be one of the reasons it is the only state to have successfully both defended itself against and engaged in hybrid warfare. Even so, the fact that the Russian solution to the Chechen problem has been to inflict considerable destruction and degradation to much of Chechnya, a 'success' achieved by large-scale conventional means, and that it still lists other states as the primary threats could indicate that even Russia itself is not yet fully aware of its 'out of the boxes' actions.

Japan has had little practical experience in the post-Second World War era of either conventional or unconventional warfare. It does however seem to have grasped the blurred hybrid concept employed by China remarkably well. The 'grey-zones' operations it has observed might indicate that it is better placed to respond to hybrid warfare because of its lack of experience of other warfare. It might be helpful to view Japan as a state that does not have any bad habits it needs to unlearn because of this lack of experience; it is capable of approaching this new problem with only limited, US-derived preconceptions. As such, its observations are less hampered by the problem of the delineation of the boxes and it has been able to describe accurately what this new phenomenon entails.

Hybrid warfare is based on the deliberate and opaque merger between conventional and unconventional modes of warfare. It does not fit neatly into either conventional or unconventional boxes. Instead it sits in its own box, which borrows elements from both, but does not adopt all of their characteristics, which means it can pick and choose which strengths and which weaknesses it will have and which it can exploit. The weak spots primarily stem from the division of threats, and responses to them, into the two boxes. Secondary weak spots emerge from misconceptions about hybrid warfare itself. A good example is the UK 77 Brigade; hybrid warfare is not just about psychological operations or a cyber-argument on social media, and yet that is what counter-hybrid operations have been deemed to be. That is not to say that international perceptions, including social and news media, are unimportant. Hybrid warfare can rely heavily on the international perceptions of the actors involved. The humiliation of one can even be one of the aims, as was the case for Israel in 2006, but it is primarily designed to advance political ambitions, not gain popularity points.

Another weak spot concerns timing. Most Western national security strategies or strategic concepts only began to refer to hybrid warfare following Russian actions in Ukraine, largely dismissing earlier examples. While this can be explained with the Euro-centric view of the states involved, it is very bad strategy. Hezbollah in 2006 or the Chechens in the 1990s did not rely on social media for their impact, nor did Russia limit itself to a cyber-war. Like every other form of warfare, hybrid warfare is specific to an environment and a timeframe in which it takes place; therefore, in order to understand its principles, it is useless and dangerous to focus on only one example. This lack of strategic forethought illustrates the problem that political structures face when predicting future security trends. All the documents analysed earlier have been produced by political organizations, be they military oriented or not. This is normal since politics is the primary frame of reference for all security-related activities. However, political structures, particularly in Western states, are particularly susceptible to misinterpretation of military-related phenomenon. This is a trend that has gained prominence ever since the end of the Cold War, when strictly strategic considerations have seemingly become less politically viable. The majority of everyday political activity in any state has to do with micromanagement of socio-economical or legal issues, largely focused on the notion of the welfare state. Such a mindset can lead to a panic-stricken political reaction when a serious security threat emerges. The political discourse which surrounds hybrid warfare is an excellent example of such a panic. Hybrid warfare has been an emerging phenomenon for decades and yet has been largely ignored by the political structures in the West, despite some earlier warnings form the security community.

The final weak spot, which also permeates most others, is the democratic system. When discussing defence planning or examples of counter-hybrid warfare, the examination in this chapter focused primarily on the guardian powers of the international order. The United States, the United Kingdom, Israel and Japan are all democratic states and even NATO can be considered a democratic organization since its members are all democratic states and its decision-making is based on consensus and unanimity. The defence planning of all these actors seeks to maintain the international order and the benefits they receive from it. Therefore, the preservation, and spread, of the democratic liberal state model has become a core national interest for the guardian powers. States like Russia and China, which do not follow this mould, perceive that they are being pressured into adhering to this logic and change their domestic systems or face potential intervention. The examination of Russian defence planning, for example, clearly shows a state which has a greater capacity to dictate which policies receive strategic priority, even if they are democratically unappealing. The best examples of this were the two Chechen wars, during which the Russian state imposed media restrictions which would be impossible in a Western state.

Open liberal democratic states, where the populace is accustomed and encouraged to participate in all facets of political life, can find it difficult to make the claim that foreign or security policy should not be subjected to wider participation to the same degree. Through public and media pressure, political leaders in democratic states are not free to base their security calculations only on strategic considerations but are forced to take account of domestic politics. While this process is not new, or indeed undesirable, the influence of domestic actors on the formulation of foreign policy has increased over the last three decades. The perception of Western victory in the Cold War only reinforced the idea that injecting more democracy into the process is not only desirable but also necessary. Interestingly, the common themes discussed above are geared towards protecting the democratic system rather than formulating long-term strategy. Countering threats posed by international terrorists, the constriction of defence spending in order to spend more on social welfare and the securitization of defence planning are all policies designed to preserve democracy, rather than strategic aims which would seek to address existential threats. Terrorism and other securitization issues are not existential threats to either the individual states or the international order. Ironically, the reaction to them, which is a result of democratic politics, and the consequential limiting of defence spending and further restrictions on the use of force are the issues which can become existential threats. As hybrid warfare is deliberately opaque and therefore difficult for even expert observers to identify, it offers actors the ability to exploit the participatory nature of democracy when this is applied to foreign and defence policymaking. Other tendencies of democratic states, specifically the aversion to casualties, and the attention they give to other non-critical defence issues, create the potential for an even greater relative advantage for the hybrid actor and can, in fact, aid them in maintaining the low level of conflict.

In summation, the theory of hybrid warfare aims to explain why and how hybrid warfare can succeed. The simplest answer is because states have allowed it to succeed, primarily through the creation of, and ideological adherence to, a rules-based quinitarian international order. Through a process of reform and doctrinal and strategic change over the last twenty-five years most states and international organizations have successfully filled the gaps in their capacity to counter conventional *or* unconventional threats. However, as is always the case in war, that only serves to increase the ingenuity of the opponent to find new weak spots and exploit them through a new kind of warfare. Unfortunately, conventional military forces or establishments are usually great lumbering beasts that are not prone to rapid change, which is perhaps the largest weak spot of them all. It is difficult to re-orientate a structured institution, especially if that institution has decades or even centuries of traditions and the reorganization would require changes to a significant number of those. This is further complicated by thinking within the framework of neat boxes. Whether it is the example of Russia or Hezbollah or the potential threat from China, unfortunately such threats are unlikely to fall neatly into either purely conventional or purely unconventional box. There are two reasons for this assertion: the first is that almost no conflict in history could claim to fall purely into one box and the second is that the Western powers have an enormous advantage in both capabilities and doctrinal history when faced with a neat boxed threat. The difference between past non-hybrid conflicts and future hybrid ones is that it is practically impossible to determine whether they are mostly conventional or mostly unconventional; they are both.

Hezbollah and state-like hybrid warfare

The Middle East as a region has been a cauldron of conflict for millennia and this condition persists to the present day. It has always been a battleground of different interests and various great power struggles and continues to be an important global arena for hegemonic contests. Since no conflict occurs in a vacuum, this is the context in which the events of the summer of 2006 will be observed. In broad strategic terms they are part of both a regional and a sub-regional hegemonic struggle. The interplay between the larger region and its sub-regions is complex, but it is important to establish it in broad strokes in order to provide a strategic assessment of the conditions in which the conflict occurred in 2006. Regionally, the United States, as the global hegemon, aims to maintain a balance of power between the various regional actors and preserve its control over this economically and politically important region. It does so through a system of close associations, friends and its own military presence in the region. The major threats to this regional order come from Iran and Saudi Arabia, which despite its close relationship with the United States wants to establish itself as the dominant regional power as does Iran. The religious Shia–Sunni divide among the Muslim population of the region is also important as both states claim to represent their respective sects. Both use direct and indirect means to influence the course of events, with Iran being particularly important for this examination because of its patronage of Hezbollah. On a sub-regional level, focusing on the territories of the Levant in a narrow sense (Syria, Lebanon, Israel and Jordan), Israel can be considered as the hegemon, particularly so since the start of the civil war in Syria which has left Israel without a sub-regional competitor of near-comparable power. Israel's position is greatly strengthened by its close friendship with the United States, which not only helps Israel but also cements the US position as the regional, and global, hegemon. When conflict occurs, it is usually because an actor wishes to challenge the status quo either directly or through a weakening of the current hegemon. Both of these forces were present during the 2006 Lebanon War and they, along with the strategic situation in the region as a whole, heavily influenced both the conduct and the outcome of the war. The aim of this chapter is to examine how the war was conducted by both sides and to apply the observations to the larger strategic overview in order to determine how each influenced the other and the relevance it holds for future wars.

The thirty-four-day conflict between Israel and Hezbollah in the summer of 2006 has been widely viewed as an important turning point in the development of modern warfare. It has also been heralded as the definitive beginning of the trend towards hybrid warfare. In the most widely referenced study of hybrid warfare, Frank Hoffman used the 2006 Lebanon War as a key case study, although the term itself has been used before, in reference to the First and Second Chechen Wars. Both of these wars will be examined in more detail in the following chapter. The main reason why the Hezbollah-Israel conflict in 2006 has been so widely studied is because it demonstrated that a non-state actor could effectively, and with some degree of success, engage a state actor almost as an equal in strategic terms. This was a departure from the norm of the classical Maoist insurgency organizations which only engage in conventional warfare at the very end, once the opposing authority is already severely weakened. That a non-state actor like Hezbollah could initiate a conflict with the region's premiere conventional power, which has managed to best all of its neighbours in a succession of wars through the decades, and not only survive but also be able to claim victory is certainly novel and worthy of careful study. Since the power imbalance between the two protagonists is so large, the secret to Hezbollah's apparent success had to lie in its novel approach to warfare, and because Hezbollah conducted both conventional and unconventional warfare in the same operation, this novel approach was termed 'hybrid warfare'.

Overview of the 2006 Lebanon War

As with any conflict, it would be unwise to begin examining the 2006 Lebanon War completely out of context. This part of the chapter will provide a concentrated timeline of events preceding the conflict as well as those that took place during the conflict. Particular emphasis will be given to Israel's 1982 invasion and subsequent occupation of much of southern Lebanon until 1985, the holding of a shallow, border security zone until the unilateral withdrawal in 2000 and the subsequent escalation of intermittent hostilities leading up to the 2006 war. The events during the war itself will be examined briefly to provide context for the more in-depth analysis in the second part of the chapter.

Lebanon has played an important role in the relations between Israel and its Arab neighbours, particularly Syria. When the Lebanese Civil War broke out in 1975, it created a breeding ground for sectarian violence. By 1976, a Syrian-led, Arab League-sponsored peacekeeping force had begun deploying within Lebanon, although the conflict continued. Within southern Lebanon, the Palestine Liberation Organization (PLO) began attacking Israel, using the lawless region as its strategic sanctuary. In 1978, Israel raided southern Lebanon in response to PLO attacks, an action which resulted in the establishment of the UN peacekeeping mission (UNIFIL) and an Israeli withdrawal. The situation did not change drastically since regional security, particularly from an Israeli perspective, did not improve. The Lebanese government was unable to regain control of the south and PLO activities continued. The continued Syrian presence in Lebanon also compromised Israel's strategic position.

Israel-Lebanon relations between 1982 and 2006

Isolated clashes which constituted a continuous campaign of violence in southern Lebanon and northern Israel continued for many years. The PLO had evolved from a purely guerrilla organization to a standing army, and in 1981 was capable of firing thousands of shells and missiles into Israel from Lebanon.[1] This upgraded the PLO threat from a terrorist nuisance to an existential challenge and Israel therefore decided to intervene. The rationale behind the invasion of southern Lebanon in 1982 was purely strategic. The official goals called for a security zone, which would push PLO units out of artillery range of Israel, a peace treaty with Lebanon and the establishment of a new political order within Lebanon.[2] Arguably, the real goals, as elucidated by Prime Minister Menachem Begin and Defence Minister Ariel Sharon, were to expunge the PLO from Lebanon and hopefully destroy much of its power, to ensure Israel's dominance in the settlement of the territorial disputes, the withdrawal of Syrian forces from Lebanon and the subsequent establishment of a government within Lebanon which would seek friendlier relations with Israel.[3] Despite the apparent differences between the cabinet-approved goals and the ones privately held by Begin and Sharon, they were not in conflict. Certainly, the unofficial set of objectives can be seen as both complementing and expanding the officially released ones.

Both sets of goals were unrealistically ambitious and, as a result, none of them were wholly achieved. Israel managed to create the security zone and it delivered a serious blow to the PLO, effectively removing it from Lebanon, but neither of those achievements resulted in accomplishing the strategic objective, the peace sought by Israel. The security buffer would prove to be a very costly commitment in the long run, and the internal political situation in Lebanon did not change, much less improve. On the international stage, Israel's standing suffered as well, in no small part because it overran positions held by UNIFIL. Despite a partial Israeli withdrawal to a narrower security zone in 1985, UNIFIL was essentially reduced to providing humanitarian aid.[4]

The most tangible consequence of the Israeli invasion was the rise of Hezbollah. Lebanon had been governed through a complex set of arrangements called the 'national pact' which attempted to create a balance of power between the Christian, Sunni and Shia groups within the government.[5] Since the beginning of the civil war, various factions had attempted to challenge that balance through appeals to outside powers. With Christian groups supported by Israel and Sunni groups receiving support from across the Arab world, the Shia felt increasingly threatened. Historically, the Shia organizations attempted to stay out of politics and adopted a posture of political passivity,[6] a stance that became increasingly untenable following the Arab renewal of the 1970s and 1980s. Following the successful Iranian revolution, Shia's in Lebanon could count on significant amounts of support from Shia Iran, as well as Baathist Syria. Since the Al-Assad family are members of the Alawite sect of Shia Islam, and have created an Alawite ruling elite in Syria, this has also been a significant consideration. Arguably, Syria's motivations were more strategic than religious, but that can also be said of Iran. For both of these states, the increased influence of Israel in Lebanese politics post-1982 had to be stemmed. Additionally, for Iran, this was an opportunity to threaten Israel by proxy without risking a direct confrontation. With Israel now a key stakeholder in the future of Lebanon, both Syria and Iran looked to the last remaining 'unclaimed' segment of Lebanese society, the Shia. With Iran providing the bulk of the money and training and Syria providing a refuge within their occupation zone in Lebanon, the grounds were set for the establishment of a Shia militia which could not only oppose Israel but also promote the rise of Shia influence in Lebanon.[7]

The final product of these calculations was Hezbollah. It was officially founded in 1985 as a direct challenge to Israeli occupation and drew its initial legitimacy from its opposition to it. Originally envisioned as a guerrilla-style terrorist organization, it later transformed into a political and social organization with a militant wing, in order to broaden its appeal and expand its support base. This process, encouraged by Syria and Iran, sought to make Hezbollah a viable political entity for the 1992 parliamentary elections and move it away from

3

2

functioning purely as a resistance movement.[8] While the transformation was successful, it was not total, and it resulted in Hezbollah gaining a kind of dual personality, becoming both a legitimate political party and a militia/resistance organization. This duality has always produced some ambiguity both within and outside Lebanon. Currently listed as a terrorist organization by numerous states and organizations,[9] it is nevertheless regarded as an important and influential organization within the Lebanese government; it won thirteen seats in parliament following the 2009 general election[10] and has two ministerial posts.[11] It also managed to secure the election of a favourable president of Lebanon after a two-year political crisis and is set to be immensely influential in the new Lebanese Cabinet.[12] The inherent difficulty of establishing what precisely Hezbollah is has translated into a great debate on how best to counter it, which continues to the present day and contributes to its ability to act as a hybrid actor.

The occupation of the narrow southern Lebanon security zone ended with Israel's unilateral withdrawal in 2000. There are several reasons why Israel decided to withdraw, the most important of which was the high cost of the continuous low-intensity fighting within the security zone. While Israeli security policy was fundamentally opposed to a unilateral withdrawal absent a meaningful security guarantee from either Lebanon or Syria, the government of Ehud Barak decided to do it. The IDF objected strongly to a unilateral withdrawal and argued, quite presciently as it turned out, that Israel would be back in south Lebanon very soon. In response, Barak argued that it would increase the international legitimacy of Israel and deprive Hezbollah of their justification for attacks.[13] That Hezbollah had managed to convince Israel's leaders that continuous presence was futile is a significant achievement for a guerrilla organization fighting the most powerful conventional military power in the region. Barak's decision sent shockwaves throughout the Middle East because it seemed that Hezbollah had triumphed where Israel's other Arab opponents had failed so often. It was not only that there was a perception that Hezbollah had defeated Israel but the biggest surprise was the irregular nature of the achievement.[14] While Arab states looked on this development with great interest, it was the PLO that embraced its lessons most thoroughly and likely attempted to duplicate the results in the subsequent second intifada.[15]

During the Israeli occupation, southern Lebanon became a strategic military release valve for Syria, Iran, Hezbollah and Israel. It was an arena in which they could directly or indirectly engage with each other when they thought it necessary without risking a major war.[16] Unfortunately for Israel it became an increasingly costly one. Since the IDF had not engaged in a major war for more than two decades, the perceptions of the acceptable loss of life had changed. This shift was not limited to Israel but was present throughout the Western world. It partially coincided with the refocusing of military thinking to operations based on technology. As the warfighting became increasingly tech-heavy there were fewer demands placed on individual soldiers, to the point where it became imperative that loses must be avoided at all cost. While it is normal for states to seek to achieve their goals with minimum loss of life, the unpredictable nature of war suggests that they cannot be wholly avoided. Aversion to losses is a staple of Western warfare, including Israel's, which, due to its small population relative to its neighbours, has always attempted to keep losses to a minimum. While admirable, such a policy can sometimes be counterproductive as it forces states to postpone the commitment of ground forces. Ironically, that can sometimes lead to higher losses because the enemy has time to prepare or it can mean that the strategic objective can no longer be achieved; the latter proved to be the case in the 2006 Lebanon War.

Timeline of the war

The conflict began on 12 July 2006[17] when a group of Hezbollah fighters attacked an IDF patrol, killing three soldiers and abducting two under cover of a mortar strike. Since Israeli policy is very mindful of such incidents, they sent in a larger patrol to investigate (it is IDF standard procedure). That patrol was ambushed as well with further loss of life as the move had been anticipated by Hezbollah. In retaliation Israel began launching air and ground raids into southern Lebanon to recover the soldiers and strike back at Hezbollah. The next day, Hezbollah began launching missiles into Israel. The missile arsenal employed used both short- and medium-range weapons, from simple 'Katyusha'-style rockets to more sophisticated Fajr 3 and Fajr 5 medium-range pieces.[18] Israel responded with an increased air and artillery campaign, striking tactical targets in south Lebanon as well as strategically important targets such as the Hezbollah headquarters in the Dahiya neighbourhood in Beirut. An important milestone during the conflict occurred on 14 July when Hezbollah launched and hit the IDF naval vessel INS *Hanit* with a C-701 anti-ship missile.[19] Although the damage was relatively limited and the corvette survived, it was a clear indication that Hezbollah had access to some very sophisticated weaponry, a fact that had not been anticipated.

Although border skirmishes had occurred since the beginning of the conflict, the IDF did not begin major ground operations until 22 July. This was due to a political aversion to risking significant numbers of casualties as well as a belief that the conflict could be won with an air campaign. These factors will be examined in more detail in the next part of the chapter. The ground campaign was slow to get under way, so most of the rest of the conflict consisted of exchanges of missile fire on the side of Hezbollah and artillery and air strikes on the side of Israel. Hezbollah employed even longer-range rockets, reaching the city of Haifa, which they had never been able to hit before. The IDF ground operation slowly built up and was eventually extended to the Litani River, in order to secure the area in missile range of Israel although no significant progress could be made. On 11 August, the UN Security Council drafted Resolution 1701, which would bring about a ceasefire and a pullback of both sides, while significantly expanding the mandate for the UNIFIL force.[20] Since the resolution did not take effect till 14 August, both sides attempted to use the last few days and manage some kind of a victory. On the last day of the conflict, Hezbollah, in a very defiant move, launched around 217 missiles into Israel.[21] After that, despite some limited violations of the ceasefire from both sides, the conflict effectively ended with both Israel and Hezbollah claiming victory.[22]

A hybrid war

The 2006 Lebanon War is often considered the first example of hybrid warfare. In his influential treatise on the subject, Frank Hoffman uses it as the primary case study and many subsequent publications have done the same. Although the term 'hybrid warfare' did not originate with the 2006 Lebanon War, it remains very closely tied to it and continues to be re-examined through the Lebanon lens even when applied to other conflicts. While it is normal for observers and scholars to attempt to distil the lessons from one conflict in order to apply them to the next, such a process is only of value if it is limited in its scope since all conflicts share a basis of similarities which stem from the basic nature of war. In order to determine the nature and extent of the hybridity of the 2006 Lebanon War, this book will examine four crucial aspects: the state-like nature of Hezbollah, its use of advanced technology, Israel's difficulties in establishing the nature of the conflict and the information war.

Hezbollah as a state-like actor

In order to determine the hybrid nature of the 2006 Lebanon War there are two basic premises which need to be established: the nature of Hezbollah as an actor in the conflict and the conduct of the war itself. To qualify as a hybrid war, the conflict had to be fought between states or very state-like actors as the conventional aspect of hybrid warfare requires a significant amount of structure and logistical support. There were two primary combatants in the 2006 Lebanon War, Hezbollah and Israel, with Syria, Iran and the United States playing secondary roles as supporters or backers. The examination will focus only on Hezbollah and Israel since it is the situation inside the actual conflict zone which is crucial to determine the level of hybridity.

For Hezbollah, the determination is not clear-cut but there are several indicators which seem to suggest that it can be considered a state-like actor even if it falls short of being considered formally as an independent state. The key question is what is meant by the term 'state-like' actor? Common definitions list a number of requirements for an entity in IR to be considered a state: population, territory, government, sovereignty and international recognition.[23] These criteria are widely adopted although often disputed, but for the purposes of this examination they will serve as the benchmark. Extrapolating from the definition of hybrid warfare,[24] which requires the practitioner to be capable of both conventional and unconventional military operations, a non-state actor is considered state-like if it fulfils enough of these criteria to be able to engage in conventional warfare against another state. The underlying assumption is that the non-state actor, by its very nature, is already capable of unconventional warfare.

Hezbollah is hardly unique in its dual role as both a political party and a militia, but its ability to engage Israel in open warfare in 2006 is not consistent with guerrilla or terrorist approaches adopted by other similar organizations (e.g. Hamas). Hybrid warfare is not practised only by non-state actors, and once such actors begin acting in such a manner, they can no longer be considered either purely terrorist or purely non-state. Hezbollah's role as a political party in Lebanese politics has already been discussed above, so in order to explain why Hezbollah can be considered a state-like hybrid actor this segment of the chapter will expand on two additional aspects of its activity: its role as a sociopolitical institution, providing social and other services to the people living in its 'territory', and its military capabilities, possessing the military and logistical organization similar to that of a state-run armed force. These criteria were chosen because they offer the clearest explanation of Hezbollah's nature and because they are crucial to its legitimacy, a fundamental component of Clausewitzian war.

Hezbollah has always taken great care to emphasize its social activities, even before it officially began its guerrilla operations. It has followed the Muslim Brotherhood model of providing social and financial support to the people in its care in order to establish a secure and loyal base for its other activities while concurrently developing the insurgency elements. The Shiite community in Lebanon was particularly susceptible to such advances since it had been largely neglected by the Lebanese government in the 1970s and 1980s, primarily because the government in Beirut was unable to provide even the basic services. To improve their situation and simultaneously rally the population around their cause, various groups began offering social and economic services on their own accord even before Hezbollah, or its earlier competitor organization Amal, was founded.[25] Hezbollah possessed a significant advantage over all other groups in this regard because it had access to the financial resources of its ideological backer, Iran. Services that were eventually organized by Hezbollah include financial aid to families in distress, pensions for families whose members had died fighting for Hezbollah, as well as other financial aid which would nowadays be associated with a welfare state (subsidized cultural and educational programmes or unemployment benefits). Hezbollah also provided subsidized or even free medical care through a system of hospitals owned and run by its members, as well as education. The latter activity in particular has been very useful for the organization in creating a base of support through indoctrination and propaganda.[26] All activities are further exploited through Hezbollah's media presence; it runs a radio station, a TV station and print media, and has a significant online following.[27] While it may be expedient for Hezbollah to couch its social programmes in terms of aiding those in need or other high-sounding rhetoric, the bottom line is the establishment of a secure and loyal base for its militant activities. The social and military activities of Hezbollah have been combined very efficiently to the point where it has gained enormous influence over domestic Lebanese politics and it has garnered wide-ranging public support even outside the Shia community. Its leadership has managed to transform this influence into both political and military capital.

From a military standpoint, Hezbollah possesses a horizontally diverse structure, based on a large number of small self-contained units capable of significant autonomy in terms of both logistics and tactical decision-making. The latter characteristic is very rare in Arab organizations (both state militaries and non-state groups) since it devolves decision-making authority to the lower echelons; a doctrine requiring extensive training and education which is more common in Western militaries.[28] The actual numbers of fighters available to Hezbollah are hard to determine, with estimates ranging from about 1,000 regular fighters and a much larger number of village fighters[29] to thousands of supporters and members and a few hundred terrorist operatives.[30] The consensus appears to be that Hezbollah has access to a significant number of well-trained 'front line' troops as well as a large number of local reserves, an impressive feat for a non-state organization. Recently, Hezbollah has been able to send hundreds of fighters to aid its long-standing patron, the Assad regime, in the Syrian Civil War,[31] indicating that it has the capabilities and the expertise to conduct military interventions outside Lebanon. As a result of suffering significant losses during the 2006 Lebanon War, Hezbollah has focused on recruitment in order to replenish and increase its numbers, some of which come from non-Shia populations, reflecting Hezbollah's high standing in Lebanon as well as in the region.[32]

While the number of fighters Hezbollah is able to call upon is disputed, their fighting ability is not. During the 2006 Lebanon War, Hezbollah units were able to engage their IDF counterparts effectively and decisively. The pre-prepared and fortified positions along the Israel-Lebanon border were also a significant asset and acted as a force multiplier for Hezbollah. Southern Lebanon, with its rugged hills and valleys, is well suited for insurgency and light infantry, which Hezbollah simply improved with the addition of fortifications. The IDF was aware of the construction effort across the border but had little intelligence on how extensive the system was. Only once the ground units entered Lebanon and encountered the bunkers did the full extent of the fortifications emerge.[33] The system of fortifications served two purposes: first, to emplace and protect the medium and long-range missile launchers and, second, to defend the villages in order to stall the expected IDF ground assault for as long as possible. By splitting up the force into small units which were capable of operating independently and were self-sustaining, Hezbollah reduced the logistical trail and made it almost impossible for the IDF to root all of them out of southern Lebanon. The ability of these small groups to survive was exemplified by the fact that throughout the conflict they maintained a steady barrage of rockets into Israel, often from behind the IDF lines.[34] The late start of the IDF ground operations in fact surprised Hezbollah as it had prepared in-depth defences to the Litani River in order to blunt the expected armoured thrust. It used the additional time to reinforce its forces in southern Lebanon to a limited degree, although that did not give it a significant advantage since the distributed nature of its forces meant that resupply or re-deployment of forces, especially in the face of Israeli air superiority, was not possible.[35]

The final aspect, which exemplified Hezbollah's military acumen, was its ability to study and learn from the IDF. Hezbollah trained and prepared in advance to exploit the weaknesses of Israeli doctrine and society, particularly the Israeli aversion to high casualties resulting from manoeuvre warfare.[36] The basic premise of Hezbollah's activities was to ensure steady rocket fire into Israel in order to frighten the civilian population and force the IDF to either wade back into the quagmire of southern Lebanon and face potentially unacceptable casualties or leave the civilian population exposed to Hezbollah's rockets.[37] The unguided rocket arsenal fielded by Hezbollah was of little or no practical use against military or other high value targets, which normally requires precision guidance, but is a weapon of choice for creating psychological pressure on the civilian population and, consequentially, the Israeli leadership. In doctrinal terms, the Israeli adoption of American-style Shock and Awe and EBO was also skilfully exploited by Hezbollah, an aspect which will be explored later in this chapter.

When compared to other insurgency organizations Hezbollah certainly stands apart. Not only does it have a political wing which gives it broad political legitimacy, it also offers social and welfare programmes in what is in essence a state within a state in southern Lebanon. By obtaining public support and legitimacy in a certain territory, which it effectively controls, Hezbollah can be said to at least partially fulfil the population, government and territorial conditions for an entity to become a state. Being recognized as a legitimate resistance movement within Lebanon allows it to combine its sociopolitical and military activities into an advanced, state-like organization. Furthermore, the demonstrated ability of Hezbollah's military forces to work as an organic combined-arms army is also more indicative of a state rather than a non-state actor. In order to engage in hybrid warfare an actor must be capable of acting in both a conventional and unconventional manner simultaneously, which is what distinguishes it from a traditional insurgency. Hezbollah has demonstrated that ability both in theory and in practice and can therefore be considered a state-like hybrid actor.

Hezbollah's use of advanced technology

With Hezbollah ability to act as a state-like actor in a hybrid context established, the next logical step is to examine the kind of technology capability available to it during the 2006 Lebanon War. When talking about non-state actors, such as militias or insurgency organizations, advanced technology, particularly advanced weaponry, is normally not a major consideration. Hezbollah, however, has been able to employ some relatively advanced weapons which would certainly be considered unusual for an 'ordinary' insurgency organization. This is a core distinguishing feature of a hybrid actor and it is directly connected to its state-like nature. In describing Hezbollah's use of advanced technology, the primary focus is going to be on the missile arsenal and communication technology. These aspects have been chosen because they represent the aspects which set Hezbollah apart the most and because they had proven very effective during the 2006 Lebanon War. Missiles are not usually the weapon of choice for an insurgent organization, and communications tend to be the Achilles's heel of either state or non-state organizations, but Hezbollah has demonstrated a proficiency in both those fields far beyond what had been seen before.

Hezbollah's missile arsenal has been a subject of extensive research and debate since the establishment of the organization. Supplied chiefly by Iran and Syria and smuggled across the Syrian–Lebanese border, it has formed the backbone of Hezbollah's tactics. In the context of the 2006 Lebanon War, the missile arsenal can be divided into two parts: the ground-to-ground rockets, such as Katyushas and Fajrs, and the anti-tank missiles. While the former was chiefly intended to scare the Israeli public, the latter could be said to have been Hezbollah's most effective weapon of the war. In terms of numbers, the organization's missile arsenal was estimated between 10,000 and 13,000 missiles of various ranges before the start of the war in 2006.[38] The majority of them were simple 'Katyusha'-style unguided, short-range rockets, with more sophisticated medium- and long-range rockets also documented, mostly consisting of Syrian and Iranian supplied stock, although Hezbollah allegedly possesses some limited production capabilities.[39] Although Hezbollah also used a shore-based anti-ship missile successfully, the fact that it was an isolated incident is not particularly useful in an examination of the use of missile technology but rather in examining the state of Israeli intelligence, which was not aware of the missile being deployed by Hezbollah.

As described earlier, Hezbollah's strategy was to lure the IDF into a pre-prepared trap in order to inflict as many casualties as possible. The dispersed nature of fortifications in southern Lebanon essentially meant that Hezbollah's units would be fighting a static tactical defence. This in turn meant that they would very likely face an IDF armoured ground incursion which necessitated the use of anti-tank missiles capable of disabling or destroying IDF's Merkava tanks and other vehicles although Hezbollah went even further and utilized these weapons for many other purposes such as destroying shelters or houses that IDF soldiers were occupying.[40] The arsenal eventually used by Hezbollah could be described as varied, since it consisted of a mixture of various Syrian and Iranian Soviet-based weapons and US-made TOW launchers.[41] The relative sophistication of some of these weapons (such as the laser guided AT-14 Kornet-E) meant that they were a threat to even the most advanced Merkava Mk 4 tanks, although that was largely as a result of the tanks inadequate protection.[42] Owning weapons and using them effectively are, of course, not the same and the lack of training has often been a crucial weakness of many of IDF's opponents through the years. However, as IDF armoured units learnt to their dismay in the closing days of the 2006 Lebanon War, Hezbollah's anti-tank teams, trained in advance use of the weapons in Iran, demonstrated the ability to use such missiles with a proficiency similar to that of a regular army. This applies to both the actual firing of the weapon and its deployment and the preparation of the battlefield.[43]

One aspect of missile warfare in which Hezbollah seems to have fallen short is anti-aircraft missile systems. At first glance this is an odd omission, given its demonstrated ability to wield missiles on land and sea very effectively, and the danger posed to its launchers and fighters by the Israeli Air Force (IAF). However, the simplest explanation for this apparent oversight is most likely the highly complicated nature of modern anti-aircraft missiles which would be capable of downing the IAF's F-15 and F-16 aircraft. While low flying and relatively slow helicopters or troop transport aircraft might be vulnerable to even anti-tank missiles, high-altitude fighter bombers are not and missile systems that would be capable of reaching such targets appear to be out of reach even for an actor as resourceful as Hezbollah. Despite an impressive sortie generation rate, and although its close air support and rescue missions often found themselves in a fusillade of IR-seeking surface-to-air missiles and small arms fire, the IAF suffered only one combat loss. IAF pilots, in an attempt to limit casualties, usually flew at very high altitudes and relied on precision guided munitions to strike Hezbollah targets and enjoyed essentially complete air superiority throughout the conflict.[44]

Communications are an important aspect of any conflict, but they are particularly important for a hybrid actor. The ability to mobilize and de-mobilize rapidly is one of the hallmarks of a hybrid force and for Hezbollah fighters in the villages and 'nature reserves'[45] it was particularly important. Its rocket units would quickly prepare and fire the rockets and then disappear from the vicinity until the danger had passed and a different unit had prepared the launchers again. For fighters within the fortified villages, it was particularly important to be able to blend into the civilian population (most of which were Hezbollah supporters if not fighters) when IDF troops broke into the defences and then be able to re-form rapidly once the front line had moved on. All of these activities required reliable but relatively sophisticated communications, and Hezbollah had established a system that seemed to have performed very well. To facilitate the communications between the groups, the organization had a system of ham radios, sophisticated call signs and even its own closed cell phone network.[46] It also maintained communications between its headquarters and field units as well as lines of communications to its backers in Syria and particularly Iran.[47] While not considered state of the art by modern communication standards, Hezbollah's network was nevertheless remarkably robust and efficient, surviving relentless air raids and even the destruction of much of its headquarters in the Dahiya neighbourhood of Beirut. Additionally, Hezbollah was also able to intercept and exploit a significant number of communications, particularly cellular communications, from within Israel, including from within the IDF.[48] As a result of all these factors, Hezbollah was able to organize its fighting teams much more efficiently and, in some cases, save them from an impending air strike while simultaneously confusing the Israeli decision-making processes. Combined with significant intelligence-gathering capabilities,[49] such assets were certainly almost as decisive to the outcome of the conflict as the fighting itself.

Israel's response

Perhaps the most well-known and studied aspect of the 2006 Lebanon War has been the unsatisfactory military and political performance exhibited by Israel before and during the conflict. There are several reasons for the difficulties Israel, and particularly the IDF, experienced at the time and this part of the chapter will examine the three most influential ones: doctrinal flaws, political and military indecision and the myopic state of the IDF. Before examining each of these factors in turn, it is important to note that the common theme with all of them was the inability of both the political and the military decision-makers to grasp what kind of a conflict Israel was facing. As argued earlier Hezbollah had prepared for the confrontation in a way that was specifically designed to counter the Israeli strengths and exploit the weaknesses of their defence doctrine. While it is normal, indeed preferable, for an actor to target its opponent's weaknesses, the impact of the 2006 Lebanon War had as much to do with Hezbollah's preparations as with Israel's shortcomings. In fact, it could be argued that most of the difficulties that Israel faced were self-imposed.

From a doctrinal perspective, the IDF defence doctrine prior to 2006 was very much of its time. It was following the US trend of turning away from conventional warfare to a mode called EBO. The core idea of EBO is that rather than viewing the opponent's government, infrastructure and military forces as discrete units, the enemy can be regarded as a single system. Actions against the system should therefore aim to disrupt the opponent's operational ability rather than focus simply on destroying its military force.[50] An example, based on Israeli interpretation, would be that a military action does not necessarily have to take and hold territory in order to secure objectives; it is enough if the territory can merely be controlled as the control of territory would produce the same trickle-down effects.[51] It was a product of the US experience in the Balkans, and in practice, it was based on the precision delivery of firepower, primarily from the air. Arguably, this made EBO suitable for low-intensity operations against technologically inferior states, where the use of precise munitions limited the number of civilian casualties while allowing ground forces to stay clear of the combat zone. The appeal for Israel can clearly be seen as the IDF had been fighting essentially a counterinsurgency campaign against the PLO and Hamas for decades.[52] In theoretical terms, leading Israeli defence scholars were arguing that the focus should be wholly switched to Intifada-style conflicts, which were more similar to low-intensity operations than full-scale war.[53] A few months before the outbreak of hostilities, the IDF Chief of Staff General Dan Halutz signed into effect the new Israeli defence doctrine, based on SOD.[54] SOD was very much a product of the IDF experience in Gaza and the West Bank. While it incorporated some EBO ideas, it aimed to take the debate even further and change the entire basis of thinking within the Israeli defence community. As it turned out, the doctrine was over-complicated and largely useless in practice, with many officers confused about the orders they received.[55]

The second consequence of EBO was the over-reliance on stand-off firepower, primarily airpower, but also ground-based rocket and artillery fire. By following the US example of believing in the ability of the air force to knock out any opponent much more quickly and with fewer casualties on both sides, Israel invested heavily in the air force, even to the detriment of other services.[56] The Chief of Staff during the 2006 war, General Dan Halutz, was a career Air Force officer who believed very strongly in the notion that air power alone can win wars.[57] This was one of the reasons why he initially declined to activate the IDF reserve troops and why he recommended to the Cabinet that a short, precision fire power intensive, campaign would be successful. While it is undeniable that the IAF was highly successful in taking out the long- and medium-range missile launchers, leading General Halutz to proclaim a premature victory on 13 July, it ultimately proved unable to destroy or neutralize the much smaller and more mobile Katyusha rocket launchers.[58] This led, towards the end of the conflict, to the decision to deploy significant numbers of ground troops as it was the only way to clear the area of Hezbollah launchers and missile stockpiles. Overall, the IAF airstrikes were estimated to have impacted only around 7 per cent of Hezbollah's military strength within the first three days of operations.[59] While that is not insignificant, particularly since it removed the more dangerous longer-range missiles, it is hardly the overwhelming success that air power proponents imagined.

When examining Israel's conduct from the perspective of military and political decision-making, it quickly becomes clear that the inherent opaqueness of hybrid warfare had produced effects. Complicated by doctrinal weaknesses, neither the top civilian nor the military leaders were quick enough to react. Moreover, Prime Minister Olmert strategic goals for winning the war were over-ambitious and unachievable against a hybrid opponent. Officially, Israel's goals were to change the strategic situation in southern Lebanon, push Hezbollah from the border to prevent future abductions of soldiers, strengthen Israel's deterrence and engender a diplomatic process that would lead to a military intervention and full implementation of UNSC Resolution 1559.[60] The resolution called for Lebanon to establish full control over its territory (including the withdrawals of Israeli and Syrian troops) and the disarmament of Lebanese militias (chiefly Hezbollah).[61] The fact that these goals were presented three days after the conflict began is perhaps the most interesting aspect as it points to the fact that Israel entered the war without clear objectives or a coherent strategy.[62] The IDF had prepared several contingency plans and exercises in the months before the war, some of which were remarkably similar to the eventual conflict. The general conclusion was that without a major ground operation the objectives could not be secured. Despite clear indications to the contrary, the political and military leadership (Prime Minister Olmert, Defence Minister Amir Peretz and Chief of Staff Halutz) decided against implementing a major ground war at first. Their reasoning was based not on strategic thinking, but on the grounds of avoiding casualties, precisely as Hezbollah had anticipated. [63]

This almost pathological aversion to casualties was certainly a major stumbling block for the performance of the IDF during the 2006 Lebanon War. History has shown that no worthwhile goal can be reached without some kind of loss. The trend in Western militaries since the end of the Cold War has been very heavily geared towards minimizing both military and civilian casualties, a process called 'post-heroic warfare'.[64] While it may be natural to want to limit the casualties of war, such thinking should not be pursued so far as to become detrimental to the actor's ability to achieve them at all. In the case of the 2006 Lebanon War, the desire to keep casualties to the bare minimum severely hampered Israel's ability to secure a clear victory over Hezbollah. The postponement of the beginning of ground operations was also partially based on this consideration, as was the prime minister's promise to bring the two abducted soldiers back home safely. On a tactical level, even the limited operations were often halted, after sustaining minor losses, over the objections of combat commanders.[65] Such action was mirrored in the perception of losses within the general population, as relatively low civilian casualties did not cause overwhelming demands for a retaliatory response. Only when it had emerged that Israel was faltering did the perception change, both within the government and in the public, essentially forcing the government to commit significant numbers of ground troops. In the later stages of the conflict, when it was increasingly clear that a ceasefire would soon emerge, Israel reversed its original philosophy and conducted a combined large-scale armoured and airborne assault towards the Litani River in order to secure at least some kind of victory, the results of which were underwhelming.[66] Both the Israeli and Lebanese home fronts were also heavily influenced by the information war between the two sides, an aspect which will be examined later.

The final issue on the Israeli side was the myopic condition of the IDF. While it is an issue that is connected to all others, it is important enough to merit its own separate examination. The term myopic is used in this case to refer to the poor state of both the professional and reserve units of the IDF, primarily its ground forces. The ground component had deteriorated from the most feared military instrument in the Middle East during the 1970s and 1980s to the point where its troops did not receive even basic instruction on how to fight an actual war, as opposed to an insurgency. Armoured units in particular had suffered from years of neglect both in terms of training and equipment, with some tank crews more familiar with patrolling the West Bank on foot than in operating tanks.[67] Expertise in armoured warfare is particularly susceptible to loss due to lack of training, much more so than infantry tactics, because it requires familiarity with the vehicles as well as tactical skills and topographical knowledge. When coupled with equipment shortages, most Israeli tanks were not fitted with active countermeasures or protective systems, and little practical experience it is no wonder that the IDF underperformed.[68] This lack of preparation was also evident in the navy during one of the most famous incidents of the war, when Hezbollah successfully attacked the INS *Hanit*. Despite the corvette being equipped with protective systems capable of defending it from precisely this kind of a strike, those systems were switched off at the time because Israel did not believe that Hezbollah possessed weapons capable of hitting a vessel patrolling offshore.[69] While indicating a failure of intelligence, by not being aware of the existence of the C-701 missile, it is also an indictment of the low level of preparation on the part of the navy. Whether the threat was known in advance or not, it is strange that a military vessel patrolling a hostile shoreline was not in full battle-ready mode.

Information warfare

Information operations or, more broadly, information warfare is increasingly viewed as a crucial and novel aspect of modern war. While certainly not novel, despite many Western military scholars and politicians proclaiming it as such, it is important – a point that was well-proven during the 2006 Lebanon War. Although information warfare is not a unique feature of hybrid warfare, it represents one of its distinguishing characteristics. Success in hybrid warfare relies on the ability of the user to avoid escalation to a large-scale conventional war, and the control of the information flow is a vital component of that endeavour. Both sides engaged extensively in information warfare, mainly in an attempt to portray the opponent as the aggressor, but also in order to disrupt each other's battlefield communications. Influencing the home front was also an important aspect as popular support is often crucial for the success of an operation. This part of the chapter will examine how these aspects of information warfare influenced the conduct of the conflict on both sides and how it impacted the conclusion and aftermath.

When Israel withdrew from Lebanon in 2000, it was seen by Hezbollah as a culmination of its eighteen-year-long insurgency campaign. As with any guerrilla operation, the publicity and public perception of the struggle were important, a lesson that Hezbollah clearly learnt. Israel, on the other hand, has always viewed the public perception of its actions, particularly in the international community, as relatively unimportant. Its view was that states which are either allies of, or friendly towards, Israel would support its actions and what the rest said did not really matter. Such thinking stems partially from the more aggressive aspects of Zionist ideology but also from Israel's strategic reality; as a small state surrounded by hostile, or at least unfriendly, neighbours it cannot afford to taper its response to aggression in order to placate international public opinion. When Prime Minister Barak withdrew from southern Lebanon, one of the reasons was to create some goodwill for Israel within the international community. At the time the policy was supported by a casualties-weary Israeli public, but in strategic terms it was breaking with decades of precedents. This shift also coincided with the doctrinal and political changes outlined earlier, and it produced a state of Israel which attempted to improve its image in the international community through restraint. However, through the process of doing so, it provided Hezbollah with a perfect opportunity to exploit this new position and bait Israel into retreating from its new posture by reacting to Hezbollah's provocation.

Hezbollah's goal in this regard was to portray Israel as the occupier/aggressor in order to strengthen its position within Lebanon and within the broader Shia community, as well as to once again demonstrate its position as a resistance movement. It could be argued that this information campaign was too effective for its own good. Believing that Israel would not react as violently as it had in the past Hezbollah launched the kidnapping operation, which led to the war. By the end, even Hassan Nasrallah, the Secretary General of Hezbollah, admitted that had he known that Israel would react as violently as it did he would not have launched that operation.[70] In a great illustration of the limits of hybrid warfare, in this aspect at least, Hezbollah lost control over the escalation of the conflict and sustained casualties not commensurate with its goals, including a significant number of its most experienced fighters.[71] While it succeeded in portraying Israel as the non-proportional aggressor, it can be argued that overall this approach was as much a failure as it was a success.

The second aspect of the information warfare during the 2006 Lebanon War concerns battlefield communications. As a non-state actor Hezbollah did not possess state-of-the-art military communication equipment but, as mentioned earlier, its communications technology was still quite impressive. On a number of occasions, it managed to intercept and decode Israeli communications which enabled it to set up ambushes of the IDF forces. Israel's intelligence services, on the other hand, proved to be a disappointment. Not only were they not aware of the quantity and type of Hezbollah's missile arsenal, but they also failed to intercept or impede its communications. Hezbollah fighters often communicated with cell phones and ham radios, which enabled them to blend better into the civilian population, leaving Israel with a difficult choice of whether or not to attack in the face of certain civilian casualties. IDF commanders were often leading their troops from far behind the front lines in bunkers filled with plasma screens, leading to some observers to begin referring to the war as a kind of 'plasma conflict'.[72] While in keeping with the times of modern technological war, it meant that commanders were wholly reliant on the information flow, which was often unreliable or incomplete. Technology cannot eliminate the fog of war and in some cases can actually exacerbate it. When these factors combined, they created a permanent state of uncertainty in the IDF command structure adding to an already confused decision-making process.

Another aspect of the information warfare was public diplomacy. This war particularly important for Israel since the policy of the Olmert government was the maintenance of international legitimacy in order to ensure that Israel's friends, particularly the United States and Europe who hoped for a constructive dialogue with the Lebanese government at the time, would not forgo their support.[73] On the other side, the conflict was also part of a larger competition between two ideological blocs in the region: the Resistance bloc (comprised of Iran, Syria, Hezbollah and Hamas, with some support from Qatar) and the more US-order leaning bloc of Saudi Arabia, Egypt, the UAE and Jordan. The latter would privately welcome a defeat or humiliation of Hezbollah in a conflict with Israel because it would weaken Iran's position, although they could not associate themselves too closely with Israel because of domestic political pressure.[74] Immediately after the start of hostilities, Prime Minister Olmert reiterated the Israeli policy of keeping the Lebanese government responsible for Hezbollah's actions, a stance encouraged by General Halutz,[75] but he switched his position a few days later in order to garner international support by dialling down the rhetoric on blaming the Lebanese state for the aggression and limiting it to Hezbollah.[76] Such an approach was a gamble since it went against historical precedents and can only be said to have been partially successful; it managed to placate the Saudi bloc as well as the United States and Europe, but it also caused confusion and raised fears of being simply Israeli propaganda.[77] A huge blow to this effort was Hezbollah's successful manipulation of media coverage. The nature of the conflict meant that Hezbollah fighters blended into the civilian population, leaving Israel with no effective means of distinguishing between the two. While civilian casualties were relatively low, reportedly around 1,100[78], for such a firepower-intensive conflict, Hezbollah still managed to portray Israeli actions as deliberate targeting of civilian populations, a tactic that led to the NGO Human Rights Watch accusing Israel of committing war crimes.[79] What is most intriguing about this tactic is not that Hezbollah resorted to it – it is the staple of insurgency organizations across the world – but the fact that Israel failed to respond to it adequately, further worsening its position vis-à-vis both the domestic community and the international public.

On the home front, both Israel and Hezbollah faced a similar dilemma. Both needed to protect their base from unnecessary casualties, maintain morale and keep the public on their side after the war was over. Reflecting their nature, the opponents relied on different approaches to achieve these goals. As a democratic and relatively open society, Israel could not completely control the information flow while Hezbollah, through authoritarian means, did have virtually absolute control; exhibiting an impressive internal discipline.[80] In terms of success, Hezbollah can be said to have managed to achieve most if not all of its information goals while Israel was largely unsuccessful. Israel's chief difficulty, as with most aspects of the 2006 War, was in the nature of the conflict itself. As the government had such difficulties deciding on clear goals and means, this was translated to the public as an appearance of indecision. Further complicating matters were several information leaks, which left the public in little doubt over the problems they were facing.[81] In addition to damaging public morale, such leaks were also an intelligence boon for Hezbollah, demonstrating to it that its hybrid approach was succeeding. In turn, it was able to use this information to shore up its own support within Lebanon. It is interesting to note that public support for the operation remained high in Israel throughout its duration and only dipped towards the end once the deficiencies were increasingly obvious. The IDF also enjoyed higher support than the political leadership, demonstrating that the public had greater trust in the military, despite its failures.[82] Tight control over the flow of information also enabled Hezbollah to manipulate that information and present a united anti-Israeli front and, ultimately, to claim victory in the conflict. Although the situation was much more complex than that, the simple fact that Hezbollah appeared more composed and better organized, while Israel seemed to be struggling, made such a proclamation much more credible among Hezbollah's supporters, sponsors and sympathizers across the Arab world.

Early hybrid warfare

As with any new concept, even those who employ it are often unaware of its potential or how successful their use of it will be. It would be incorrect to claim that Hezbollah decided to fight a hybrid war against Israel in July 2006. It simply decided that the time for a more serious confrontation had come and it had developed a strategy suitable for just such an occasion. Both sides were aware that a conflict was inevitable as pressure had been rising throughout the spring of 2006. It was even clear that a kidnapping attempt would be the most likely choice for Hezbollah to spark off a confrontation.[83] What was not predicted was the way in which Hezbollah engaged in war. Exchanges of rockets and artillery between Israel and Hezbollah or between Israel and Hamas were not a new occurrence, but now Hezbollah had coupled that with a sophisticated defence network, manned by well-trained, well-equipped and motivated fighters. While still technically a militia force, their organizational skills, advanced weaponry and mobility made them resemble a standing army, ironically almost more so than the IDF at the start of the war. Hezbollah fighters were also able to disperse and blend into the civilian population when pressed and required the minimum amount of relatively primitive and inexpensive communications technology to re-assemble. However, Hezbollah was also capable of utilizing state-of-the-art signals interception equipment.

The hallmarks of Hezbollah's brand of hybrid warfare, as illustrated previously, are conventional state-like behaviour, tactical innovation and adaptation, information warfare and the use of technologies not commonly employed by insurgencies. It managed to successfully employ all these factors simultaneously and in a controlled way to achieve its political goals. The fact that the IDF was not prepared for such a conflict and reacted incorrectly made matters easier for Hezbollah, but it in no way detracts from its achievements. While considered an overall success by Nasrallah, the campaign did illustrate the limitations of a hybrid approach, particularly when used by a non-state actor. Limited wars are a constant balancing struggle to prevent unwanted escalations, and in this case Hezbollah, at least partially, failed, although it could, and did, still claim a public relations victory. As a non-state actor Hezbollah lacked some instruments of state (such as international recognition and the associated diplomatic and economic measures) which could have enabled it to prevent Israel from escalating to the point it did. Being largely dependent on Syrian and Iranian aid also limited its options in this regard as it was essentially viewed as part of a larger, regional competition between Israel and Iran. While not simply an Iranian proxy, Hezbollah still cannot claim to be a completely independent actor which implies that escalation against its actions is perceived as striking a blow against Iran, which was one of the rationales behind Israel's apparent overreaction. In the information sphere, Hezbollah took full advantage of modern media outlets, and the global public's thirst for breaking news headlines, to influence a much larger audience that it ever could before and succeeded in humiliating Israel. This was one of the aims of the conflict. Perhaps the greatest legacy of the 2006 War in technological terms was the importance placed by Israel on developing a defensive anti-missile system, a process which culminated in the deployment of the Iron Dome system in 2011. While at present the system is primarily positioned to intercept rocket fire from the Gaza strip, it is also being deployed in northern Israel to deter Hezbollah.[84]

As mentioned earlier in this book, one of the key issues with hybrid warfare is that Western militaries tend to think in terms of discreet boxes. In practical terms, the IDF can be considered one such force, but with one distinguishing characteristic. While most Western militaries are still predominantly geared towards a conventional war, the IDF, particularly in the years just prior to the 2006 conflict, had been adapted almost completely for unconventional warfare. Had Hezbollah followed the strategy of the PLO or Hamas and focused solely on an unconventional approach, it would have been highly likely that Israel would have quickly prevailed because the IDF would be in the same relatively advantageous position it enjoys against the Palestinian guerrilla organizations. A non-state actor therefore had to develop conventional capabilities in order to engage a state's nominally conventional armed forces successfully. This reversal of traditional roles illustrates the flexibility of the hybrid warfare approach, as well as that of Hezbollah. It further demonstrates the dangers of focusing exclusively on one 'box' or the other, as that inevitably leads to a deterioration of capabilities. In many ways it was lucky for Israel that the war occurred when it did, particularly in respect to the transformation of the IDF. Had that transformation been completed, Hezbollah might have been capable of defeating Israel in a limited conventional war on a narrow and shallow front, to disastrous effects for Israel's security since its deterrence capabilities would have been severely reduced. Given the developments in the region since 2006, particularly the civil war in Syria, the rise and fall of the Islamic State, the uncertainties over the future of Iraq, and the Kurdish question, it is clear that the IDF will have to retain the bulk of its conventional capabilities. To its credit, Israel conducted two in-depth inquiries (the Meridor and Winograd Commissions) into the 2006 Lebanon War and, while it has gone to great lengths to implement the findings and correct the deficiencies, a great debate still continues on what changes are required. The 'Dahiya doctrine', presented in 2008, was a return to pre-2006 firepower-intensive campaigning that held Lebanon responsible for Hezbollah's conduct, while omitting SOD elements.[85] Although it might have been comforting to return to a purely conventional approach after a period of turmoil, it did not address the problem of hybridity. However, the latest IDF doctrine, presented in 2015, is geared towards countering both conventional and unconventional warfare and could theoretically be deployed against a hybrid threat.[86] Whether the doctrinal changes Israel has made are correct remains to be tested in practice. The pressure in southern Lebanon has decreased in recent years as most of Hezbollah's attention has shifted to the war in Syria where it has played an important role in keeping the Assad government in power. It has also spent the years since the 2006 War re-arming and solidifying its position within the Lebanese government. Despite the relative calm, another confrontation between the two adversaries remains highly probable.

Russia and hybrid warfare

This chapter will examine the Russian approach to hybrid warfare. This case study seeks to determine what influenced the Russian hybrid warfare strategy and how it is applied. Its most recent, and most visible, example is the ongoing operations in Ukraine, which began in 2014. The Ukrainian crisis is important not only because it represents the culmination of the Russian development of hybrid warfare but also because it is the conflict which cemented the concept of hybrid warfare into the lexicon of strategy.

Russia represents a unique case for the study of hybrid warfare because it is not only a practitioner but also a target of hybrid warfare. While the bulk of the chapter will be devoted to hybrid warfare in Ukraine, two other crises will also be included, in order to better understand Russian strategic options and choices. To begin, the chapter will examine the earliest example of hybrid warfare, the Chechen wars (1994–6 and 1999–2009), followed by the Russo-Georgian war (2008). The inclusion of the Georgian war is based on the fact that it not only is a precursor to Russian actions in Ukraine (both politically and strategically) but also represents a useful stepping stone for an examination of the evolution of Russian hybrid warfare.

At this point, it is important to note that the term 'hybrid warfare' is a Western invention and, as such, it does not have a direct Russian counterpart. Some literature refers to the Russian equivalent as being 'non-linear warfare' while other sources use the term *gibridnaya voyna*.[1] The latter term does exist in Russian sources but refers to what in the West would be termed 'colour revolutions'. It would not serve a useful purpose to introduce even more new and difficult-to-define terms into the research dedicated, in part, to clarifying hybrid warfare. For this reason, when examining the Russian use of conflict and coercion in this chapter, it will be referred to as hybrid warfare.

Prelude to Ukraine

Chechen wars

The two wars in Chechnya represent both the low point of the post-Cold War Russian military decline and the beginning of the Russian military renaissance. The aim of this chapter is not to describe the wars in Chechnya in great detail. While there were a number of contributing factors (political, economic and strategic) that led to the wars, the focus here will be on the tactical and strategic lessons that Russia has learnt during these conflicts and has employed to great effect in subsequent crises. Exactly how these factors were employed, for example, in Ukraine, will be examined in the main part of the chapter.

From a hybrid warfare perspective, the First and Second Chechen Wars mark a significant landmark. William Nemeth's book on the future of war uses Chechnya as a case study and is generally viewed as the origin of the term 'hybrid warfare'. One criticism aimed at Nemeth's work is that he focused too much of the research on giving the Chechen perspective. While it is true that it was the Chechens who engaged in hybrid warfare, the fact is that some of their approaches were adopted by the Russian forces, or they modified their doctrine to better fit the conditions. It was in these wars that the Russian forces exhibited the first signs of hybridity. Since Russia has now emerged as the world's premier hybrid warfare state, it is important to understand where and how that transformation began. This chapter will build on the assumption that, while hybrid warfare did indeed begin in Chechnya, it had not achieved its definitive form during the conflict. A form of warfare can be likened to a biological organism which requires time to develop fully. The Chechen wars merely represent the first step towards a more complex hybrid warfare strategy, which Russia would eventually deploy in Ukraine two decades later.

When the Chechen Republic of Ichkeria[2] declared independence, on a wave of similar declarations throughout the Soviet sphere, in October 1991, the Soviet Union was in its death throes. The climate was somewhat conducive to such a declaration since there were far more vital parts of the crumbling state which the government in Moscow wanted to preserve. The new Russian president Boris Yeltsin largely tolerated the nationalist regime of Dzokhar Dudayev but the latter seems to have politically overstretched when he began advocating full secession from the newly formed Russian Federation.[3] By 1992, the Chechen Republic was able to negotiate the withdrawal of federal troops from its territory, and the transferal of equipment to the Chechens, and was the de facto sovereign, even though Russia never recognized or even acknowledged its independence.[4] Between 1992 and 1994 Chechnya became a conduit for large amounts of illegal trade to and from Russia that not only exposed the Kremlin's political weakness but also opened a porous border into the Russian heartlands.[5] When the situation throughout the rest of the new Russian southern borders had relatively stabilized by 1994, Yeltsin, facing domestic unpopularity and the spread of instability from Chechnya to the rest of the North Caucasus, decided to deal with the separatist Chechens. After a failed coup in November 1994 by a group of Russian-backed Chechens (reminiscent of the 1961 Bay of Pigs invasion), the Russian armed forces invaded Chechnya in December of the same year with the aim to restore it to the status of a component republic of the Russian Federation.[6] Chechen resistance did not abate despite the death of Dudayev in a missile strike in April 1996, if anything, it actually hardened. The political situation for Moscow worsened after a terrorist attack in Russia. When one of the most famous Chechen commanders, Shamil Basayev, seized the hospital in Budyonnovsk in June 1995, and managed to force Moscow to negotiate a ceasefire, it became increasingly clear that Russia was fighting a war it could not win. The fact that Basayev was able to return to Chechnya with his fighters was a further blow to Russian public and military morale.[7] The First Chechen War ended with, from the Russian perspective, a humiliating ceasefire in November 1996. The May 1997 Moscow Peace Treaty formally ended hostilities and granted significant autonomy, amounting almost to a de facto recognition of independence, to Chechnya. With greater autonomy, however, came greater challenges. The biggest challenges the Chechen government faced were the rise of fundamentalist Islamic groups, which had gained considerable prominence in the first war, and a complete economic collapse of the state. Although the entire North Caucasus region is historically Muslim, Chechen independence was predominantly a nationalist policy, not a religious one. However, during the first war, an increasing number of Islamic volunteer fighters came to wage a declared holy war against Russia; the most infamous of these was the warlord Khattab whose goal was not an independent Chechnya but rather a Caucasus Islamic caliphate.[8] The new, Moscow-recognized, government of Aslan Mashkadov failed to curb extremist influence and the economic situation did nothing to improve people's faith in their government. Chechen society and state became increasingly divided along ethnic and religious lines, leading to a collapse of government and the rise of banditry and corruption.

Such an increase in instability in the Caucasus region could not be tolerated by Russia. If the situation in Chechnya continued to deteriorate the problems would spread throughout the rest of the region, which already had historical grievances against Russia. The sense of unfinished business also permeated Russian decision-makers, particularly the military high command.[9] Although Yeltsin continued largely to ignore the issue, the newly appointed prime minister Vladimir Putin grasped it as an opportunity to gain prominence, especially with presidential elections due in the year 2000.[10] When the Second Chechen War began in October 1999, it was the result of a series of apartment bombings blamed on Chechen rebels and a cross-border raid by an extremist group, led by Basayev and Khattab, into neighbouring Dagestan. These events also provided Russia with an opportunity to blame the resumption of hostilities on the Chechen government and present itself as merely defending its territory and people.[11] Correspondingly, the second war was designated as a counter-terrorist operation by official Russian sources. It proceeded quite differently from the first war. If the First Chechen War represented the low point of Russian post-Cold War military performance, the second signalled its rebirth. Not only were federal forces much better prepared and equipped, the intervening years had desperately weakened Chechnya. Even using terrorist 'spectaculars', like seizing the Dubrovka theatre in Moscow in October 2002, or the school in Beslan in September 2003, did not help the Chechen cause. On the contrary, they badly damaged the image of Chechnya across the world, which, post-9/11, no longer saw them as freedom fighters, but merely as terrorists.[12] A tactic that worked surprisingly well in the first war, embodied in the successful raid on Budyonnovsk, had turned out to be a fiasco. The main reason for the failure of the terrorist approach was a more hard-line, non-negotiating stance by Putin, compared to Yeltsin. The perception of such actions in the wider public had also changed. The Beslan tragedy was even called 'Russia's 9/11' by various sources, both in the immediate aftermath and later. This might partly be a result of closer cooperation between Russia and the United States on the GWOT,[13] which came about in the aftermath of 9/11, as both states were seemingly fighting a common enemy. The terrorist spectaculars proved to be the last major acts of the Second Chechen War. Although major military operations were proclaimed finished by the end of 2000, the subsequent counter-terrorist operation was only declared completed in 2009.

Hybrid warfare in Chechnya

Warfare in Chechnya has been noted for its brutality and large-scale destruction, but underneath the surface, as noted by many observes, it was a foretaste of a different kind of conflict. Unlike the US experience in the First Gulf War, which was a conventional interstate conflict, Russia's experience of post-Cold War warfare was much more revealing in how future warfare will be waged. This trend has culminated in what is now called hybrid warfare. In order to ascertain which factors made the Chechnya experience so distinctive, five important elements will be examined: information operations, the use of advanced technology, the rapid and sudden mobilization and de-mobilization, the semi-conventional nature of Chechen forces and the policy of Chechenization.

Information operations played an important role in the Chechen conflicts, even taking into account the technological limitations of the time. Both sides made use of it, with varying degrees of success, but it was the initial Russian failures in this field which led to Russia, rather than the Chechens, gaining more valuable lessons for the future. The first part of the information warfare landscape was the public presentation of the conflict itself. During the First Chechen War, President Yeltsin, as part of his democratic image, did not impose any kind of effective media restrictions on the conflict. As a result, the whole world could see the destruction wreaked on Chechnya and the embarrassing shortcomings of the Russian forces. This was the first televised war for the Russian military and it would seem that no procedures were in place to control the flow of information. The Chechens, whose leaders tended to be rather flamboyant, managed to portray their struggle in anti-imperial and national liberation terms,[14] which resulted in widespread public support for their cause, even in the Western world. The psychological impact of the successful Chechen campaign went beyond NGO and media support. Since the Russian forces were largely made up of conscripts, who rotated in an out of the area, their stories were widely available to the Russian home front. This caused widespread demoralization and created a war-weary public that was already sceptical of Yeltsin's reforms and threatened to end public support for any government action. Clearly, on a strategic media level, the Chechens vastly outperformed Russia.[15] However, it was a lesson that was not lost on Vladimir Putin who, as soon as the Second Chechen War began, took tight personal control of the operations and instituted a complete lockdown on all information in and out of Chechnya.[16] Only select reporters from friendly news outlets (almost exclusively Russian media) were permitted to report from the field, and those reporters who did dissent were faced with increased hostility and lack of cooperation. This combination of information control and direct involvement was also used as part of Putin's wider political move to reduce the power of Russia's oligarchs.[17] At a time without social media, such control was easier to achieve, but more important than its direct impact was that the experience taught the Kremlin that such mechanisms can be of great use.

The use of advanced technology has always been a staple of any conflict as all sides would naturally gravitate to obtain the best and most advanced capabilities, which could often, but not always, tip the scales. In this respect, both Chechen wars are something of an exception. Before the conflict began, the Kremlin pulled out many of the troops stationed throughout the, soon to be former, southern borderlands of the Soviet Union.[18] Strategically, the military doctrine in the early days of the Yeltsin administration was chaotic. With the old Soviet priorities of opposing NATO forces in the Northern European Plain now irrelevant, the number one threat became ethnic and nationalist movements within the new Russian Federation.[19] However, despite fitting the threat profile, Chechnya was given a lower priority as relations with Ukraine, Georgia and Azerbaijan, among others, took precedence. As a direct result of this, Chechnya came into possession of an arsenal of heavy equipment left behind by the withdrawing troops after it declared independence in 1991. When the war began both sides were very similarly equipped and, relative to its size and budget, the Chechen force was somewhat modern. Particularly important were stockpiles of anti-aircraft and anti-armour missiles, as well as handgun and rifle ammunition and stocks of Rocket Propelled Grenades (RPGs), a favourite weapon of the Chechens. While these quickly dwindled due to the difficulties of resupply, they provided the Chechen armed forces, effectively a militia formation, with the capabilities of a conventional army. However, the key use of advanced technology was in the sphere of communications. The Chechen combat units proved remarkably adept at using modern satellite and mobile telecommunications to coordinate their efforts. Sometimes these means proved to be even more reliable than Russian military communications. Additionally, the heavy and active online presence allowed Chechen forces to dominate domestic (both Chechen and Russian) and foreign news, providing videos of attacks, interviews with prominent leaders and their own news channels. Often, they would hijack the Russian news signals and substitute their own, an approach that allowed them to keep the Chechen public informed of their actions, policies and goals.[20] Since these actions reached into Russia proper as well, they were able to shape the media profile of the conflict among the Russian population. Such methods proved to be cost effective as well, with conventional weaponry being more expensive and ultimately less effective in bringing an end to the war.[21]

On the Russian side, the first war saw the use of old Cold War era weaponry and equipment, which proved to be woefully inadequate. What proved particularly problematic was the use of heavy munitions at a rate with which Russian manufacturing simply could not keep up, the result being that Russian forces had to use increasingly older and unreliable artillery stock.[22] The situation was somewhat improved by the time of the second war, particularly on an organizational level. More importantly, although modern equipment was still in short supply, the Russian armed forces had absorbed the bitter lessons and employed these capabilities in a new way, better suited to the assigned task, using better and more effective tactics. Conversely, the Chechens had either used up or lost their best equipment during the first war and were increasingly reliant on homemade weapons or on raiding Russian supplies.[23] They were also limited to the same tactics they used the first time, which were a shock to the Russians then, but would not be again.

The most important of the hybrid features in Chechnya was the ability of the Chechen combat formations to mobilize and de-mobilize quickly and efficiently. Historically, Chechen society has always been separated into family-based clans for whom warfare was a constant fact of life. This was used to great effect by the military commanders who organized small clan-based units, which were personally loyal to their commander, often shared a family bond and were in essence already pre-trained for guerrilla warfare.[24] Many Chechens were veterans of the Soviet armed forces, with significant numbers of them trained as snipers.[25] The historical and cultural 'training' the Chechens received by the very nature of their geographical reality made them a perfect fit for such roles. However, their key feature was the ability to blend into the civilian population and later be able rapidly to organize, carry out an operation and either disappear into the mountainous countryside or blend back into the population. This was greatly aided by the use of reliable communications and the fact that their surrounding population shared close bonds with the fighters and were therefore willing to protect them. The Russian forces often found it impossible to distinguish between fighters and civilians, with the unfortunate consequence that large portions of the Chechen population were subjected to harassment, interrogation, internment or execution. In the long term, such heavy-handed approaches were counterproductive and merely increased the support for the fighters, an issue that was, at least theoretically, addressed during the second war.[26]

Additionally, the nature of the Chechen force itself is very important in understanding the hybrid nature of the conflict. When Dudayev proclaimed independence in 1991, he set out to create a coherent military. To that end, he nominally organized a number of the clan militias, who were loyal to the regime, into the Chechen state's armed forces. Although the precise nature of their structure is difficult to ascertain, a safe assumption is that these forces retained their previous organization in practice, particularly the fact that they were still loyal to their local leaders, rather than a central government authority. This can be seen by the fact that during even the most crucial battles, individual, proven commanders were able to act on their own or ignore orders. The Chechens used this de-centralization to great advantage and developed a 'swarming' tactic to engage superior Russian forces. With highly mobile, well-armed and, above all, very motivated groups of fighters acting in concert with one another, they were able to outmatch a conventional army.[27] The ability to attain such a significant amount of coordination from the varied groups without a highly centralized 'high command' was impressive.

It effectively produced a fighting force that, from the outside, resembled guerrilla fighters but was in reality able to act as a conventional army. It was precisely this dual, semi-conventional nature of the Chechen forces that is so important to the development of hybrid warfare. The same units were able to act as large formations in stand-up battles, perform rear-guard actions during retreats, besiege villages and fight in urban Grozny while being simultaneously able to perform small unit ambushes of Russian columns or carry out hit-and-run attacks on outposts or isolated garrisons. The former nevertheless required a somewhat centralized command and logistical structure, as exhibited during the retaking of Grozny in 1996, although these structures were much smaller and looser than in any conventional force while the latter showcased high mobility and independent initiative of combat commanders. It is important to note that Chechen forces in any individual engagement rarely exceeded a few hundred fighters; a notable exception is the retaking of Grozny which featured a coordinated attack by an increasing number of fighters, beginning with about 1,600 and reaching up to 6,000 towards the end.[28] Evidently, while they strategically acted as large organized formations, tactically they stuck to their small unit approach. As the Russians discovered, the two combined into a formidable force unlike anything that the Russian, or earlier Soviet, armies had encountered before.

The only slightly similar previous experience that soldiers and commanders on both sides had was the campaign in Afghanistan (1979–89).[29] Afghan mujahedeen, however, fought like a classic insurgency force, avoiding conventional battles and instead focused on a guerrilla approach. While the Russian forces in Chechnya employed many of the tactics they had learnt in Afghanistan, it took them almost a decade to come to grips fully with them and apply them successfully, mainly due to a lack of reform following the breakup of the Soviet Union. Further complicating matters was the fact that the Chechens, many of whom were Soviet army veterans, knew the tactics their opponents were using. A particular Soviet favourite, using transport helicopters accompanied by heavy attack helicopters for ground support to airlift units behind enemy positions rapidly was heavily exploited by the well-equipped Chechens, who, thanks to their rapid mobilization and movement, were able to turn landing zones into helicopter kill zones.[30] The lack of a professional, non-commissioned officer (NCO) class meant that the Russian conscript army, which entered Chechnya, was forced to improvise and learn during the heat of battle.[31]

During the First Chechen War the tactics used by the Chechens were largely a reflection of their strategic reality. They would never be able to defeat Russian forces in a conventional war and a protracted guerrilla campaign would never be able to guarantee independence, their ultimate goal. Nor is Chechnya, with its small population and confined territory, a good location for a guerrilla campaign against an opponent with an unmatchable numerical superiority. The Chechens therefore made do with what they had, but in the process of doing that, they created a novel type of warfare. However, by the time of the Second Chechen War the Russians began using these same elements to conduct their operations. This demonstrates the importance and impact of the Chechen way of war.

While they learnt from their opponents, the Russian forces also added a very important element, which would prove effective in many subsequent campaigns: the policy of Chechenization. The term 'Chechenization' refers to the idea that the majority of the fighting, particularly during the insurgency stage of the conflict, would be delegated to pro-Russian Chechen groups, led by Akhmad Kadyrov, and later to his son Ramzan. This approach was made possible by the defection of a number of prominent Chechen leaders and their units to the Russian side at the start of the second war. The idea behind Chechnization was threefold: to take advantage of the split within Chechen society between the traditional nationalists and the more militant Islamists, to provide the former an honourable and simple way of laying down their arms or switching sides and to add some much-needed legitimacy to the new pro-Russian Chechen government.[32] From the Chechen perspective, such a policy introduced a similar problem that the Russian forces had faced, namely the difficulty of identifying the enemy. Internecine conflict of this kind is often barbaric, but with massive support from Russia, the pro-Russian Chechen forces were able to present themselves as a more acceptable alternative to the majority of the population, who were not overly enthusiastic about the rise of radicalized Islamic groups, but at the same time did not want to see a completely Russian-dominated Chechnya. Close personal and family ties in this case worked both for and against the Kadyrov forces; they helped to convince some clans to switch sides while permanently alienating others.[33] In the end the combination of local forces, massive military, logistical and financial support from Russia, and the internal societal factors proved to be a winning combination. The use of local, proxy forces, has since established itself as a staple of Russian hybrid warfare. Such uses of local forces are of course not new; the history of the Cold War is full of examples of so-called proxy wars, but it is their combination with other forms of warfare that makes it an important element of a hybrid strategy.

When the Second Chechen War officially ended in 2009, the country itself was well on the way to relative prosperity, aided by a big infusion of federal funds. Ironically, in order to keep the Kadyrov regime in power and to maintain peace and security, the Kremlin had to delegate a significant amount of autonomy to Grozny, resulting in a situation where Chechens are now freer than they had ever been throughout two centuries of Russian rule.[34] Considering the conflict began largely because of the Chechen nationalist idea of full independence, it could be argued that they had achieved at least a more realistic version of that goal. That such an aim was achievable against an opponent whose military and political power could never be matched by them is even more impressive. The wars did cause enormous damage in Chechnya. Grozny was declared the most destroyed city in the world in 2003,[35] and almost half of the pre-war population had either fled or been killed.[36] So if the strategy employed by the Chechens can be said to have ultimately been successful, the cost of that success was very high. From a hybrid perspective, the first use of hybrid warfare can be declared a partial success, but it also clearly demonstrates the fact that once the threshold of large-scale conventional war is breached, a hybrid strategy can incur costs which bring into question its original rationale. From a Russian perspective, the first encounter with an albeit embryonic hybrid opponent provided valuable lessons which Moscow has clearly remembered. By modifying their approach in Chechnya to mimic certain aspects of the Chechen forces it could be argued that the Russians created their first, equally embryonic, hybrid force. With the greater resources of a major power and the corresponding political and military capabilities, Russia has been able to develop a hybrid strategy for its newfound force and its next field test was not far away. In fact, the second Russian use of a hybrid approach took place just across the Chechen frontier in Georgia.

Russo-Georgian War

The five-day war in August 2008 between Georgia and the breakaway republics of Abkhazia and South Ossetia, which were supported by Russia, generated much debate, particularly for such a small and limited conflict. The main reason behind such extensive coverage and study is the wider implications of the war, rather than the operations themselves. The conflict has now been recognized as major milestone in the deterioration of the West's relationship with Russia (particularly NATO–Russia relations) and signalled a clear escalation of the post-Cold War era of Russian activity in its near abroad.[37] Previous conflicts, like the wars in Chechnya, were largely internal in nature. Intervening in South Ossetia, however, meant war with a sovereign, independent and internationally recognized state, Georgia,[38] which had slipped from Moscow's control.

Before examining, briefly, the timeline of the war, it is important to note a number of other events that had preceded it. Three in particular, are crucial to obtain an in-depth understanding of the actions of both sides. NATO's intervention in Serbia in 1999 and the creation of the 'state' of Kosovo, already viewed with deep suspicion by Russia, was further compounded by the partial international recognition of Kosovo in February 2008. The election of Mikheil Saakashvili, part of the so-called Rose Revolution, as the president of Georgia in 2004, was at first viewed by Russia as a welcome break from his predecessor, the anti-Russian Eduard Shevarnadze. Saakashvili, however, continued with an increasingly pro-Western stance as well as a very aggressive policy towards the breakaway republics of South Ossetia and Abkhazia. The situation was further complicated by the Russian suspicion that his ascent to power was funded and favoured by the West, particularly by the United States.[39] The final event, which made confrontation almost inevitable, was the proposal tabled by US president George Bush at the Bucharest NATO summit in April 2008, wherein he argued for Georgian and Ukrainian membership. For Russia, this was one NATO expansion too far, while the Georgian government seemed particularly empowered by this show of support.[40] Unfortunately for them, they seemed to have interpreted the move as tacit approval for their bid to settle the outstanding territorial disputes; uncontested borders being one of the conditions for NATO membership.[41] Frequent and friendly visits by numerous high-ranking US officials, including the president, only reinforced Saakashvili's convictions, despite their obvious flaws.[42]

Abkhazia and South Ossetia became autonomous entities after the breakup of the Soviet Union, although Georgia has maintained that they are part of its sovereign territory. This has led to many conflicts and border skirmishes throughout the decades, to the point where a daily exchange of gunfire was a normal occurrence, despite the presence of UN observers and Confederation of Independent States (CIS), as well as Georgian, peacekeepers.[43] The increasingly nationalistic political sentiment in Georgia only exacerbated problems. From a Russian perspective, both regions provided them with leverage over Georgia as well as a limited buffer zone. They are a classic example of a frozen conflict, which both sides would periodically use to try and antagonize the other. However, with the drastic change of Georgian politics after 2004, the situation became increasingly tense. Combined with the events in the wider region, including the wars in Chechnya, and the US lobbying for Georgian entry into NATO, the otherwise provincial dispute had the potential to become a major world crisis.

The actual fighting began on 7 August in 2008 when Georgian troops, pre-positioned for an invasion, began shelling the South Ossetian capital of Tskhinvali. The Georgian plan was rapidly to capture the city, as well as the Roki tunnel, which was the most direct way into Russia. The Georgian army, relatively well equipped and trained, planned for the entire operation to last only a few hours. As a result of this, the Georgian plan did not include the possibility of the entry of Russian troops.[44] Because any combat operations against the autonomous regions would rely on rapid deployment, the Georgian military wanted its fighters to have some familiarity with local geography. Prior to the commencement of hostilities, many Georgian soldiers served as peacekeepers in this region and Georgian army units were rotated in and out of the force with very high frequency especially for this purpose.[45] Surprisingly, their much vaunted training did not seem to amount to much, as they were almost immediately bogged down and never came close to capturing either the capital or the important roads to Russia. The South Ossetian militia, due to limited training and outdated equipment, could never hope to defeat the Georgians. Ultimately, however, they would not need to as Russia had assured both South Ossetia and Georgia that any Georgian military incursions into the breakaway region would trigger a Russian intervention.[46] Considering the balance of forces, it is remarkable that they managed to hold back the Georgians for as long as they did, even before the Russian reinforcements arrived. The rapid strike against South Ossetia, by far the smaller and weaker of the two territories, was part of a larger bid by Saakashvili to deal with both separatist entities and would likely have been followed by an attack on Abkhazia as well.

Russian troops entered South Ossetia in the early hours of 8 August first as a small forward tactical group, designed to capture key points and hold them until the main force arrived. Despite some Russian ineptitude and problems with ageing equipment, they very efficiently rolled back the Georgian military and caused them to retreat into Georgia proper in a complete rout. Supported by numerous airstrikes and the use of concentrated artillery, as well as a naval task force, which landed troops in Abkhazia and neutralized the Georgian navy, the Russian troops then advanced across the border towards the Georgian capital Tbilisi.[47] The goal was not to capture the city, but to destabilize and hopefully force the Saakashvili government out of power. A side bonus of this move was the raiding of the Georgian military and supply bases, which were placed near the South Ossetian border. By the time a ceasefire was declared on 12 August, the Georgians suffered massive equipment and supply losses. The fact that they suffered such horrendous losses after the fighting had mostly drawn to a halt was even more embarrassing.[48]

Politically, the conflict was seen as a boon to pan-European institutions like the EU and the OSCE, since France, the mediator for the talks, was holding the rotating Presidency of the Council of the European Union at the time.[49] Russia had sent an important message to its competitors in the Caucasus region as well as NATO. Unfortunately, as later actions would suggest, the United States in particular did not hear or understand that message as their policy towards Georgia did not change, even with a new administration in power,[50] and NATO still lists Georgia as a prospective member state.[51] The biggest impact of the Russo-Georgian War was the political aftermath and the clear delineation of spheres of interests in Eastern Europe; it also signalled that a resurgent Russia was willing to resort to war to defend what it perceived as its core national interests. While that is not unusual, the fact that the borders of the EU and NATO had been pushed so close to Russia over the preceding two decades now meant that the national interests Russia was willing to defend so aggressively, were located in a geographically very constrained area (in effect limited to Belarus, Ukraine, Moldova and Georgia). This lack of a 'buffer zone' for geopolitical manoeuvring went largely unrecognized in the West, despite repeated warning from prominent individuals with extensive knowledge in such matters. The consequences were not long in coming.

Hybrid elements

The 2008 Russo-Georgian War was not in itself a hybrid conflict. The vast majority of operations were purely conventional, focused on combined-arms tactics and large-scale conventional forces. There were, however, some hybrid elements present during the war. Most of them had been present earlier in Chechnya, but had been further developed and refined in their use and acted as a stepping stone to the much larger conflict in Ukraine. Three elements in particular are very relevant: information operations, cyber warfare and the use of local separatists and proxies.

In contrast with information operations in Chechnya, which only began after the start of the conflict, an information war between Russia and Georgia had been escalating for years. Both sides attempted to twist facts and events to spin news reports in support of their own narratives. Ever since South Ossetia and Abkhazia became semi-autonomous, Georgia had threatened to reintegrate them, by force if necessary. This rhetoric expanded to a policy of hostility towards Russia, who was backing the breakaway republics. As the situation deteriorated, both sides staged border incidents or lambasted the other in news outlets. President Saakashvili took this policy to a whole new level by combining it with a desire to become a NATO member, and gain official US support for his irredentist policies and for modernizing the Georgian armed forces. By claiming that Russia was behind the escalation of the conflict in 2004 and 2006, as well as any other developments that might not be seen as beneficial to Georgia, he combined the information conflict with an actual physical threat.[52] Most realistic observers would agree that Georgia had no practical way of defeating Russia in an open conflict, and yet that is what Saakashvili was apparently trying to achieve. Imagining US support where no actual commitments existed seemed to have become almost a pathology in the Georgian government.[53] Russia undoubtedly took advantage of the situation by increasing the pressure on Saakashvili who, eventually, and mostly by his own fault, manoeuvred his way into a corner.

A particularly important narrative was one surrounding the question of which side actually started the war. Of course, such questions are never easily answered as they are closely connected to a larger debate on what constitutes sufficient action to be called a war. The simplest way is, of course, if a war is officially declared, but that has disappeared from modern conflict trends. The alternative is to determine, in some way, when open hostilities began. In the case of the 2008 Russo-Georgian War, it has been argued persuasively, although not without controversy, that it was in fact Georgia who fired the first bullet.

That fact was not apparent at first and, to an alarmingly large degree, Western sources almost immediately began condemning Russian incursions and widely believed the Georgian version of events.[54] The story Saakashvili was spinning was that Georgian actions were in response to the presence of Russian troops in South Ossetia, who had undertaken an offensive intervention.[55] This stance conveniently ignored the fact that Georgian troops had been amassing at the border for a number of days beforehand and that Saakashvili's rhetoric was inflammatory. These factors caused both the South Ossetian and Russian governments to put their forces on high alert.[56] After the war was over the EU ordered the Report of the Independent International Fact-Finding Mission on the

Conflict in Georgia (RIIFFMCG) to be conducted by the career Swiss diplomat Heidi Tagliavini. It was precisely the muddled nature of the information coming from both sides that prompted the EU to commission the report. While by no means exonerating Russia from any wrongdoing (the report also contained a detailed and damning account of Russian human rights abuses), it did establish that the conflict was initiated by Georgia.[57] Nevertheless, despite the RIIFFMCG report or even members of Saakashvili's own government testifying to this effect,[58] some states simply refused to adapt their stance, particularly East European states like Poland and the Baltic republics. In light of the crisis in Ukraine, the Georgian government has only intensified its manipulation to this effect, as did Saakashvili when, after his second presidential term expired in 2013 and he left Georgia for fear of criminal prosecution, he was governor of the Odessa oblast in Ukraine from May 2015 until November 2016.

As mentioned earlier, Russia is by no means innocent of manipulating the flow of information. In fact, if part of their strategy was to portray Saakashvili as an aggressive and impulsive warmonger, they can be said to have been very successful. Russia had countered increased Georgian troop presence on the South Ossetian and Abkhazian border by deploying additional troops as peacekeepers, but capped it at 3,000, the highest number allowed by the Moscow Treaty.[59] Perhaps the most important aspect of the information war for Moscow was not the process itself, but how it played out in the foreign press. By immediately believing the Georgian version of events and dismissing Russian official press statements, Russia was left with little to lose in the public relations battle with the West. Even after the EU report was published, a large number of states, and public opinion in many others, still condemned Russia as the aggressor. For Russia then, the lessons were clear: first, the initial press narrative was crucial and second, some Western states would, regardless, always blame Russia for conflicts on its periphery , while others would meekly stand by.

Another aspect of the war was the use of cyber warfare. What the terms 'cyber warfare' or 'cyber operations' precisely mean is difficult to determine as most actors do not seem to have any sort of useful definition. Both the US and UK governments, for example, have so-called cyber strategies, policy documents specifically related to cyber threats, but neither contains any technical definition. Part of the problem stems from the general overuse of the term 'war', particularly in the public sphere, where it is used primarily for dramatic effect.[60] Briefly, cyber warfare is usually defined as damaging actions by states or other actors upon a target's computers or information networks through the use of various cyber means.[61] These operations take place in a specific battlespace of 'cyberspace' which consists of networked information technology and the included data.[62] Definitional quagmire notwithstanding, cyber operations are an increasingly important component of modern, including hybrid, warfare. They are not, however, a defining characteristic of hybrid warfare, despite many arguments to the contrary, merely one element among many which can help identify a hybrid conflict.

In the case of the 2008 war, both the Russians and the Georgians had been engaged in an escalating cyber 'feud' for years, but during the conflict itself both sides attempted to shut down the opponent's news and government websites in order to impede or influence the spread of information. Although the use of cyber warfare is usually associated with impact on the flow of information, the term itself is much broader and can produce effects on four levels: physical, code, regulatory and the level of ideas.[63] It is precisely the potential for a real-world consequence by cyberattacks that makes the idea so intriguing, whether it is the Stuxnet virus, damaging Iranian nuclear centrifuges,[64] or a malware designed to overload an oil pipeline,[65] part of which runs through Georgia.

Despite no definitive links between cyberattacks during the 2008 war and the Russian government, the fact that most actions coincided with troop movements on the ground, would suggest at the very least a tacit approval of actions by private individuals with some limited level of coordination. Such a mode of operation is perfectly suited to a hybrid strategy since official deniability, however tenuous, is not only useful but necessary to prevent unwanted escalation. The conflict also demonstrated that a combined conventional and cyber-attack during military operations can have a disastrous effect on the opponent's ability to communicate and coordinate its forces. The 2008 Russo-Georgian War is usually considered to be the first example of the use of cyber capabilities in conjunction with conventional operations and, at least for the Russian side, the combination had proven very effective. Georgian communications were severely disrupted to the point that the cohesion of the entire invasion force had broken down, a factor that contributed to the general rout.[66] While it would be wrong to claim that cyber operations proved decisive, they demonstrated that, if used effectively, they can provide an important edge in the crucial moments of battle.

In another similarity with Chechnya, the Russian forces incorporated proxy and local forces, particularly in the early stages of the conflict. Despite Russia lifting the arms embargo in 2006, these forces were under-equipped and poorly trained; they nevertheless proved sufficiently strong to delay the Georgians while suffering relatively minor casualties. Once sufficient numbers of Russian troops arrived, they took over the majority of offensive operations while local forces guarded the rear.

More interesting is the presence of the Chechen Vostok battalion, at the time still part of the Russian military intelligence service. While it gained some notoriety for its often brutal actions in Chechnya both during and after the second war, it was used in South Ossetia in clean-up operations. Due to the complex ethnic makeup of the South Caucasus there were a number of Georgian enclaves located in South Ossetia. When the Georgian armed forces invaded, they quickly moved to take control of those enclaves, partially because some of them were located in strategically important areas but mostly to provide Georgian troops a safe haven from which further operations could be launched. Correspondingly, once the Georgian military began its rout, most of the civilians from the enclaves followed suit. A combination of South Ossetian and Russian troops (including the Vostok battalion) were used to clear those enclaves of any potential threats.[67] While the Vostok battalion has often been accused of human right violations and even war crimes, the fact that most Georgians had abandoned the enclaves before these troops got there meant that these operations were not particularly noteworthy. It was disbanded, in fact, along with the Zapad battalion[68] soon after the end of the Russo-Georgian war. The Vostok battalion later re-emerged during the fighting in Eastern Ukraine where it was originally comprised of veterans of the disbanded unit until it eventually became a kind of multi-ethnic mercenary force.[69] If that is indeed the case, it would mean that Russia has been using the same proxy units across three conflicts, in relatively similar circumstances. One reason why the unit was selected to perform such tasks was that it provided Russia, and particularly the Russian military, with deniability in what could have been very brutal and politically damaging operations. The principal idea behind clean-up operations in South Ossetia might have been based on military logic, to flush out any remaining Georgian fighters, but it also had the potential to escalate into an ethnic cleanse of Georgian enclaves, something in which the conventional Russian military forces could not openly engage.

Hybrid warfare in Ukraine

The most famous example of hybrid warfare, and the one that thrust the concept into widespread use, is the Russian operation in Ukraine. The conflict itself is important for a number of reasons; chiefly because it re-introduced the possibility of open hostilities on the European continent, but also because it signalled the end of US-NATO hegemony in the region, leading to a return of hard power politics. From a hybrid perspective, the conflict represents the maturation of Russian hybrid warfare approaches and could potentially be used as a template for future uses by other states. That being said, it is important to note that the Russian situation vis-à-vis Ukraine was unique and offered several advantages that other states might not have. Rather than think of Ukraine as a case study which can simply be transplanted into every other part of the globe, it is merely the lessons and the approaches that other actors might consider valuable; with the understanding that the strategy should be adapted to changing circumstances.

Build-up to February 2014

No crisis ever occurs in a vacuum. As with previous cases of Russian hybrid warfare, the examination of its use in Ukraine will be preceded by a brief historical timeline and strategic framework, both of which are key in understanding the events leading up to the uprising in February 2014 as well as its aftermath. Since this case study represents the main part of this chapter, the historical narrative will be more extensive and include a general overview of the state of affairs in Ukraine since its independence.

In general terms, the post-Cold War history of Ukraine could best be described as an era of duality. There are a number of splits present both within Ukrainian society and in its politics. There is a clear West/North versus East/South divide which is based on language, culture and political affiliation. A key feature in understanding the politics of Ukraine is the internal tension over the very nature of Ukrainian statehood, the contest between a monist and a pluralist state. Richard Sakwa describes the two aspects as corresponding to

> the long struggle in Ukrainian history between those who assert that the country is an autochthonous cultural and political unity in its own right, and those who believe that common ancestry in Kievan Rus … means that they are part of the same cultural, and by implication, political community.[70]

Monism therefore represents a very nationalist vision of Ukraine while pluralism argues that it is the un-homogenous characteristics of Ukraine that give it strength. While on its own this is not unusual in many European states, it has been elevated to an existential crisis within Ukraine by political mismanagement. The monist and pluralist camps do not directly correspond to trends of unitarism against federalization but, like Ukrainian politics in general, they are very clearly geographically divided. The monist approach is favoured in the Western and Northern Ukraine, as well as in Kiev, while the pluralist approach has its base in the East and South. These geographical divisions do however correspond to the tendency to favour a unitary or a federalized Ukrainian state, respectively.[71]

The Western/Northern parts of Ukraine tend to be more Western leaning, or at the very least more anti-Russian while the exact opposite can be said for the Southern/Eastern regions. In practice, the most visible division between the two approaches is over the role of the Russian language and culture within Ukraine. On paper, the divide seems to follow the same geographical lines, but with the added complication that Russian tends to be the language of higher education, business and even conversations at home across the majority of Ukraine. Up to 80 per cent of Ukrainians, which must include the more nationalist west and north, use Russian as an everyday language as opposed to Ukrainian.[72] Despite this, the monist nationalist governments, which have dominated Ukrainian politics, maintain that such a policy is crucial for the creation of a Ukrainian nation state. While the argument that making Ukrainian as the sole official language might appear, in principle, to aid the creation of a monist Ukrainian nation, the consequences of policies based on such thinking alienated most of the Russian and other ethnic minorities as well as a significant number of pluralist Ukrainians; in many ways ensuring that the monist vision of a unitary Ukraine was always going to be in peril.[73] The internal divides within Ukrainian society and state have manifested in a number of ways throughout the period since independence, even in foreign policy and regardless of who was in power. They are a constant and must therefore be taken into account when forming a theoretical framework within which to examine the Ukrainian crisis.

Ukraine became an independent state following a referendum on its independence in December 1991. The period immediately following independence was very tumultuous in terms of domestic politics. There was a big divide between the drive for a more Western-oriented market economy and the continuation of old communist practices.[74] Neither side prevailed and Ukraine has remained, to this day, in a state of indecision, which has largely become an entrenched system. Ukraine's first president, Leonid Kravchuk, was able to manage the east–west internal division relatively well, although in economic terms his presidency was dismal.[75] Perhaps the most important legacy of his tenure in office was the so-called Budapest Memorandum, which offered Ukraine a guarantee of its territorial integrity in return for its relinquishing the Soviet-era nuclear arsenal and maintaining the status of a neutral state. The memorandum was signed by the leaders of Russia, the United States, Ukraine and the United Kingdom,[76] although it was not intended as a formal treaty and was therefore not ratified by any of the states. The agreement was very important as it essentially established a Western guarantee of Ukrainian territorial integrity vis-à-vis Russia which has in actual fact proven to be inadequate. Kravchuk's successor Leonid Kuchma was the more Western-oriented. Although he started off as the pro-Russian candidate when he was campaigning against Kravchuk's policies, Kuchma shifted his stance after his second election victory. He enjoyed a good relationship with US president Bill Clinton with Ukraine becoming the third largest recipient of American foreign aid.[77] This foreign aid was to prove problematic in the long run. In 2003, Kuchma also announced Ukraine's desire to become both a member of NATO and the EU, although he soon realized that membership in either was an unrealistic prospect.[78]

For Ukraine, 2004 was to prove the most important year in the period between its independence and the beginning of the conflict with Russia in 2014. If the previous decade was indecisive in terms of the balance between a progressive and conservative path for Ukraine, the early years of the new century saw a definitive rise in support for a more liberal, market-oriented Western democratic approach. The fact that during Kuchma's presidency corruption in Ukraine had reached unprecedented levels was one of the main reasons for the push for reform.[79] Events came to a head in the 2004 presidential election. With Kuchma barred from a third term by the constitution the contest was between the reformist bloc, led by the populist figures of Viktor Yushchenko and Yulia Tymoshenko, and the prime minister and establishment favourite Viktor Yanukovych. After an election rigging debacle which proclaimed Yanukovich the winner, protests erupted across the country. After intense negotiation, mediated by the EU, another election was agreed and held. This time it was Yushchenko who won, with Tymoshenko becoming the prime minister.[80] The so-called 'Orange Revolution'[81] had swept in and brought very high expectations with them. Unfortunately, they were to prove unrealistic. The old political system and the power of the oligarchs remained, and the situation was not aided by the bickering and in-fighting between Yushchenko and Tymoshenko. She was dismissed from her post of prime minister after only eight months and government instability was to remain a trademark of the Yushchenko years.

As a very pro-Western (or rather anti-Russian) politician, Yushchenko attempted to move Ukraine firmly outside of Russia's orbit. His approach was twofold, strengthening the political and economic bonds between Ukraine and the EU and NATO, and also a more nationalist domestic policy.[82] Both of those were to prove to be divisive within Ukraine and only further angered and alienated Russia. While it is possible to see why Yushchenko attempted such an approach, it nevertheless seems recklessly dangerous for a state like Ukraine essentially to attempt to ignore the wishes and concerns of an immensely more powerful neighbour with which it shared a common history, not to mention a very close economic relationship. There are certain similarities which can be drawn between Yushchenko and Saakashvili on this matter; both came to power through a 'colour' revolution and both seemingly assumed that Russia would simply stand by as they did whatever they wished. In both cases this was to prove a dreadful miscalculation. Among Yushchenko's most anti-Russian policies was the recognition of Ukrainian 'national hero' Stepan Bandera, who was a controversial nationalist and Nazi collaborator,[83] as well as the campaign to designate the Holodomor as a genocide perpetrated against the Ukrainian people.[84] The issue of Ukrainian becoming the sole official language of the state was also raised again. While the constitution did provide for the protection of other minority languages, it relegated Russian to an 'other' language. There are large populations of Russophone people in the eastern and southern Ukraine,[85] for whom this was a worrying turn of events.

In attempting to build up a national Ukrainian consciousness Yushchenko made two errors. First, the Ukrainization policy alienated large segments of the society. As it was seemingly done in an attempt to join the EU, it tainted the EU association process with a very radical nationalist hue. In turn, this meant that those worried about his policies were more likely to support politicians who advocated closer ties to Russia (the fact that those regions did not vote for him anyway made this decision easier). Secondly, by upsetting the internal balance of a pluralist Ukraine, he permanently disrupted the relations both within and outside of the country. The two previous presidents, whatever their other faults, were clear on the problem of Ukraine's split personality and attempted to balance the competing sides whether in domestic or foreign policy. Yushchenko's many governments, in a drive for rapid reform, ignored that divide and attempted to paper over the splits and pretend as though they did not exist, which only made the problems worse. The fact that he also managed to deepen the economic crisis, by alienating powerful oligarchs as well as Russia, meant that by the time of the 2010 presidential election Yushchenko was no longer a viable candidate.[86]

The election of Yanukovych in 2010, in what most observers agreed was a relatively free and fair election,[87] was mostly a consequence of the disunion among his opposition. He was completely reliant on the Russian-leaning parts of Ukraine for his political support and accordingly most of his policies reflected that reality. That is not to say that Yanukovych was always amenable to Russia. His relationship with Vladimir Putin[88] was very poor and the Russian president preferred to deal with Tymoshenko.[89] It would seem, based on his major policy decisions, that Yanukovych wanted to return to the old balancing act between Russia on one side and the EU/NATO on the other.[90] It could have worked, as the popular support for NATO membership was decidedly low across Ukraine.[91] However, his attempt to steer Ukraine towards a non-aligned status, which was codified in 2010,[92] was undermined by his continuation of the corrupt domestic policies which were dominated by the country's oligarchs. Closer association with the EU was bound to put that system under immense pressure; with closer ties came greater demands for reform and transparency. Russia offered him an easier way out, with a $15 billion direct loan and a significant reduction in gas prices. When Yanukovych cancelled the signing of the Association Agreement with the EU in November 2013, it was not so much an attempt to align with Russia as it was, ironically, given later events, an attempt to preserve the system and his place in it.[93]

The abrupt decision to halt association with the EU seems to have resonated within Ukraine more than anyone had anticipated: four months of increasingly violent protests followed, centred on Kiev's Maidan square, although similar protests were occurring in all major population centres. On 21 February 2014, Yanukovych made a deal, endorsed by the EU, with the opposition leaders in parliament to restore the revised constitution, assemble an interim government of national unity and hold early elections in December.[94] There are severe doubts as to whether either side could actually be satisfied with this agreement. The opposition within parliament was much more moderate than the increasingly right-wing protesters, who largely rejected the proposal and demanded that Yanukovych immediately step down, while Yanukovych clearly felt that his position was untenable and fled Kiev the next day.[95] Upon his departure, parliament voted him out of office, in complete disregard to the constitution, and set an earlier date for new presidential elections.[96] Russia immediately responded by denouncing the interim government as a coup and questioned its legitimacy. Given the circumstances of its creation the Russian position has considerable validity even though the new Kiev authorities were immediately widely accepted in the West.[97]

Seizing of Crimea

The Crimean peninsula has played an important role in the histories of both Russia and Ukraine. It had been a Tatar polity and later part of the Crimean Mongol Khanate throughout the middle ages. The Russian Empire conquered and integrated Crimea into its fold in 1784 and it remained in Russian hands until 1954, when administratively it became part of the Ukrainian Soviet Socialist Republic, a constituent republic of the Soviet Union. At the time, this also transferred ownership and administration of the city of Sevastopol and its naval base. However, with a later change in the constitution Sevastopol, along with its naval base, became an 'object of all-union significance'; a 'republican' city that was directly administered by the federal government, rather than the regional administration.[98] When the Soviet Union collapsed in 1991, the issue of Crimea and Sevastopol came up in discussions over territory. Yeltsin, however, did not press the matter as he assumed that the newly established CIS would essentially mean that things would not change on the ground. The status of Sevastopol was never properly addressed even though it should legally have come under Russian administration.[99] For strategic and geopolitical reasons Sevastopol was immensely important to Russia as it represents the only major 'warm water' port for the Russian navy and is the home of its Black Sea Fleet. The two sides signed an agreement on the partition of the fleet and their respective basing rights in 1997.[100] Among other provisions, it gave Russia the right to use the Sevastopol naval base until 2017 and to station up to 25,000 troops in Crimea. This issue proved contentious particularly during the Yushchenko years, when Ukraine was pursuing closer NATO integration and the government presented the idea that the basing right was not to be expected in perpetuity. Partly, as a result of that and partly to help an economically unstable Ukraine, when he was elected president in 2010, Yanukovych signed a new agreement, known as the Kharkov Accords, extending the use until 2042 in exchange for a significant reduction in the price of natural gas from Russia.[101]

When the Yanukovych regime was overthrown in February 2014 it presented Russia with a dilemma. Not only was Ukraine in internal turmoil, but the Euromaidan movement, which had spearheaded the uprising, was also decidedly anti-Russian and, as is common with populist movements, it became more and more nationalist.[102] It seems that at first Putin and the rest of the Russian leadership were distracted by the Sochi winter Olympics,[103] and Russia did not react as quickly as it could.[104] When the situation in Ukraine deteriorated further with the flight of Yanukovych, Russia's hand was forced. In Crimea the parliamentary assembly met on 26 February to discuss loosening ties with Ukraine, a goal which the semi-autonomous Crimea had been pursing in one form or another ever since 1991, but the lack of a quorum meant that no decisions were reached. On the morning of 27 February, masked and uniformed troops, without any identifiable insignia began taking control of government buildings, including the parliament in Simferopol, the capital of Crimea, and deposed the appointed Crimean prime minister. The parliament later voted, in a secret session, to install a new prime minister Sergei Aksenev and to arrange a referendum on the sovereign status of Crimea.[105] The next day, groups of armed soldiers took control of Simferopol airport and began setting up checkpoints on major roads and blockading Ukrainian military bases.[106] Officially, they were called pro-Russian local militias, but their equipment and the precise timing and organization of these operations suggested that they might have been Russian troops. They came to be known as the 'little green men' in Ukraine, while in Russia they were referred to as the 'polite people'. The groups were later identified as Russian Special Forces and Crimean riot police.[107] Under a military lockdown a referendum was held where the people of Crimea apparently overwhelmingly voted to join the Russian Federation, a decision that was quickly accepted by the Russian legislature and made official.[108] The results of the referendum are widely regarded as rigged and although the annexation of Crimea is generally unrecognized in the world, the fact on the ground has become that Ukraine had lost Crimea in a largely bloodless operation to Russia.

In an extremely well-organized and executed example of hybrid warfare, Russia used its favourable position in Crimea to secure its key strategic prize in the region. There are three important aspects to the Crimean operation that need to be examined: the use of the 'little green men', information operations, and the overall strategic rationale.

Using masked and unaffiliated troops was a perfect adaptation to the circumstances in Ukraine at the time. Not only did it provide Russia with some degree of international deniability, but it also generated a significant amount of confusion on the ground over who was directing the operation. In a chaotic environment, where the central government did not exist, Ukraine's regional oligarchs began setting up their own security forces.[109] Other groups also began to form across the political spectrum, in what was perceived as a national showdown on the future course of the country. Part of the Russian defence of its actions in Ukraine was the protection of the Russian population in Crimea. While this fear was certainly exaggerated, it is not wholly without merit. Crimea contained the largest concentration of Russian speakers and Russian citizens within Ukraine and the anti-Russian Euromaidan tide was turning increasingly violent, particularly once government control completely failed. Later events in Odessa demonstrate the hatred that had been stirred up by the movement.[110] By using un-attributable forces, Russia took advantage of this situation. Neither the local population nor the government in Kiev could ascertain with a sufficient degree of certainty who was behind these forces until it was well too late. The confusion did not last long, but it gave Russia the crucial hours it needed.

Out of all the various tools employed by Russia during the entire conflict in Ukraine, it is the information operations that achieved the most attention internationally. It was precisely this unexpected propaganda offensive which brought the term 'hybrid warfare' into everyday use. As mentioned before, while control or influence over information is an important aspect of hybrid warfare, it is not its crucial component. In fact, the conflict in Ukraine should be used as an example of how dangerous it is to fixate on a single aspect of a poorly understood concept to the detriment of practical policymaking. Two aspects of this are particularly noteworthy. The first is the use of the media by Russia to gain an advantage in the crucial moments, immediately before and after the operations were underway, and the second is the Western response to these events. Heavily influenced by the media, which stirred up domestic audiences calling for action, their immediate response resulted in little but the embarrassing revelation that the West was caught completely off-guard and it could not figure out a practical way to respond to the situation.[111] In the end, it resorted to lambasting Russia for misrepresenting the truth, and applied pressure through international institutions. Owing to Russia's veto in the UN Security Council, wide-ranging sanctions were not possible, so the United States, and much more reluctantly, the EU, imposed economic sanctions on Russia.[112] They also engaged in an information operation of their own in a bid to paint Russia, embodied in the form of Vladimir Putin, as an unreliable aggressor with no regard for international norms or morals.

A key argument in the information war was the labelling of Russia as having planned these operations in advance. Many international actors have pointed to the rapid deployment of Russian troops, and the dates inscribed on the back of the campaign medals for the troops involved,[113] as evidence that operations against Ukraine were envisaged beforehand. Such accusations are fundamentally misguided as any sensible state would have any number of contingency plans prepared, particularly for a region that is so important to its national interests. Considering the timeline of events, Russian military planners would have had up to four months to prepare for several possible scenarios, although it is far more likely that some preliminary plans were created even before events in Kiev started spiralling out of control in October 2013, after the Orange Revolution or the Russo-Georgian War, for example.[114] As the number of troops involved was relatively small, about 3,000, and most of these were either Special Forces units or units already based in Crimea, it is not outside the realm of possibility that, even absent a pre-made plan, they could have been deployed with very little notice.[115] The Russian military training doctrine, which puts great emphasis on snap drills with minimum notice and the relatively high levels of professional soldiers among the units stationed in Crimea, would certainly support such an argument.

Rather than blaming Russia for planning deliberately to carve up Ukraine, emphasis should be given to the fact that the situation in the country left Russia with virtually no other options. It could not stand by and face the very real threat of the new Ukrainian administration cancelling its basing rights and, by actively pursuing NATO integration, not only removing Russian influence but possibly turning Sevastopol into a NATO base.[116] Such a dramatic change in the balance of power in the Black Sea region would effectively relegate Russia to a minor power in Eastern Europe, a situation that would in no way increase the security of the region. It could be argued that Russian assertiveness in fact saved NATO and the EU from extending their reach so far as to completely upend the balance of power in Europe. In an era of modern information technologies, which allow the broader public to get engaged in and provide increasing pressure on foreign policy, such assertiveness could only be achieved through a hybrid approach. By adopting a hybrid approach, Russia sowed confusion within Ukrainian and Euro Atlantic decision-making circles, and it avoided a large-scale conventional response. Whether such a response would actually materialize if Russia had invaded in a classic conventional manner is not strictly relevant, just the possibility of escalation would deter such an attempt.

From a strategic standpoint, Russia had two goals in the Crimean operation: first, to take advantage of the instability within Ukraine and ensure that its use of the Sevastopol naval base was never in doubt again and, second, to avoid, to the greatest possible degree, the international condemnation and reaction to such action, including a Western military intervention in support of Ukraine. A purely conventional approach could not achieve the first goal as it would likely have rallied the divided Ukrainian polity, since nothing motivates people better than a common enemy. It also carried a very high probability of causing a general war in Europe. An unconventional approach, an insurgency or a sponsored uprising for example, might have delivered the first goal but it would have taken too long. The turmoil would not last forever, and once the central government had regained control, they would have done everything in their power to supress it. It would also very likely have resulted in some kind of peacekeeping mission or a military intervention to prevent the conflict from spreading outside of Ukraine. Either of those approaches had the potential to incur costs which would make it unappealing to even the most fervent hawk. A hybrid approach, as it was demonstrated, managed to achieve Russia's political goals with incredible ease, speed and decisiveness. In terms of costs, it is fashionable to claim that the economic sanctions have impacted the Russian economy and leading politicians in a major way. Not only does that position not make sense in political or economic terms, but it is also strategically misguided. Compared to the strategic costs of a war, even if it was limited to only Ukraine and Russia, at best an unlikely scenario, the consequences of economic sanctions are almost insignificant.

Conflict in Eastern Ukraine

While certainly connected to the events in Crimea, the conflict in Eastern Ukraine, also known as the Donbas region,[117] should not be viewed as a direct continuation of it. Both were part of a larger struggle for Ukraine and had similar roots but were relatively independent of one another, both in terms of time and motives. In hybrid warfare terms, the Donbas operation should be viewed as another aspect of a Russian hybrid strategy, but one with significantly different geopolitical goals than the seizure of Crimea.

Events in the Donbas began escalating in the weeks following the annexation of Crimea, although local resistance in Lugansk and Donetsk had been present since the start of the Maidan movement. Eastern Ukraine is the most industrialized and pro-Russia segment of Ukraine, not including Crimea, as well as being the political base of pluralist and regionalist parties, including Yanukovych's Party of Regions. Larger protests began in March 2014, including in Kharkov, Ukraine's second largest city, but from the start these were dealt with much more severely by the Kiev authorities. Law enforcement units, supported by armed gangs of thugs, would disperse and suppress any kind of anti-Maidan protests, usually with considerable brutality. While suppression was relatively successful in Kharkov, it backfired in the more rural Lugansk and Donetsk, where protest began turning into rebellion.[118] Local armed groups began forming and seizing government buildings, soon to be replaced by much better organized and equipped groups which resembled more professional, albeit irregular, forces.[119]

At this stage it was difficult to determine whether these units were Russian trained, equipped or backed as the region did have the potential for the formation of such groups even without outside assistance; large segments of the population had served in either Ukrainian or Russian militaries or local militias and there was no shortage of weapons. Additionally, the early successes of the militia groups can be ascribed to the degraded state of the Ukrainian Armed Forces. By the time the 2014 crisis came about, the military had been largely neglected by Kiev for most of the twenty-three years since Ukraine gained independence.[120] The forces were in such a poor state that the government had to issue a call for private donations to supplement the Army's financing, simply to help to pay for the most basic of supplies.[121] By April insurgents had occupied a number of important government and administration buildings and on 7 April the so-called Donetsk People's Republic was proclaimed, followed by a neighbouring Lugansk People's Republic on 27 April. A conflict erupted between government forces attempting to regain control of the breakaway regions and the local militias. At first, it seems, Russia was not eager to get drawn into the fight, but as the separatists began to lose ground, particularly after the failed attempt to seize Donetsk airport in May 2014, Russia became more assertive. They began training and filtering through volunteers as well as providing limited amounts of equipment, although to what extent this began before August is difficult to establish and is almost certainly exaggerated by Kiev.[122] The shooting down of flight MF17 on 17 July was a significant development as it more or less confirmed that Russia was supplying weapons to the rebels as nothing in their initial arsenal was capable of reaching a high-altitude aeroplane. Criminal charges brought against the individuals deemed responsible further show that although they all had ties to Russia, though they were not outright members of its armed forces.[123] Ultimately, the conflict in the Donbas became a frozen conflict. Russia was unwilling to commit large numbers of its own troops, although they did provide advisers[124] and stationed large numbers of units along the Ukrainian border to act as a deterrent. In the later stages of the fighting, some of those troops entered Ukraine as 'volunteers'.

The conflict in Donetsk and Lugansk shared few similarities with Crimea, and the Russian response should be viewed in this light. Both were part of the same geopolitical confrontation, but the motives and methods behind them were different. Russia did not want to annexe Eastern Ukraine, but it wanted to maintain leverage over Ukrainian politics by supporting the regime's opponents and strengthening their, and its own, negotiating position vis-à-vis Kiev.[125] In terms of hybrid warfare, the Donbas operations were characterized by the use of information warfare, use of proxy forces and a conventional deterrent posture. As with Crimea, Russia again made use of extensive information operations to both discredit the Kiev regime and to assert its view that it will protect Russians (not limited to just ethnic Russians but all those who shared its position). It attempted to counter the accusations coming from Kiev and the West over an invasion of Ukraine, although, as it learnt in Georgia, the West, and particularly the United States, will sooner believe the anti-Russian Kiev government than reports from either Russia or even the OSCE observers who could find no evidence for the presence of significant numbers of Russian troops.[126] Certainly nothing that could be described as an invasion was reported. After a period of stagnation, the conflict in the Donbas began flaring up again in late 2016, when it became obvious that the Minsk agreements would not be implemented. Since then, it has become another classic frozen conflict, escalating and de-escalating depending on the political relations between Russia and Ukraine. Interestingly, over the years there occurred a number of assassinations of high-profile rebel leaders with no apparent culprit. This mystery has led to speculation that it is in fact Russia that is eliminating unsavoury and warmongering individuals which it cannot control. If that is indeed the case, it is an example of the necessity to have a firm control over the proxy forces employed in order to prevent the conflict from escalating on its own.[127]

By using local proxies in the Donbas, Russia actively attempted to prevent exactly the kind of invasion it was being accused of committing. Anti-government and anti-nationalistic tendencies were present in the region long before the crisis began, and Russia merely took advantage of the situation once the underlying tensions flared up. As with Chechenization, such use of proxy forces led, effectively, to a civil war within Ukraine and the brutality of the conflict is just further confirmation of this. On this occasion the nationalistic fervour of the Kiev government and its supporters, who viewed ethnic Russians in the Donbas as traitors, arguably exacerbated the severity of the conflict even more than Russian policy did in Chechnya. Russia also supplied the separatists with weapons and other supplies, although never to the degree they expected. Rather than establish a no-fly zone to prevent the Ukrainian air force from overpowering the separatists on the ground, Russia seems to have decided to give them advanced anti-aircraft missiles, which led to the unintended shooting down of a civilian airliner. Separatist or insurgent forces do not normally have access to this kind of weaponry; by their very nature they rely on lighter weapon systems. In doing that, as well as helping them organize a centralized command structure, Russia essentially turned them into forces much more closely resembling a conventional army. This is in keeping with a hybrid warfare approach, and it did help reverse the tide of conflict. Additionally, by placing significant numbers of Russian forces on alert and moving them closer to the Ukrainian border Russia added its own conventional weight behind them. Such a move not only reinforced proxy forces but also discouraged any thoughts of

Western intervention or even supplying arms to Ukraine. Given the dilapidated state of the Ukrainian military, Russia could be reasonably sure that even with limited support the separatists could hold their own and by influencing them it would maintain an influence over Ukrainian politics, certainly Russia's most important geopolitical goal in the region.

It is important to note, however, that these proxy forces were not 'little green men'. They were not members of the Russian military nor did they act in the same way. The operation in Crimea was surgically precise and executed without a glitch, whereas the conflict in the Donbas has an aura of amateurism. They also did not fill the same role. Proxy forces in the Donbas are more like the South Ossetian militia from the Russo-Georgian war: under-equipped and under-trained local units who view the conflict in local terms rather than grand strategy.

Hybrid strategy, like any other strategy, must be flexible enough to take advantage of opportunities which might present to the actor. Ukraine in 2014 presented Russia with several opportunities, although the circumstances, a complete collapse of a neighbouring state, were certainly not desirable. The importance of a hybrid strategy was particularly illustrated by the fact that no other conventional or unconventional approach could have achieved the goals for which Russia was aiming.

Hallmarks of Russian hybrid warfare

When comparing the Russian hybrid warfare in Ukraine with previous cases in Chechnya and Georgia, there is certainly no shortage of parallels. Four key aspects stand out: the blurring of conventional and unconventional warfare, information operations, the use of proxies and the use of advanced technologies by forces that would not normally be in possession of them. It represents the culmination of the Russian hybrid warfare approach and the apex of hybridity in a global sense.

There has been a sizeable debate in academia over Russian motives for its actions in Ukraine. While such debates can often be useful when examining new phenomena, this particular one was unfortunately skewed by the insistence of many that the primary cause was Putin's personal desires or world views:[128] a desire to restore either the Soviet Union or the Russian Empire, for example. The arguments for this position simply do not stack up, as alluded to earlier, and the opposition is clearly in the right. It is all about geopolitics and the changing world order. Russia has been on a resurgent course ever since the downturn of the early 1990s and has begun to reassert itself in Europe, while selectively challenging the US hegemony globally. The mark of a good strategy is the ability to transform tactical advances into strategic and political gains, at which Russia has been enormously successful. Reducing the debate to, essentially, name-calling is perhaps more an attempt to distract from the lack of understanding of the Russian hybrid approach. Collectively, the West has been unable to grasp how to manage an actor that denies it the ability to respond either in a clearly conventional or a clearly unconventional way. In other words, its response has been constrained by the quinitarian nature of the international system and its lack of flexibility. Ironically, for Russia this was an approach developed out of necessity and hard previous experience rather than clairvoyance. It has been selectively successful in applying the lessons it learnt in conflicts like Afghanistan and Chechnya. The 2008 Georgian War presented the opportunity to test them out.

An important document in the study of Russian hybrid warfare is the so-called Gerasimov doctrine. The publication is named after Valery Gerasimov, the Chief of the General Staff of the Russian armed forces, who published an article on a possible vision of future warfare in February 2013.[129] While by no means an actual doctrinal document, it is nevertheless a very useful exposé on the current state of research into new forms of warfare within the Russian military. The key points he outlines are the blurring of lines between the states of war and peace[130] and the changes to the rules of war, with the growing importance of non-military means of achieving political goals.[131] It would be a gross exaggeration to view this article as somehow predicting events in Ukraine, as it does not specifically mention hybrid or non-linear warfare. What it does provide, however, is an insight into the transformation within the Russian military, including dealing with a new reality of war: that wars no longer fit into neat boxes. It is easy to point out that this is hardly new information, but as a previous chapter has demonstrated, Russia's Western competitors have certainly not grasped these changes to the same degree in their policy declarations.

A key and consistent feature of the conflicts examined here is the blurring between conventional and unconventional warfare, which represents the very core of hybrid warfare. Unlike the United States or NATO, whose post-Cold War military experience has largely focused on interstate conventional warfare, Russia has had to adjust to a different reality. The only conflict in which Russia could be said to have engaged in traditional, conventional warfare was the 2008 conflict with Georgia, although, as examined above, even that war cannot be so neatly categorized. If anything, that conflict only confirmed the lesson of Chechnya which demonstrated that the requirements for the use of conventional force have shifted, and it was no longer applicable for an increasingly large number of scenarios, either because it could not produce results or because it came with too steep a price. The 'little green men' are the best example of the opaqueness inherent in hybrid warfare, being drawn from conventional forces and acting as insurgents, but with a precise purpose and organization only found in state-organized armed forces. The lack of insignias might have provided a banal level of deniability, but it provided enough of it at a crucial time for the approach to be wholly vindicated. In a management-oriented Western political environment it might be easy to claim outright that one was sure from the first instant that they were Russian troops, but that assuredness is not easy to translate into strategic certainty. When the price of guessing wrongly is potential nuclear war, such declarations should be treated with the utmost reservation. The blend of conventional and unconventional warfare within a hybrid approach is not designed to replace conventional warfare and deterrence; it is meant to operate in the grey zone between certainty and guesswork and to provide the actor just enough leeway, no matter how banal or ridiculous it may appear in hindsight, to achieve their goals without breaching the threshold of outright war.

An archetype of hybrid warfare?

The final part of this chapter will be dedicated to establishing in what way, if any, the Russian hybrid approach in Ukraine can be duplicated elsewhere. Without question the scope of exact replication is very limited. The seizure of Crimea was predicated on the fact that there were 12,500 troops already in situ[132] and that the peninsula, due to its geography, can be separated from the mainland with relative ease, limiting retaliatory options. It also contained the largest concentration of ethnic Russian and Russophone population of any region within Ukraine,[133] and it had a long history of demands for greater autonomy. There are no other areas in the world where such a combination of factors can be seen; therefore, it follows logically that a Crimea-style annexation is unlikely to be repeated. The same cannot be said about the use of the little green men on their own. The situation in Crimea merely meant that they could be deployed with extraordinary speed, which does not preclude the possibility that a similar event could not be orchestrated somewhere else. It would simply take more time to do so. A popular idea is that the large ethnic Russian minority within Estonia could serve as a basis for the next use of the 'little green men',[134] but in a hybrid context they would become proxy fighters, since they are not members of the Russian armed forces nor do they have the required training. Eastern Ukraine-style hybrid warfare, with the use of proxies and resulting in a frozen conflict, is more plausible as an example and can also be used in a wider variety of regions and settings.

More important than specific aspects of Russian hybrid warfare is the concept of a hybrid strategy as a whole. If the use of hybrid warfare by the Chechens and the Russians in Georgia can be considered a mixed bag, it has been remarkably successful in Ukraine. The principle of achieving political goals through a means that can avoid foreign (usually Western) military intervention provides the opportunity to disavow knowledge or participation in such actions, incurring only a reasonable strategic cost is certainly appealing. Before 2014, most military thinkers would agree that gaining territory within another state can only be done through a conventional invasion. Russia has proven that with a controlled and carefully choreographed hybrid operation, a state can stay below the threshold of conventional war (the Chechens' mistake) and achieve disproportionately significant goals. The annexation of Crimea was completed when Russian troops did indeed move in, in a conventional manner, but by then Crimea was officially already part of Russia. Although it would be wrong to credit Russia with single-handedly upending the logic of force, it is fair to say that it came across an alternative approach; an approach that has traction in professional and academic discourse as well as in the real world. States usually fight new wars in the same way they fought the last one, as strategic prediction is one of the clearest examples of Sisyphean work. When changes occur, it is therefore not unusual for the innovative state to be equally surprised.

At the beginning of the conflict in Ukraine, Russia could not be said to have possessed a full-fledged hybrid strategy; rather it had a better understanding of the trends in the conduct of war and a greater insight into Ukrainian internal divisions. It combined previous experiences with strategic opportunities and experimented with a different approach which led to success. Although the conflict in the Donbas continues, as of time of writing, the Russian approach can now be summarized in a coherent strategy. In its basic form, it can be said to have become an archetype of hybrid warfare which is not merely theoretical and has also been proven in the field. While other actors might emulate and adapt the concept to suit their own particular needs or their strategic environment, the basic premises to a successful hybrid approach have been established.

South China Sea and non-kinetic maritime hybrid warfare

Following the previous two chapters which examined hybrid warfare on a state-like and state level, the third and final case study will introduce hybrid warfare into a separate domain while maintaining the state level of analysis. This chapter will examine how a switch to a maritime domain affects the conduct and strategy of hybrid warfare in an environment that is fundamentally different from the previous examples. While operating on land, whether the actors are states or state like, the rules of warfare are relatively straightforward and simple. People can easily imagine what a land war looks like based on either their personal experience or historical records or epic cinematic portrayals. Even when such operations are incredibly complex, such as the Battle of Leipzig in 1813, or take place on a gigantic scale, the German invasion of the Soviet Union in 1941, for example, they are still somehow more accessible than the great naval campaigns. This is partly a result of the confined geographical space that limits warfare on land, and partly because, while there have historically been many great land powers, there have been relatively few states that could claim to have been great maritime powers. The sea has always been a much more formidable obstacle to human endeavour than any feature on land, and it presents a unique set of challenges.

As a result, land and air domains of war tend to dominate the debate on the nature of war and are the most studied aspects of conflict. This is particularly true of the debate surrounding new and future wars which often includes the space domain or the cyber arena, but largely neglects the maritime domain despite a geographical scope encompassing over two-thirds of the planet's surface. Hybrid warfare is distinct in this regard since it potentially includes and/or combines all domains of warfare. The goal of this chapter is to introduce the complexities of the maritime domain into the debate surrounding hybrid warfare, an aspect that has received far less scrutiny than its land and air-based counterparts. As a prime and current example of hybrid maritime warfare, this chapter will use the South China Sea (SCS) as a case study in order to determine the real-world applications of maritime hybrid warfare. More specifically, the examination will focus on Chinese actions and activities in the region.

Structurally, this chapter will begin with a brief overview of the maritime domain and situate hybrid warfare into the naval context. It will define what hybrid maritime warfare is, illustrate what its key distinguishing characteristics are and situate it within the definitional context of this book. The main body of the chapter will examine how the maritime environment impacts the conduct of Chinese hybrid maritime warfare with an analysis of the case study of the SCS based on three main aspects: island building, the maritime militia and lawfare. Since the process of Chinese political and strategic manoeuvring within the broad area of the SCS has been occurring in a very large and widespread geographical area and over a long time period, only some of the most illustrative examples will be used to support the theoretical examination. The final part of the chapter will sum up the similarities and differences between the land and maritime domain-based hybrid warfare and determine how relevant the level of kineticism is to hybrid warfare in each separate domain.

The maritime domain

It is not an exaggeration to suggest that the sea has been a major feature in the conduct of human activities since the dawn of civilization and, as such, it has also played an important role in the conduct of war throughout history. Conflicts in the maritime domain are fundamentally different from any land- or air-based operations. Not only are there often no obvious geographical features delineating the maritime domain, but the pace of operations is also much slower and usually occurs over longer distances. Often, maritime operations which impact a certain part of the world might not even take place in the waters next to it. In terms of capabilities, the maritime domain is also in a league of its own in terms of expense and the knowledge required. It is relatively easy to train a soldier to fire a gun or to drive a tank. Pilots go through arduous training and their aeroplanes are technically complex and expensive, but they are still relatively few in number and only one or two pilots are generally required to operate a plane. Ships, on the other hand, require large numbers of trained sailors and officers to operate them and tend to stand out as the most expensive assets in any state's arsenal. Naval warfare certainly stands apart as the most complicated and expensive way of conducting war and its rules differ significantly from those of other domains.

Before proceeding to examine the maritime domain in more detail, it is important to clear up the nomenclature. Various sources use various terms, such as sea power, maritime power or naval power, when describing the conduct of activities connected to the sea. The term 'sea power' was first coined by Alfred Thayer Mahan in his famous study on the subject but, unhelpfully, he never offered a concise definition of the term. Mahan's broadest meaning of sea power is a type of contest between nations which occurs on the sea, and which could result in a war,[1] with its key components being geographical position, physical conformation, extent of territory, number of population, character of the people and the character of the government.[2] For the purposes of this book, a more modern definition, distilled from the work of Geoffrey Till,[3] will be used. Sea power, in its broadest meaning, refers to the use of all available assets to utilize the sea and influence behaviour at or from the sea. However, as this volume is primarily concerned with the strategic and tactical employment of hybrid warfare, a narrower definition pertaining simply to the military activities of a navy is also required. Till places sea power into the context of national power and describes it as being comprised of both civilian and military maritime capabilities which lead to both naval (military) and commercial operations.[4] Naval power is therefore a component of sea power, primarily concerned with the activities, organization and employment of navies.[5] Put simply, based on the aforementioned definition of sea power, naval power merely limits the available assets of an actor to its naval forces.

The reasons for the importance of the sea can be connected to four broad attributes, stemming from the sea itself: the sea is a source of resources, a medium of transportation, a medium of information and a medium for dominion.[6] The interplay between the uses of the sea, and the importance assigned to each of them by the actors concerned with its use, determine the nature and use of navies, both military and civilian. Unlike some of the theories and approaches examined in earlier chapters, where control over territory can be achieved indirectly, in the maritime domain it is still predominantly ships at sea that determine which actor will reap the benefits of the maritime domain. In fact, modern sea power has moved even beyond that, to effects which can be achieved *from the sea* rather than simply *at sea*.[7] As such, the modern approach to sea power covers the geo-strategic and economic spheres to a much greater degree than either land or air power, a fact that is reflected in its relative complexity and impact.

Maritime strategy

Maritime strategy is the key link between, and a major component of, sea power and naval power. It deals with the connections between politics and policy and how they pertain to the conduct of operations on the seas. At its core, maritime strategy is 'the principles which govern a war in which the sea is a substantial factor'.[8] Building on this, Corbett further connects maritime strategy and foreign policy, in a Clausewitzian way, by stating: 'The paramount concern, then, of maritime strategy is to determine the mutual relations of your army and navy in a plan of war.'[9] In other words, naval operations will almost always have impact on the general conduct of conflict and will likely influence events in other domains (land, air, etc.) as well as serve a grand policy objective. Without the policy objective, maritime strategy, and the resulting implementation of sea power, is unlikely to produce results. As with any other forms of strategy, maritime strategy is difficult to articulate and implement successfully, but tends to yield great results if executed correctly. The complexity of the maritime domain itself is what makes maritime strategy, arguably, the most difficult. It is often indirect and rarely decides conflicts on its own. Whereas an army can capture a capital, or crucial ground, thus bringing a conflict to an end, naval battles, although often a deciding factor, do not directly end conflicts. Similar to airpower, sea power aids the actor in achieving its policy goals but its effects are often ancillary.

Naval forces

In addition to defining terms which deal with sea power at a strategic level, it is useful to clear up a point about naval capabilities. While it may seem self-evident, the definition of naval forces is particularly relevant in the case of the SCS and, consequentially, for hybrid warfare. The key question is: What constitutes a naval force or, which vessel can be called a warship? The term 'naval force' in this context is being used to describe an actor's military capabilities, which pertain to the sea; in other words, what constitutes the actor's navy. This is important for two reasons. First, conventional naval forces have capabilities which are unique to them, in terms of weapons, platforms and personnel. Second, the inclusion or exclusion of a certain naval asset from being a constituent of a naval force has both practical and legal consequences. The problems are similar to those associated with distinguishing combatants and non-combatants on land. Different types of vessels will be treated differently by opponents and their use will reflect this. There are clear differences between, for example, naval warships and coast guard vessels. Some states may also have maritime police force or customs vessels which, again, tend to be distinct from either coast guard or naval vessels. The key question is that which of these forces can be said to constitute an actor's (usually a state) naval force.

While there are no clear-cut answers to these questions, a useful starting point is to examine how international law has attempted to address these problems. The most widely accepted definition of a warship is given by the 1982 Convention on the Law of the Sea (UNCLOS), which defines a warship as

> a ship belonging to the armed forces of a State bearing the external marks distinguishing such ships of its nationality, under the command of an officer duly commissioned by the government of the State and whose name appears in the appropriate service list or its equivalent, and manned by a crew which is under regular armed forces discipline.[10]

However, as with most aspects of international law, there is a problem with implementation. This definition relies on the states themselves to clearly mark which vessels are considered warships and therefore part of a naval force. Some states, such as the United States, consider coast guard vessels as warships,[11] but that is not universal. The UK coast guard, for example, works almost exclusively as a sea rescue service and is neither a law enforcement or military organization, although it is a uniformed service.[12] China's coast guard is also technically not a military organization, although there are concerns over its militarization[13] and it would likely be subsumed under the People's Liberation Army Navy (PLAN) during wartime. These examples illustrate the key concern, that individual states consider the various maritime capabilities at their disposal quite differently which can cause problems when different types of vessels meet at sea in a disputed area. How the disputed or unclear legal status of ships ties into the context of maritime hybrid warfare in the SCS will be further examined later in the chapter.

Maritime hybrid warfare

As a subdivision of hybrid warfare, maritime hybrid warfare still comes under the same definitional umbrella as its land-based counterparts but presents an additional level of complexity in its employment and strategy, largely stemming from the nature of the maritime domain itself. This part of the chapter will define what the term 'maritime hybrid warfare' means and address the crucial distinguishing factors that differentiate maritime hybrid warfare from other kinds of hybrid conflicts. With the strategic debate so heavily dominated by land and air warfare proponents, there are relatively few examples of attempts at defining maritime hybrid warfare. The most important of these comes from

Admiral James Stavridis, the former NATO Supreme Allied Commander (SACEUR), who defined the key components of maritime hybrid warfare as being conducted in littoral waters, making use of not-directly identifiable, possibly civilian, vessels, which would be crewed by 'little blue sailors', and armed with a variety of concealable weapons.[14] This definition, while illustrating some crucial aspects of maritime hybrid warfare, falls into the same trap as the majority of others and simply lists the various components rather than addressing the core conventional/unconventional nature of hybrid warfare. The definition used in this chapter will be based on the overall definition of hybrid warfare presented in this book while utilizing some aspects of the one offered by Stavridis.

Maritime hybrid warfare in the broad sense is defined as hybrid warfare which takes place at or from the sea and is conducted primarily through maritime capabilities. Since this chapter will focus primarily on examining Chinese actions in the SCS, Chinese maritime hybrid warfare can specifically be defined as actions of a hybrid actor which employs conventional forces (navy), irregular units (coast guards, militia, civilian fishermen), and other activities (island building, lawfare), brought together through a carefully controlled, opaque merger of conventional and unconventional modes of warfare. The limited nature of hybrid warfare is especially pronounced in the maritime domain. Not only does an actor employing maritime hybrid warfare seek to maintain the level of conflict below the threshold of escalation to conventional war, it must also stay below the threshold of major disruptions to the good order of the seas in order to maintain the usability of the sea for extraction of resources and trade for the actor. As over 90 per cent of all global trade is carried by sea,[15] any and all disruptions as a result of hybrid maritime warfare must be carefully controlled. If an actor's actions were to escalate beyond this, these actions could prove economically and diplomatically extremely damaging even without escalation to open conflict. The goal of maritime hybrid warfare is to gain significant influence or control of the sea without having to resort to conventional war. However, unlike land hybrid warfare, the process is much more painstaking and slow because maritime strategy takes longer to implement and any new capabilities that are required take longer to build than their land-based counterparts. Maritime hybrid warfare is therefore based on a series of small individual steps or stages, each of which does not upend the maritime balance of power on its own and protects the actors use of the sea under the status quo for as long as possible.

The examples of Chinese activities outlined earlier will form the basis of the examination later in the chapter, but they represent an interesting blend of conventional and unconventional warfare. While some aspects, such as the use of navy vessels to escort or intimidate other vessels, fall clearly into the conventional aspects, the remaining activities are all unconventional to a greater or lesser degree, largely depending on their use. It is interesting to note that China has historically been inclined to use conventional warfare in the SCS and has only recently turned to what can be termed as a hybrid approach. In January 1974 China clashed with Vietnam over the control of the Paracel Islands group in a naval engagement that involved small naval vessels on both sides and ended with some of the Vietnamese vessels sinking with over 100 sailors killed or wounded.[16] While the operation did include fishing trawlers, the dramatic escalation to a shooting war and the use of warships suggests that this was not a hybrid conflict. When compared to the 2012 Scarborough Shoal stand-off, a similar contest over sovereignty in an important area of the SCS which will be examined in more detail later, the 2012 events seem to be of much less consequence since they did not involve casualties or shooting.

In addition to the 'standard' aspects of hybrid warfare, Chinese maritime hybrid warfare is characterized by a strong influence of legal manoeuvring. The complex legal environment associated with the rules of the sea is an important feature of sea power. This refers not only to the aforementioned difficulties with clearly identifying warships but also to the conduct of state actions on a grand scale. Questions of legality and legitimacy play an important role in modern IR, and this is particularly the case with hybrid warfare. The hybrid actor must always be conscious of where the legal norms draw the lines which, when crossed, could result in an overwhelming conventional response from the opponents, probably the status quo actors, most likely Western states. In the context of sea power, these norms and regulations are especially important since brinkmanship is much more difficult at sea because there is a lack of flexibility. Soldiers on land can be grouped as desired, or operate individually, and it is unlikely that a single soldier crossing a border will lead to an outright war. At sea, however, the smallest discreet naval unit usually carries several sailors and bigger weapons than those used on land. Traditional navies therefore lack a certain degree of controlled escalation, an issue that can be resolved by using smaller vessels, which might not be strictly military.

China seems to be particularly adept at this and to further muddy the waters it is using competing legal claims as a cover for expanding sovereignty. The purpose of the artificial islands, beyond their immediate tactical value, is to demonstrate and expand Chinese de facto sovereignty over large swaths of the disputed island groups. Artificial islands do not create legal rights or expand territorial waters;

however, by changing the status on the ground China is seeking to circumvent any legal obstacles to its interests in the region. Since there is no clear sign of a forthcoming resolution of the territorial claims in the region, China is free to proceed essentially as it wants. If there is ever a concerted push to resolve the issue, China will be in a much stronger position both diplomatically and geo-strategically, the benefits of both it can also enjoy in the meantime. Such obfuscation and deliberate misuse or exploitation of law is called 'lawfare' and will be further examined in the last part of the chapter. It is clearly an important instrument in China's hybrid arsenal since it not only allows it to achieve its own goals but, by claiming that its actions are legal under the same legal provisions it is challenging, it also is able to isolate itself from Western reprisals.

Maritime hybrid warfare is a much slower-moving type of conflict and therefore much of it occurs in the form of a hybrid threat, a state of anticipation in which kinetic confrontation is imminent, or perceived to be imminent, but has not yet fully materialized. The hybrid nature of the threat, particularly its opaqueness, is its key distinguishing characteristic and it serves a different purpose than a conventional threat. A conventional threat is designed to signal the opponent in order to deter or intimidate them. A hybrid threat is designed to confuse and to obscure the eventual limited escalation to hybrid warfare. Whereas in conventional and unconventional thinking an actor wants their threats to be known for them to be effective, a hybrid threat is subtle and is as un-attributable as possible in order not to compromise the threshold of escalation.

At this point it is important to note that the theoretical situating of maritime hybrid warfare described earlier has been accomplished from a Western perspective. Much as in the case of Russia, Chinese interpretations of hybrid warfare are significantly different. While there is a general lack of Chinese sources on security matters due to the secretive and closed nature of the government system, some sources have made significant impacts and the chief among those is *Unrestricted Warfare*. The book was written by two colonels in the People's Liberation Army and published in 1999. Since its translation into English[17] the book has caused some consternation in the security community because of its perceived foresight into how China could use underhand means to strike at the United States in times of dispute without directly challenging it for dominance. Some of the proposed means include cyber hacking, attacking financial institutions, terrorism, influencing the media and conducting urban warfare.[18] The authors argue that these are the means that a weaker state must undertake in order to challenge a powerful one, particularly one like the United States, which is heavily reliant on high-technology warfare. The underlying premise is that in this kind of warfare, everything is permitted because if the challenger limits themselves to fighting by the same rules, which are imposed by the hegemonic superpower which therefore greatly benefits from it, it is destined to lose.[19] While this is an interesting concept, the public perception in the West seems to view this publication as a kind of master plan for Chinese global domination. This is clearly an over-interpretation. *Unrestricted Warfare* is an interesting exposé on the course of modern warfare from a Chinese perspective and it illustrates several important and well-known weaknesses associated with the Western way of war. It observes warfare from the perspective of globalization and is in fact closely related to what in the West is called the Revolution in Military Affairs.[20] The lack of official Chinese recognition of this work as a basis for foreign or defence policy means that it cannot be counted as the definitive source of Chinese thinking on hybrid warfare. Therefore, notwithstanding its value as illustrating an alternative perspective, it will not be utilized further in the chapter.

Chinese operations in the South China Sea

In order to distil the essence of what constitutes hybrid maritime warfare, it is useful to begin by looking at how it is currently being conducted in practice. The most important and interesting occurrence of what could be described as maritime hybrid warfare are Chinese actions, both strategic and tactical, in the SCS. As this is an ongoing, contemporary case study, there are several caveats that need to be established before an in-depth analysis can begin. First, the SCS is a vast and loosely defined geographical area located between China, Vietnam, the Philippines and Malaysia. Geographically, the focus of this examination will be on the groups of islands and features within the northern and central areas of the so-called 'nine dash line';[21] chiefly the Spratly Islands group, the Paracel Islands group and Scarborough Shoal. Secondly, since the timeline of events and their significance cannot be easily established, individual events will be used as examples to demonstrate the ongoing conflict and tensions within the SCS, although a straightforward historical narrative cannot yet be created.

The examination of Chinese activities in the SCS will be divided into three key aspects: island building, the maritime militia and lawfare. These have been chosen because they represent the most important distinguishing features and provide the clearest examples of how hybrid maritime warfare works when combined into a logical and strategic whole.

Island building

The most visible and the most controversial Chinese activity is undoubtedly land reclamation. Through this process China has created over 3,200 acres[22] of new land on the various features over which it claims sovereignty within the island groupings in the SCS. While Chinese land reclamation has received a great amount of attention both within the region and globally, it is important to note that China is not the only actor engaged in land reclamation in the SCS. Vietnam and Taiwan have also enlarged their territorial holdings; although with reclaimed land of 120[23] and 8 acres,[24] respectively, they do not match China in either scale or intensity.

The three most extensive reclamation projects are Subi Reef, Fiery Cross Reef and Mischief Reef, all of which are located within the Spratly Islands group. All three features have been significantly enlarged and now feature long runways, aircraft handling facilities, large port facilities and water and fuel storage.[25] While China has exercised control over these features for decades in some cases, for a long time they were either undisturbed or contained only small bases. The latest wave of reclamation and construction, which is the largest to date, began in 2014 and was officially announced as completed by mid-2015. During this time, significant diplomatic pressure was placed on China because of its activities, and the timing of the halt could suggest that it bowed to international pressure. Given subsequent developments, this seems unlikely, and the reason why China stopped island building in 2015 was simply due to the fact that it had fulfilled its reclamation objectives,[26] with on-shore construction still continuing at the time of writing. In 2017 China launched a new land reclamation dredger, the largest in Asia, which has once again raised concerns that another wave of island building might be imminent.[27] While the unilateral expansion of features has generated significant interest and debate, there is disagreement over what China's ultimate goal might be. The two most likely explanations are that China is constructing military outposts in order to project power throughout the SCS, and that it wishes to gain access to the natural resources which are, or might be present, in the area, chiefly fish and oil. Of course, these two interpretations are not mutually exclusive.

Officially, China has always maintained that the expansion of its land claims in the SCS was primarily for civilian use and aimed at improving the living conditions of personnel stationed there. It particularly emphasized the use of these islands as bases for maritime search and rescue operations, safety of navigation and scientific research.[28] While these claims cannot be dismissed out of hand, the facilities could, at the very least, be considered multipurpose. Even if they are primarily used for scientific research or other civilian purposes, islands with 3-kilometre-long runways could very easily become forward military staging areas since they are able to accommodate almost any aircraft, including heavy-lift transports as well as fighter and bomber aircraft,[29] a point further demonstrated in May 2018 when the Chinese air force landed an H-6K strategic bomber on Woody Island.[30] At a joint press conference in September 2015 with US president Barack Obama, Chinese president Xi Jinping touched upon the issue of the militarization of the islands under construction. In an often over-interpreted reference, he presented the Chinese official position by stating: 'Relevant construction activities that China are undertaking in the island of South – Nansha Islands[31] do not target or impact any country, and China does not intend to pursue militarization.'[32] This latter reference to militarization has largely been interpreted as a pledge, but there is nothing in the statement which would support such an assumption. Furthermore, the term 'militarization' itself is so broad that it could include a whole host of various activities. China has deployed various anti-aircraft and anti-ship missiles on Woody Island, part of the Paracel Islands group, including the sophisticated HQ-9 anti-aircraft missile which is similar to the Russian S-300 system. It has further complemented them with the YJ-62 anti-surface missiles with both systems being deployed shortly after the United States sailed a warship through the area as part of its Freedom of Navigation programme.[33] While the Paracel Islands occupy a different part of the SCS, and would therefore not be covered by Xi's remarks, the danger is that this move could signal further militarization of the newly created islands.[34] While the new islands in the Spratly Group have been observed to contain anti-aircraft guns and missile point defence systems (CIWS), so far there has been no clear evidence of permanent offensive or defensive long-range missiles being deployed there. In May 2018, China placed both anti-ship and anti-aircraft missiles on its artificial islands in the Spratly Islands group.[35] However, it remains unclear whether these were permanent emplacements or merely a temporary deployment as part of the large naval exercise conducted in April 2018.[36]

Whatever the official Chinese position might be, prominent international security actors are certainly leaning towards the conclusion that these outposts, once completed, will effectively come to represent what US Admiral Harris termed, the 'great wall of sand'.[37] Whether these islands would actually add to China's security remains in doubt, since they are seen as very vulnerable outposts, located far away from the Chinese mainland and therefore reliant on long lines of communication. Their presence also encourages other claimants in the region to increase their military footprint in the SCS to counter Chinese ambitions. While none of the other states in the area could militarily compete directly with China, they are increasingly turning towards Japan and the United States to provide additional counterbalance. With local allies willing to shoulder their part of the burden, the United States might be more inclined to intervene should Chinese actions breach the conflict threshold. At this stage, in military terms, at least, Chinese island building can be seen as pre-positioning for a possible future conflict. It would also lead to an increased coast guard and militia presence in the area, while giving the PLAN the option to maintain some distance from the region so as not to unduly provoke China's SCS neighbours, while providing it with pre-positioned facilities for a future military deployment, should that be deemed necessary.

While the militarization debate continues and its results and implications might be a cause for concern in the medium and long term, there is a probable shorter term reason for Chinese land reclamation operations. One of the main reasons behind the pursuit of sea power by any sea-faring state is resource extraction. The world's oceans are some of the most important sources of food and energy resources, and the SCS is particularly valuable in this regard. The area contains some of the most abundant fishing grounds in the world and recent surveys have shown that it could contain significant deposits of oil and gas. However, there are significant problems with both fish and oil production in the area. The quantities of oil and gas reserves currently estimated to exist below the SCS vary significantly from 5 to 125 billion barrels of oil and between 70 and 500 trillion cubic feet of natural gas.[38] While the highest estimates are largely seen as unrealistic, there are some proven reserves which could help the states in the area, particularly China, alleviate some of their energy demands. Most of the known reserves are currently not financially viable so the best estimate of proven supplies is around 11 billion barrels of oil and 190 trillion cubic feet of natural gas, with the majority of them located in undisputed territory.[39] With offshore oil exploration and production of one of the riskiest and most expensive forms of energy extraction, the relatively small amounts of oil and gas in the SCS might not be worth it, at least not for China which imports 2.7 billion barrels of oil every year.[40]

Fish, on the other hand, are certainly a vital SCS resource. Fisheries not only provide an important source of food for the approximately 2 billion people living in the coastal areas but also provide a source of income for the local communities.[41] About 12 per cent of all global catch comes from the SCS, although since many states in the area do not have adequate monitoring capabilities this number could be higher.[42] With some fish stocks now falling to 5 per cent of their levels in the 1950s, over-exploitation, coupled with the necessity to harvest fish as a source of food, could lead to serious competition and possibly open conflict.[43] China, with the largest fishing fleet, has the greatest potential to use up as much of the remaining resources as possible and, with the artificial islands which China claims form a basis for extending its Exclusive Economic Zone (EEZ), it now has bases for fishing vessels much closer to the richest fishing grounds. With so many overlapping claims and a competition for a dwindling resource, there has been a marked escalation in disputes over fisheries in which fishing vessels are often used as proxies to assert maritime claims without open, military conflict.[44] In the case of China, these vessels are often also part of a maritime militia which gives them additional weight in maritime disputes. It is to the explanation of the nature and role of China's maritime militia that this book now turns.

Maritime militia

China's maritime militia is one of the most under-studied and least understood factors of China's influence over the SCS, but at the same time it is one of the most significant. Consequentially, its successful use also means that the maritime militia is one of the greatest causes of concern for actors who are threatened by Chinese strategic expansion. In this regard, the maritime militia could be considered a type of hybrid force and its employment would therefore be considered an act of hybrid warfare.

Unlike the PLAN or the China Coast Guard (CCG), the maritime militia is not an active duty military or uniformed service. As its name suggests, it is an irregular force, designed primarily to complement the military services in time of war. However, unlike the land militia component, China's maritime militia has moved beyond simply providing a pool of reserve units and has gained active responsibilities. While there is a lack of official sources on what precisely the responsibilities of the maritime militia are, some key areas have been identified. The four core roles of the maritime militia can be split into pairs. The first pair is usually associated with what would traditionally be considered militia activities and comprises: supporting the front, by assisting the PLA and the PLAN through logistics, concealment and mine warfare, for example,[45] and emergency response, such as dealing with search and rescue at sea as well as providing assistance during natural disasters.[46] The second pair of responsibilities and activities is more recent and also diverges more significantly from its traditional role. The maritime militia conducts 'rights protection' missions, involving law enforcement, as well as island landings and working in disputed areas, in order to 'display presence, manifest sovereignty, and coordinate with the needs of national political and diplomatic struggles'.[47] It is a role it shares with the CCG, although the precise relationship or delineation between the two is difficult to ascertain and likely depends on the situation. Lastly, the maritime militia is also prepared to conduct independent missions such as anti-air missile defence or sabotage. Particularly important in this regard is the militia's ability to aid in intelligence gathering, surveillance and reconnaissance since they can conduct these activities during the course of their normal duties.[48]

With such an array of responsibilities, it is clear that the maritime militia is the key component in China's maritime hybrid warfare. However, these responsibilities would only have a meaningful impact if the militia had corresponding capabilities and it is to these that the examination will now turn. The principal capabilities of the maritime militia are its crews and ships. All Chinese militia units are divided into two main categories, an ordinary reserve and a primary force. The ordinary reserve is comprised of all eligible male citizens, while the primary force is comprised largely of demobilized active duty troops which receive dedicated resources and training.[49] All members of the maritime militia fall within the primary force, receiving more frequent training and acquiring more advanced skills.[50] Maritime militia units tend to be smaller and more specialized than their land-based counterparts, and there is even a corps of elite maritime militia units beginning to emerge within their internal structure.[51] Officially, these militiamen are not connected in any way with the Chinese government and have continuously been described as civilian fishermen.[52] Their command structure is based on a grass-roots approach, following a dual civilian-military structure, common to Chinese decision-making, from the provincial level downwards. The key decision-making body responsible for the activities of the militia is the National Defence Mobilisation Committee, which, at the state level, is under the command of the Central Military Commission, China's supreme governing council for military matters.[53] Most decisions related to the day-to-day running of the militia are therefore relegated to the local level while mobilization commands and instructions are passed on from above. Most militia units are established by commercial fishing companies, which then coordinate their efforts with the local People's Armed Forces Department[54] further 'muddying the waters' surrounding the precise composition and command and control structure of the militia, but clearly these units are not completely disconnected from Chinese government authority despite the official stance.

The Sansha City[55] maritime militia, operating the closest to some of the most disputed and valued areas of the SCS, is a good example of how Chinese maritime militias are formed and operate. It is particularly interesting because the job listings from the fishing company that organized the units favoured military veterans and has committed to paying them a salary. This is significant because normally militias do not receive a salary. They are paid from the income of their fishing haul and receive compensation for the time spent on militia duties when they could not fish. Offering salaries could mean that China is looking to professionalize the most crucial militia units and, more worryingly, that the commercial fishing companies could merely be a front for the Chinese government.[56] The fishing vessels themselves also set the militia apart from ordinary fishermen. In a recent wave of modernization, Sansha City has received eighty-four new vessels between 2015 and 2016.[57] Furthermore, these vessels possess features not commonly found on normal fishing vessels, such as strengthening rails welded to the outside of the hulls which mitigate collision damage. They are also equipped with mast-mounted water cannons and are capable of more sophisticated manoeuvring, despite being larger than normal fishing vessels, including a shallower draught which would enable them to pursue other vessels into shallower waters.[58]

With the theoretical principles of the Chinese maritime militia established, it is useful to examine how they are implemented in practice. Three incidents, involving maritime militia vessels within the SCS, have been selected because they best illustrate the activities and roles of the maritime militia. The first and most important is the 2012 'Scarborough Shoal incident', the second is the Chinese reaction to the passage of the USS *Lassen* past Subi Reef in October 2015 and the third is the incident surrounding the USNS *Impeccable* in March 2009.

Scarborough Shoal is a maritime feature which is part of a territorial dispute between China, Taiwan and the Philippines. The stand-off which began on 10 April 2012, resulted in China exercising de facto sovereignty over the feature ever since. During the incident, twelve Chinese fishing vessels, several of which were maritime militia vessels as well, were intercepted by a Philippine navy frigate responding to reports of illegal fishing. Some vessels were boarded and inspected, but further militia vessels were summoned to the area preventing the frigate from carrying out its mission.[59] After a tense two-month stand-off, which saw both sides commit more vessels, including naval ships, and escalate diplomatic activity, all vessels vacated the area following an apparent US-brokered agreement. However, Chinese vessels returned almost immediately and Beijing has denied that any deal ever existed.[60] The initial role, played by the maritime militia, is significant because it was perceived as the extension of Chinese sovereign claims in the disputed region. The rapid Chinese response with bigger, more heavily armed vessels also indicated that these were not ordinary fishermen who had strayed outside their usual fishing areas. Through a combination of deception and opaqueness, combined with a show of force, China had therefore gained control over a strategically important feature. The maritime militia were able to incite the stand-off and communicate the events which allowed other Chinese maritime protection vessels to then intervene. While they were not equipped to handle the Philippine Navy, they played an important role in seizing the Shoal at the end of the stand-off, thus illustrating both the strengths and weaknesses of maritime militia.

The incident involving the USS *Lassen* is not as complex, but it is indicative of a trend on how China is dealing with the US presence in the SCS. The destroyer USS *Lassen* was conducting a Freedom of Navigation Operation (FONOP) when it sailed past the disputed Subi Reef in the Spratly Islands group on 27 October. The Freedom of Navigation programme is based on the 1983 US Oceans Policy, which roughly aligned US policy with the Law of the Sea Convention (UNCLOS), even though the United States is not a signatory. At its core, the document asserts that the United States will follow the spirit of UNCLOS, particularly pertaining to a state's right to grant or deny passage or overflight of foreign vessels in its territorial waters or EEZ, but will ignore such claims if it deems them excessive or when such restrictions would upset the 'balance of interests'.[61] Essentially, the United States reserves the rights to exercise innocent passage for its planes or ships even in the territorial waters of another state, as provided for in UNCLOS, even if the state in question has implemented restrictions. The US DOD publishes a yearly report on claims it considers excessive and these form the basis for the conduct of FONOPs. In the case of China, for example, the excessive claims include claimed jurisdiction over the airspace in the EEZ, prohibition of survey activities by foreign entities and the requirement of prior notification for military ships conducting innocent passage through Chinese territorial waters.[62] The USS *Lassen* was exercising the right of innocent passage in disputed waters over which China claims jurisdiction (outside its territorial waters but within the claimed EEZ) in a move designed to protest Chinese island building in the region.

While such waters would normally be freely accessible to any vessel, and artificial features do not extend a state's territorial waters, China is attempting to coerce other actors to accept de facto territorial waters around its reclaimed islands by forcing them to behave as if they were within its territorial waters.

The key difference between territorial and other waters is the range of activities that, particularly naval vessels, are allowed to conduct. While the *Lassen* did sail through disputed areas, it restricted its activities only to those which would be permissible in territorial waters, a move which could send mixed signals as to the US position.[63] For most of the destroyer's journey through the SCS it was shadowed from a distance by PLAN vessels, but when it passed Subi Reef it was harassed by maritime militia vessels. While they did not engage in direct provocation or ramming, given the difference in size and armament such actions would be largely pointless, they clearly demonstrated displeasure at the presence of the US ship in non-kinetic ways and, at least symbolically, asserted Chinese jurisdiction over the waters.[64] As mentioned earlier, Subi Reef is one of the features in the Spratly Islands which China has enlarged through land reclamation and is seen as a potentially important base in the area; therefore, it would be important for China to keep foreign vessels as far away as possible or, alternatively, treat these features as part of Chinese territorial waters.

A further example of what the United States claims are Chinese excessive restrictions, relate to survey activities. In 2009, five Chinese vessels, including two fishing maritime militia vessels, harassed the US survey ship *USNS Impeccable* and even attempted to sever its towed array while coming within 25 feet of the vessel and performing dangerous manoeuvres, such as halting in its path and forcing it to perform an emergency stop to prevent collision.[65] As the earliest of the three incidents examined here, it has the added value of providing data that enables an examination of changes which have occurred since the incident in how the maritime militia operates. Their actions were perceived to be based on the prohibition of survey activities, which are primarily aimed at, but not limited to, natural resource extraction. Since the *Impeccable* was likely gathering acoustical data which could help the US track Chinese submarines in the area its actions were perceived as provocative by China.[66] The whole incident can then be seen as an act of coercive diplomacy, with which China wished to send as clear a signal as possible that it will not tolerate US interference within the areas of the SCS over which it claims jurisdiction.[67] While that in itself is not significant, the fact that this form of coercive diplomacy did not involve an actual warship is important. The perception of the use of military power as a means of coercion carries with it certain consequences, such as public outcry (both domestic and international) or possible escalation. By using non-military means, China is attempting to circumvent those consequences while still attaining its goals. Furthermore, it is transferring the burden of dealing with this ambiguity to the other parties involved by offering them little else but militia fishing vessels as direct opponents. The added legal difficulties which this presents will be explored later in the chapter.

In addition to the maritime militia, China has also been using the Coast Guard as an alternative to naval vessels. This is a trend which is present throughout the region, with Japan, Indonesia and the Philippines all increasing the role of their respective coast guards. The main reason behind this reliance on coast guards is that they represent a less militaristic, and therefore less threatening, alternative to navies. A foreign vessel caught fishing illegally in one state's EEZ being processed by a coast guard cutter is a significantly different image than if the same vessel was apprehended by a naval frigate. It is also less likely to spark a major political confrontation between the parties. Coast guard vessels are also better equipped for this kind of work, since their role is primarily law enforcement rather than military. While there is sound logic behind the increased role of coast guards it is important to note that the lighter touch of coast guards can also be a weakness, precisely because they lack certain qualities of sea power.

Two incidents between Indonesia and China in the Natuna Sea in the spring of 2016 offer an interesting contrast between the use of law enforcement and naval vessels. In both cases (March 2016 and May 2016) Indonesian vessels attempted to prevent Chinese fishing vessels from encroaching in the Indonesian EEZ. In March, the fishing vessel was intercepted by Indonesian law enforcement vessels and was being towed to port when a CCG vessel rammed and freed the captive fishermen.[68] Following this incident, the Indonesian government decided to give the primary responsibility for patrolling the EEZ to its navy. In May of the same year, and in almost identical circumstance, the CCG cutter stayed well clear of the Indonesian frigate as it was in the process of arresting and towing the Chinese fishing vessel.[69] While this example does not conclusively prove the utility of coast guards over naval vessels, it does demonstrate that the states around the SCS are struggling to address adequately the issues stemming from the opaqueness of China's maritime operations. In an environment where over- or under-reaction might have adverse consequences, using a correct strategy is crucial. This task is further complicated by a complex legal situation, which is the next topic this chapter will examine.

Lawfare

An important aspect of hybrid warfare concerns the legal and regulatory nature of the international system. While largely un-enforceable, international legal norms nonetheless possess a certain degree of legitimacy and support and therefore can be of use to a hybrid actor. The impact of international (legal) norms is particularly influential in liberal democratic states, where public support for military operations is not only important but often difficult to raise and maintain. Since much of the Western world tends to be legalistic in its approach to IR, the exploitation of legality and legitimacy could be a powerful tool for an opponent. While some previous parts of this book have touched upon the question of international law, it will be emphasized particularly in the context of the SCS as, unlike in previous examples, its use and application differ significantly when combined with a maritime environment.

The origins of the term 'lawfare' are difficult to trace but the popularization of the term is often attributed to an article by Major General Charles Dunlap. In it, he defines lawfare as 'the strategy of using – or misusing – law as a substitute for traditional military means to achieve an operational objective'.[70] Dunlap further defines lawfare as 'the exploitation of real, perceived, or even orchestrated incidents of law-of-war violations being employed as an unconventional means of confronting American military power'.[71] This definition can be expanded beyond the United States, as a means of any weaker power challenging a stronger one, and it is precisely this relation between stronger and weaker powers that lies at the heart of lawfare. Most definitions of lawfare come from international legal scholars who on the whole seem to be reconciled to the idea that challenges can be made through legal avenues in lieu of waging war. In, fact Dunlap encourages court challenges as a way of fighting lawfare and discouraging future misconduct.[72] However, in the world of IR, such logic might not automatically apply. An alternative definition of lawfare sees it as 'a weapon designed to destroy the enemy by using, misusing, and abusing the legal system and the media in order to raise a public outcry against that enemy'.[73] In essence this view sees lawfare as part of strategic communications or propaganda. Strategic communications, usually viewed as communication through words or deeds in pursuit of national strategic objectives,[74] are increasingly seen as crucial aspects of modern warfare, and presentation of actions as being legal or illegal is an important part of such a debate. Some lawfare scholars question whether there is a difference between a legal form of lawfare and an illegal one.[75] In the international arena such a question can only be answered in the negative, because it is purely a matter of perspective. What is deemed legal lawfare – that is, lawfare which uses international law for the benefit of the actor through different interpretations, and illegal lawfare, in which an actor claims to have suffered by the application or breaches of international legal norms in order to discredit them, will differ greatly depending on which actor defines them. One of the main criticisms levelled at the international legal system is that it has been set up by the Western liberal democracies for their own benefit. Their own inconsistent and sometimes opportunistic interpretation and application of these norms only reinforces this view. Rising powers like China, India and Russia have publicly announced that they seek to change the Western-centric, liberal world order which they perceive as too invasive and prejudiced against them.

With that in mind, the definitions of lawfare espoused above do not adequately cover the lawfare element of hybrid warfare because they all follow the basic assumption that international law is something that should be followed. While this is a valid legal position, the concept of hybrid warfare is designed specifically to challenge or obfuscate the existing order in such a way that allows the hybrid actor to attain its goals without inviting the wrath of the West. Therefore, a broader definition is required in order to encompass the full spectrum of the use of lawfare within a hybrid context. It is important to note at this point that the following definition is not a legal but a strategic one, and it only seeks to define lawfare to the extent necessary for its understanding in a hybrid concept. For the purposes of this book lawfare will be defined as the application or misapplication of international legal norms with the aim of providing the hybrid actor with an advantage in achieving its political objectives. Such an advantage could be very specific, confusing an individual commanding officer on the correct legal course to take in combat for example, or very broad, such as using the promise of international legal cooperation as a stalling tactic. The limited nature of hybrid warfare itself provides constraints on the breadth of lawfare that can be employed in this manner as an outright or blatant breach of international legal norms might result in a Western military intervention. Of course, hybrid warfare is designed to be ambiguous and one of the reasons for this is to avoid precisely this kind of scenario. Lawfare is merely an additional component which aids in this opaqueness by questioning whether an action can really clearly be identified as illegal. Conversely, other hybrid actions can aid in shielding an actor from punishment for breaking an established legal norm, if that is its political objective, making lawfare a possible end in itself. In an environment like the maritime domain, where legal norms are particularly complex, lawfare can produce impressive results.

In the context of the SCS this chapter will examine two strands of Chinese lawfare. The first strand will illustrate how China is using the cover of international law as a defensive measure to confuse its opponents on the legality of its actions, while the second will demonstrate a possible offensive use of lawfare as a means of pressuring other states into accepting the Chinese point of view. These two approaches are used both concurrently and separately by China, as will be demonstrated by examples focusing on the legal status of the maritime militia, the interpretation of UNCLOS pertaining to land reclamation, and the use of international agreements as a strategic stalling tactic. Since most of these topics have already been covered above to a certain degree, the examination will focus fully on their lawfare aspects.

The precise legal status of the maritime militia has long been a bone of contention with any actor dealing with China in the SCS. Their quasi-military nature means that they cannot be treated solely as fishermen, but the reality at sea is that that is what they are for most of the time. Chinese maritime militia represents a textbook hybrid force and is similar, in many ways, to Hezbollah fighters, described in Chapter 5. On paper, these vessels are civilian fishing boats, owned and operated by private enterprises and crewed by civilian personnel, that is non-active duty military. Just because they are part of a militia unit does not immediately rob them of their civilian status, otherwise every state with a military draft system would be almost bereft of civilians. What makes maritime militia members different is the fact that they not only receive military training and equipment but also operate either fishing vessels or militia vessels. Militia ships are armed not just with water cannons but also with light personal weapons and even heavy machine guns, although those are detachable and therefore not always present. Militia crews are issued PLAN uniforms, which they would presumably wear when engaging in 'militia business' and take them off them when doing 'fishing business', although Chinese officials have claimed that crews wear military camouflage uniforms for sun protection.[76] Such a distinction might be relatively simple on paper, but when confronted with a situation like this at sea, the commanding officer of a vessel facing the militia would legitimately be confused. It is precisely this kind of confusion that China is seeking with its ambiguous approach. Should such a vessel come under attack China would undoubtedly claim that they were innocent fishermen, while the reality might be quite different. Public opinion would likely side with the seemingly weaker side, the fishermen, rather than whichever actor engaged them, even if they had done so for legitimate reasons. Such a scenario is not only unthinkable but also similar to the one imagined by Admiral Stavridis;[77] it has in fact occurred before, both in violent cases (1974, 1988) and in the similarly tense but non-kinetic stand-off in 2012 at Scarborough Shoal.

Chinese island building through dredging and land reclamation has caused many fears and worries not only in the region but globally. While the states immediately adjacent to the SCS see potential Chinese military bases on reclaimed islands as a direct threat to security, the global impact stems from the importance of the SCS as a maritime thoroughfare for commercial shipping. Island bases at strategic points in the Spratly and Paracels groups could enable China effectively to monitor, if not outright control, the sea lanes. While it is unlikely that China would want to disrupt shipping, most of which goes to its ports in any case, there is a degree of power and prestige associated with being the guardian of important sea lines of communication. If that were to happen, it would render the US presence in the area meaningless in the Chinese view. The mere threat of Chinese influence over the flow of goods through the SCS could give it leverage over all the other states in the region, including Japan, South Korea and Taiwan, all of which are vitally dependant on it. In order to stake its permanent claim to the islands, and to gain a certain degree of legitimacy for enforcing its sovereignty and rights over these areas, China has declared significantly excessive maritime claims over these features. On paper, these seem to stem from the thrust, if not the letter, of UNCLOS and China is engaging in a certain degree of alternative interpretation. While it is a signatory of UNCLOS, it seems that China has decided that certain provisions should not be so strictly binding for it. For example, under UNCLOS, artificial islands do not generate any rights whatsoever[78] and maritime features outside territorial waters do not extend those territorial waters beyond their 12 mile limit.[79] While islands owned beyond the 12 mile limit of the state's coastline also generate the same amount of territorial waters in relation to their position[80] and therefore also extend the EEZ, this does not apply to rocks[81] or submerged features.[82] While the legal regulations clearly give it no rights on or around its reclaimed islands in the SCS, China is nevertheless managing to convince or pressure its neighbours into acting as if that was the case.

Another aspect of this legal wrangling is the Chinese establishment and enforcement of an air identification zone in the East China Sea. By creating the requirement to register with Chinese air control for all aircraft passing through, it is demonstrating that it is administering this part of the world, possibly as a precursor to claiming sovereignty over it.[83] This pattern of expanding international legal regimes to suit its strategic needs is being repeated in the SCS through the application of rights generated by the Chinese-claimed features. Additionally, China has asserted the moral high ground when addressing protests from Washington by pointing out that the United States has not ratified UNCLOS. While this argument might not be very persuasive, it represents a relatively successful form of lawfare since it nevertheless provides some political legitimacy for Chinese claims. After all, lawfare does not need to be perfect or universally accepted, it just needs to work for long enough to enable the hybrid actor to achieve its goals.

A recent ruling by the Permanent Court of Arbitration on a case brought by the Philippines against China over the disputed claims established that China has no historical rights to claim the majority of the SCS within its claimed 'nine dash line'.[84] It also ruled that the Chinese claims of legal right stemming from their possessions are unfounded.[85] While the decision was lauded at the time as a major legal victory against China, the fact that China had immediately declared it would not abide by it effectively rendered it toothless. The aftermath of the decision has even witnessed a hardening of the Chinese stance on the matter and, paradoxically, a rejection of a legal-based solution in favour of a reliance on traditional power instruments.[86] It even managed to negotiate with the new Philippine president Rodrigo Duterte, who is considered much more pro-Chinese than his predecessor, effectively to shelve the ruling in the name of improved relations and trade. Duterte's positive stance on China would have made the ruling, considered a legal victory, a political problem for him in the long run so he refrained from referring to it, apart from a cursory acknowledgement upon the ruling being announced.[87] Overall, while the legal status of the disputed areas was at least partially addressed, the status on the ground remained effectively the same.

The final observation, based on the earlier analysis, focuses on the strategic implication of Chinese actions. When both the offensive and defensive lawfare are taken into account it is clear that the end goal for China is the exertion of influence in the SCS, as close as possible to de facto sovereignty. While such behaviour is normal for a rising power, the way China has gone about this suggests that it is not ready conventionally to challenge the regional hegemon (the United States) or any of the regional minor powers. Whether it is buying time to build up its military capabilities or simply wants to avoid trade disruptions, China seems to be on the strategic offensive. In the realm of international law, China seems to be using stated commitments to various legal agreements, such as UNCLOS or the Code of Conduct, as a means of de-escalation and stalling. The Code of Conduct is an ASEAN agreement first proposed in 2002 as a means of limiting and de-escalating the tensions arising from disputed claims. While formal code is yet to be formulated, the issue has been raised twice (in 2012 and 2017) in response to an increase in Chinese activities. China first committed itself to this process in 2013, as a way of calming the waters after the Scarborough Shoal incident, and has reaffirmed its commitment in 2017 after raised tensions over its island building.[88] It would appear that China is using the international legal framework to appear as though it will cooperate with the other parties in the SCS, but only when it worries that the tensions have escalated too far. Such agreements tend to dampen concerns and lower the public's interest in the matter for some time and they are also not legally binding. While other parties are then mollified by China's apparent participation, China is using up the time to strengthen further its position. The longer the territorial disputes remain unresolved the more the advantage shifts to China which is exercising de facto control over the area in the meantime. As international law, like any other form of law, is supremely concerned simply with the formal legal declaration, such disingenuous stalling tactics seem to produce excellent results. When coupled with the Chinese misuse of UNCLOS, described above, the potent combination represents the archetype for a successful lawfare campaign.

Kinetic and non-kinetic warfare in the maritime domain

The term 'warfare' itself often carries with it an implied kineticism of action, concomitant with the images of war. However, in the context of hybrid warfare the primacy of kinetic warfare is somewhat eroded and non-kinetic means, such as information warfare, cyber warfare and economic warfare, transform from being considered force multipliers to becoming a force in their own right. This is not to say that hybrid warfare does not possess a kinetic component, the conventional side of hybrid warfare still requires its inclusion, but it does illustrate that in the real world of low-level conflicts within the opaque grey zone, non-kinetic approaches are crucial. The level of kineticism within hybrid warfare can differ significantly, depending on the circumstances and is directly connected to the nature of the domain in which it is waged. Examinations of hybrid warfare in the previous chapters focused on examples of kinetic hybrid warfare, but they were also focused primarily on the land domain where kinetic approaches are dominant. This chapter examined hybrid warfare in the maritime domain and established that non-kinetic hybrid warfare has become the preferred way of engaging in coercion and geo-strategic competition.

In the case of China, the vast majority of its actions in the SCS are non-kinetic in nature, in the sense that they do not involve the launching of torpedoes or missiles, or the firing of bullets or shells. Limited kinetic manoeuvres occur when militia vessels ram their opponents or employ water cannons, but for the most part kineticism is merely a background threat. PLAN's use of warships also suggests that they are following a non-kinetic approach. Its ships, planes and submarines regularly patrol the SCS but tend to stay away from active engagement in disputes, although they can often be seen on the horizon. Therefore, while naval ships still contribute to maritime hybrid warfare, in the case of China they have taken a back seat and act merely as the last line of deterrence against the escalation by another actor. The primary burden is shouldered by the coast guard and especially the maritime militia. China's maritime militia represents a textbook hybrid force which is capable of acting as a, albeit limited, conventional naval force, with the training and equipment required for such activities, while also blending into the background as fishermen. Using legal ambiguity, they are effectively immune from kinetic actions of foreign navies, except in times of war. However, hybrid warfare aims to remain below the threshold of large-scale conventional war and in this grey zone, China's 'little blue men' represent the perfect tool.

Island building through land reclamation has been the most visible aspect of Chinese maritime hybrid warfare, and it is also non-kinetic in nature. While the process caused unmeasurable environmental damage which consequentially caused economic damage to all the states surrounding the SCS, it was not conducted in a militarized way. Certainly, such assertive and unilateral action represents a possible threat, and the installation of airstrips and defensive gun emplacements only highlights the potential for military influence. However, as of time of writing, no kinetic military action has been launched from Chinese bases in the Spratly and Paracels group, although the maritime militia have utilized them as bases of operations. The value of the islands is in their strategic position and utility. China does not need to militarize them heavily because they are not conventional tools of power projection but rather hybrid ones. Their mere existence gives China the ability, and in its opinion the right, to administer and contest the control of large swathes of the SCS with all the corresponding economic and political benefits. Even the islands themselves operate as a hybrid unit in as much as they are currently predominantly used for civilian purposes and 'blend in' with the other islands in the region but could easily be mobilized by deliveries of military equipment and troops by air, a fact demonstrated by the exercises in April 2018. The defensive capabilities confirmed to be installed in the Spratly Islands do not represent a kinetic challenge, although the same cannot be said of the sophisticated missiles placed on Woody Island in the Paracels. Should China use Woody Island as a template for the future, then these island bases would become formidable conventional power projection sites, possibly capable of deterring even the US Navy. However, such actions would be inconsistent with a low-level hybrid approach and would most likely result in an escalation that would reverse some of the goals China has already achieved. Temporary and rapid mobilizations of the islands, on the other hand, would provide China the ability to gauge the response of the guardian powers towards any future, more permanent, deployments. Such exercises would also give its forces in the region valuable experience, should China seek to escalate the pressure in future.

Presently, it seems that China is employing maritime hybrid warfare in order to strengthen its position within the East and Southeast Asian regions. Like any other hybrid actor, China is seeking limited gains through means that enable it to obscure its actions so as not to provoke an overwhelming response. It is also utilizing lawfare in an attempt to avert significant and damaging legal condemnations from the West which could lead to interventions, either diplomatic or potentially military, while simultaneously hiding behind those same legal norms in order to deflect criticism and to play for time. Throughout history China has always been a patient power and its calculated advance into the SCS is another example of this characteristic. The slow pace is a result of the environment in which these actions are taking place and the Chinese desire not to upset its regional competitors unduly, so as to prevent them from joining together in opposition, probably with US backing. A hybrid approach is the most suitable under these circumstances and, although it would be presumptuous to claim that China has a fully formed 'hybrid' strategy, its actions follow a pattern that is consistent with what, in Western nomenclature, would be called as such. It is very likely that China itself is not yet fully aware of the potential of hybrid warfare and is testing the waters to see how its opponents respond and where the lines of escalation are drawn. In the short and medium term, this moderate trend is likely to continue, but in the long term it is highly probable that the balance in China's hybrid warfare will tilt from predominantly non-kinetic to kinetic as it will seek actively to rebalance the prevailing regional order.

Conclusion

A clear appreciation of the complex character of strategy is vital to the understanding of the contemporary world of conflict and the processes and phenomena which occur within it. And yet, it is one of the most often misused, or misapplied, terms in contemporary political, security and international relations discourse. International competition, coercion and particularly conflict cannot be adequately studied or researched without examining them from a strategic perspective. This has been the guiding theme of this book. Understanding phenomena like hybrid warfare is essential to obtain a more profound understanding of security and the ways in which it can be achieved. As the previous chapters have pointed out, nothing occurs outside a specific context. This is also true of the research itself. Therefore, the best way to begin the conclusion of this examination of hybrid warfare is to link it back to the context in which it began, a context that is almost entirely strategic. As an analysis in the realist tradition, the aim of this book has been to examine a complex phenomenon in a strategic way; for example, as an utilization of coercion for political objectives. This not only serves an academic purpose but can also be of practical use to policymakers and defence planners.

The present tome set out to create a unified definition of hybrid warfare. In an environment already overflowing with new terms, the problem is often that not enough time and effort is devoted to defining and explaining them properly. 'Hybrid warfare' is an example of such a term but, unlike many others which had failed to gain traction, it has managed to endure. However, for a phenomenon to be properly studied, it is not sufficient to merely observe that it exists, or that it is mentioned in academic and non-academic literature. To address this issue, this book sought to create that missing link between the phenomenon itself and its practical implications. In order to answer the two critical questions 'what is hybrid warfare and how does it work', this book looked at the existing literature on the topic. However, none of the published definitions of hybrid warfare appeared to actually answer this question. If the question is broken down into its two parts, some definitions do give at least a partial answer as to *how it works* but fail to say *what it is*. After going through the research process, a very clear answer to both parts of the question can now be offered. Hybrid warfare is a distinct form of low-level conflict, spanning the spectrum of capabilities. It works as a deliberately opaque merger of conventional and unconventional warfare, conducted under the central authority and direction of a state or state-like actor.

The most often used criticism of hybrid warfare is that it is merely a new term for something that has always been going on. Actors will always seek out the weaknesses of their opponents and engage them asymmetrically, since that is the most obvious and easiest way to achieve one's objectives. Deception, diversion and concealment are also not new but have been a staple of warfare since its beginning. Using unconventional means in lieu of conventional ones in order to gain a tactical advantage is equally obvious, as is the reverse. This book does not challenge any of these assumptions. However, the problem of using such arguments to claim that there is nothing new about hybrid warfare is the same as the problem with the existing definitions of hybrid warfare. They all focus on specific aspects or traits of hybrid warfare, rather than its character. No individual component of hybrid warfare is new in and of itself, the novelty of hybrid warfare is the way they are brought together. This is not an outlandish proposition as some critics of hybrid warfare have made it out to be. When reduced to the basic constituents, there is no differentiation between types of warfare. As Clausewitz put it, at its base, it is a duel on a larger scale.[1] The number of ways in which one international actor can engage another is always limited due to several factors, including, but not restricted to, available technology, cost, capabilities and the will to use any of them. As a result of this, the novelty or staleness of individual components is irrelevant. What makes a difference however, is how these components are combined. This research went even further to examine what makes hybrid so interesting by examining the context in which it occurs. It is not merely a product of the actors which use it but also an adaptation to the larger international system in which it is used. This, of course, refers to the way both conflict and coercion have come to be perceived in the modern international order.

It is a characteristic of the international order that it is systematically averse to a large-scale conflict. The reasons for this are twofold. First, the international order as we know it today emanates from the legacy of the two world wars, including the advent of nuclear weapons and was, at least on paper, designed to prevent a repeat of such tragedy. Secondly, any system, international or otherwise, tries to prevent systemic instability because that could lead to its demise. In the arena of international politics, internal instability of the international order usually takes the form of conflicts or coercion of various kinds. Therefore, it is only logical that the system itself would seek to mitigate their use or, failing that, their impact on the system as a whole. Since the international order is Western-oriented, the attitudes of Western great powers reflect those of the system. Over the last two decades, the Western world, and by extension the international order, has shifted towards reducing the use of military power as a tool of international politics. While such a trend has decreased the number of large-scale conventional conflicts which would pose a threat to the system, it has created the environment where lower-level conflicts are not only possible, but actually preferred.

In order to explain this new environment better, the book introduced the notion of the quinity. By combining the traditional Clausewitzian idea of the trinity and the principles of the contemporary international order, the quinity describes the circumstances, conditions, restrictions and correlating opportunities for actors within and on the fringes of the international order. Under such circumstances, the added appeal of hybrid warfare is that it can produce results which would normally require a large-scale conventional conflict, but without the complications that would arise from that. From the perspective of Western guardian powers, the quinity illustrates the problems associated with intervention and response to such low-level conflicts. The reality of the quinity means that Western actors must make great efforts to keep allies together, not only for additional legitimacy but also in order to fill any gaps in capabilities. These efforts are of course in addition to gaining, and maintaining, support at home, which is often not an easy task in a liberal democratic state. The additional quinitarian requirements are, in essence, a reflection of the democratic values and structures of the guardian powers. Such high demands for legitimacy can delay possible action and induce undue limits and caution in response to hybrid actions by competitors. Competitors, who are not bound so tightly by the structures of the quinity, can take advantage of this by obfuscating the fundamental rules of the international order; so long as their actions do not escalate to the point where the conditions required for a quinitarian response would be fulfilled. In this context, therefore, democracy, and its corresponding legitimacy requirements, can be argued to be a constraint on the ability of guardian powers to respond effectively against instances of hybrid warfare. This is further complicated by the political structures which all democracies possess and the transparent and representative nature in which they function. While in domestic politics greater transparency and representation are viewed as essential, in foreign policy this is not always the case. Particularly when dealing with conflict situations requiring a rapid response, a decision-making process which includes too many actors is ineffective. This argument similarly applies to large alliances and international organizations such as NATO and the EU. Both organizations have experienced problems associated with slow decision-making when a large number of members have a say and also hold the same weight of decision-making power. Whether it is the crisis in Libya, Syria or Ukraine, the response has always been slow in coming, if a decision was made at all.

Such problems are not particularly new as other 'new wars' concepts have made similar observations. The commonality of concepts like Three Block War, 4GW or Compound War lies precisely in the presupposition that interstate conflict is in decline. This then leads to the logical, although erroneous, conclusion that conventional warfare is losing its relevance as a tool of international coercion. The three aforementioned concepts see the future battlefield as that of peace or nation-builders fighting remnants of oppressive governments through counterterrorism or COIN. Fortunately, institutional inertia and a political unwillingness to reorganize military forces completely towards unconventional warfare has generated a substantial backlash to such notions. Only states which already enjoy the security and deterrence which substantial conventional power, often complemented by nuclear forces, can generate could have developed these concepts. In practice this meant that they were limited to the Western world and, to a degree, to the international order. However, other actors in the world did not see this as a viable way to fight future wars, but rather as a weakness which can be exploited. Hybrid warfare bridges that academic and practical cognitive dissonance between the decline of large-scale conventional war and the continued need for the pursuit of national goals which can only be achieved by orthodox military power. Unlike the other competing concepts, hybrid warfare is not limited just to the conventional or the unconventional 'box'. This does perhaps make it more challenging to analyse adequately but it also makes it a much more potent threat.

It would be erroneous to think of hybrid warfare as a kind of wonder weapon which can prevail against any opponent in any situation. History has shown many times that such a tool does not exist. Hybrid warfare has several weaknesses, primarily the need to control its escalation. Further than that, it is an approach that can only be used sparingly because it is based on opaqueness. While this opaqueness offers great potential, it also means that it will diminish with repeated use. Essentially, hybrid warfare has a very steep curve of diminishing returns. The more often one actor uses it, the clearer it becomes and the less effective it will be. This also links into the perennial problem of escalation since a non-opaque version of hybrid warfare is simply normal warfare. Precisely where the usefulness of hybrid warfare ends depends, naturally, on the actor which uses it. If the perceived and expected gains are worth the risk, then even a less-than-ideal hybrid approach is still preferable to a purely conventional or unconventional one.

Strategic considerations of the cost of war are the key. Importantly, the term 'costs' does not refer only to the economic costs of an operation, but rather to the overall strategic and political costs as well. For example, the economic costs of re-integrating Crimea into Russia have been estimated at $9 billion, with the economic sanctions imposed on Russia as a result of its intervention adding to that figure. From a purely financial perspective then, Russian actions could not have been worth the gains. However, from a strategic perspective, the seizure of Crimea cemented Russia's place as the dominant power in the Black Sea region, guaranteed the continued use of the Sevastopol naval base and sent a clear message to NATO and the EU that their continued eastwards expansion will no longer be passively accepted. The conflict in the Donbas region of Ukraine further reinforced the latter point while giving Russia direct influence over domestic Ukrainian politics. While some analysts have argued that these relatively slim moral or pride-based gains are still not worth Russia becoming an international pariah, this line of argumentation is pointless. Thucydides wrote about states going to war for prestige, fear or self-interest[2] in the fifth century BC; therefore, the idea that states can go to war over prestige or honour is hardly novel. Arguably, for Russia it was a combination of all three of those that led to its decision to intervene in Ukraine. Ultimately, it is down to Russia to decide what matters to it, and its strategic calculations are not driven by economics alone.

When expanding the horizons of hybrid warfare, this book looked at the case of China. The chapter on Chinese maritime hybrid warfare not only demonstrated how a different domain affects the conduct of hybrid warfare but also expanded on the notion of hybrid warfare as a tool of revisionist powers. The Chinese example made it clear that China is using the framework of the prevailing international order to its best advantage. While using lawfare, and the ambiguous legality surrounding the maritime militia, might be less impactful than the Russian approach of outright military intervention, it might prove to be more successful in the long run. If it is easy to see a scenario of diminishing returns with Russian-style hybrid warfare, that downturn in efficiency is not so clear in the Chinese example. Certainly, it would have a much flatter curve spanning a longer time period. On the other side, it also takes longer to implement and reap any rewards. As with any tool of coercion, it ultimately comes down to the strategic culture of the actor using it. Hybrid warfare is therefore a very wide-ranging concept, which is not limited by cultural, philosophical or political differences. As it is based on sound strategic logic, it can be used by almost any actor with the capabilities and the will to carry it out.

One of the major drawbacks of modern thinking about future conflict is its presumption that it is going to be primarily conducted by non-state actors. While not entirely false, this assumption stems from a relatively limited experience of Western states in the post-Cold War era. The rise of international non-state terrorism and the resulting US GWOT reinforce this line of thought. More recently, the focus seems to have shifted from terrorism to cyber warfare and political disinformation, although terrorism still looms in the background. In the Western world, this is largely as a result of Russian hybrid warfare and the response to it represents one of the best examples of what can occur when a term is misused. The two trends appear to follow a similar path. In both cases the emergence of a phenomenon has resulted in Western policymakers attempting to draw rapid and important conclusions and solutions, often based on incorrect or incomplete information. This is not helped by the unfortunate trend in academia, again boosted by the debates surrounding terrorism, of a much more relaxed approach to definitions. While debating the finer points of one definition or another might be of interest to academics, it is not helpful to concrete policymaking. This same error has now been repeated in relation to hybrid warfare. The value of a precise and concise definition lies not only in the fact that it informs an actor of what hybrid warfare is and what it is not. It also places it into the correct context and gives a certain amount of predictability. Definitions should therefore be as instructive as possible, rather than as broad as possible. Encompassing the totality of warfare in one definition is an exercise in futility, so precisely defining the relevant types of warfare is not only sensible, it should be actively pursued. Additionally, the false equivalency between approaches to terrorism and hybrid warfare is further problematic because the two phenomena are not directly comparable. Hybrid warfare is a much broader phenomenon whereas terrorism denotes a single type of tactic. Moreover, terrorism can be a tool of hybrid warfare, but it is not its defining characteristic.

In the example of Hezbollah in the 2006 Lebanon War, this dichotomy between terrorism and hybrid warfare is not only apparent but has actually been used by Hezbollah as a tactic in its own right. As Israel had so much experience in combating insurgents using terrorist tactics, it had geared much of its defence doctrine towards that type of conflict. When the time came to confront Israel, Hezbollah actually reversed its own doctrine and used a hybrid approach to gain an advantage. This is not to say that Hezbollah did not use terrorism in the 2006

Lebanon War, but it was not the sole, or even the main, tactic. By broadening its operational doctrine, it managed to engage Israel from a position of relative strength, since the IDF was so focused towards counterterrorism operations that it had neglected its conventional capabilities, most significantly in the ground forces. In doctrinal terms, Israel in particular followed the trend towards a post-definition world, perhaps more so than any other state at the time. By basing its defence doctrine on a post-structuralist philosophical approach to security, it not only went a step further down the terrorism line, it also attempted to change fundamentally how national defence was organized and, above all, how it was presented and perceived. This was a legacy of a time when debates on terrorism dominated national security and in Israel's case it made a certain degree of sense considering that it was constantly dealing with instances of terrorism. However, such a narrow approach has clear weaknesses, and Hezbollah not only accurately determined where those weaknesses were, it also managed to exploit them fully. In this case, it cannot even be claimed that such observations can only be made in retrospect since there were plenty of warnings voiced at the time.

In purely strategic terms, such an unbalanced approach to national defence is also clearly fraught with danger. As in any field of military endeavour, specialization can produce great results, but if it is done too intently, it can become detrimental as it encourages opponents to take advantage with an asymmetrical approach which neutralizes the specialization. A full-spectrum approach is always preferable in order to avoid such occurrences, but this is an expensive proposition in terms of both financial and manpower requirements. Much has been made about the fact that all conflicts throughout history have been asymmetrical to some degree. Hybrid warfare does not challenge that asymmetry; it is as asymmetrical as any other type of warfare. Its key strength lies in the ability to utilize the full spectrum of capabilities but do so while staying below the threshold of large-scale conventional war. From a Western perspective this is something that has doctrinally been deemed almost impossible, or at least impractical, so various states have specialized, to a greater or lesser degree, in various combinations of capabilities. Hybrid warfare is not a specialization, it is merely a lower-level type of conflict.

As previously mentioned, the 'new wars' debate had largely focused on non-state actors. Here, hybrid warfare departs further from the established norm in as much as it is an approach that cannot be used by non-state actors, as they are traditionally understood. Classical insurgencies, terrorist groups, liberation movements and other such actors are almost purely asymmetrical, meaning that they tend to focus on the most asymmetrical approach they can achieve in order to gain as much relative advantage as possible against their opponents. This creates the same problems with specialization that states face. Overcommitting to one form of warfare or another gives an actor certain advantages, but also comes with weaknesses. Non-state actors are, by their very nature, limited to using unconventional means so they can overcome the inherent weaknesses of that by simply refusing to engage in a conventional conflict. On the other hand, states often do not have a choice in the matter. They must engage a non-state actor if it represents a sufficient threat even if they must do so on unfavourable terms. Logically, states then seek to change those terms to suit their strengths, and non-state actors can do nothing but press their advantages in the hope that they can degrade the state's combat effectiveness faster that it can change the nature of the conflict. Hybrid warfare, on the other hand, does not have this limitation. As it is always comprised of both conventional and unconventional warfare, the problem of specialization never arises; therefore, the only question is whether the conventional or the unconventional aspect of hybrid operations is given more emphasis at any given time. Adjusting the emphasis from one form or another is much easier than fundamentally changing the whole approach from conventional to unconventional, or vice versa. However, this does present a very obvious limit to the type of actor which can make use of hybrid warfare. Traditional non-state actors cannot develop hybrid strategies because they are fully committed solely to unconventional warfare. Conventional warfare requires extensive logistical and bureaucratic support and is much more expensive that its unconventional counterpart. It also tends to utilize advanced technological capabilities which are almost impossible to obtain, or create, for any routine non-state actor. Therefore, the character of hybrid warfare itself means that it can only be used by states or very state-like actors.

One such state-like actor is undoubtedly Hezbollah. While variously described as a terrorist organization, political movement or a state within a state, it is clearly not a traditional non-state actor. Not only does it hold and administer its own territory within Lebanon, it also governs the population, raises taxes and provides social and other services. Its nature would probably best be described as a sociopolitical movement with a militant wing, rather than any of the above terms. While it might not be recognized as an actual sovereign state, in terms of hybrid warfare it does not need to go that far. The key requirement for becoming a state-like actor is the ability to wage conventional warfare, at least to a degree sufficient for conducting hybrid warfare. Hezbollah proved that it possesses that capability during the 2006 Lebanon War. However, the number of state-like actors is not likely to rise significantly due to the following two factors. First, the 2006 Lebanon War was not an outright win for Hezbollah and even its own leadership later admitted that they would not have launched the operation had they known what the costs would be. Second, there is a trade-off for a non-state actor pursuing conventional capabilities which makes it a more prominent threat and, consequentially, target. For most of these organizations, replacing or toppling a state is not their aim and an attempt to do so through conventional means would almost certainly result in failure. A hybrid approach is only option for certain non-state actors who can make use of it. For others, it actually represents a path that could lead to their defeat or destruction because they would gain the visibility and power of conventional capabilities, but without the corresponding utility. In essence, they would present a bigger threat and a bigger target than they need, or want, to be.

When observing hybrid warfare through the theoretical lens of international relations, several characteristics are noteworthy. For such a relatively low-level type of warfare it causes significant ripples throughout the system but stops short of changing the balance. Additionally, unlike some other contemporary trends in warfare, such as terrorism, it cannot be said to challenge fundamentally the Westphalian system of nation states. It is not specific to culture, religion or political leaning. From a theoretical perspective, it is a tool of national interests and high international politics, unconstrained by political ideology. In essence, hybrid warfare is a tool of realpolitik exploiting the liberal tendencies of the international order. Its goal is the advancement of core national interests which the international order would normally prevent from being attained. This is best demonstrated not by the actors using hybrid warfare, but from the reaction to its use by the great powers of the international order. Taking Ukraine as an example, the West has, almost to the last, focused on berating Russia for its breaches of international norms and values. The most common view of the situation is still that Russia had somehow betrayed the system, and that it is seeking to continue doing this in order to either destabilize Europe or re-create the Soviet Union, or both. In terms of response, the focus on propaganda, cyber activities and political rhetoric is also symptomatic of the liberal and constructivist approach. The EU's answer to what you do when Russia annexes a chunk of Ukraine is to condemn Russia for not following the EU's value system. Of course, Russia is not immune to the issues connected to the public perception of its actions. However, using a hybrid approach enables it to limit the impact of the negative perception. If anything, Russia actually acted in a restrained manner. The complex legal relationship between Ukraine and Russia following the breakup of the Soviet Union could, arguably, give Russia a claim on Crimea which it could pursue through purely conventional means, and with some justification. Certainly, it could have seized Sevastopol, which was the most prized asset Russia wanted to reclaim.

An important question in regard to Russian hybrid warfare has been the possibility of Russia, or some other actor, using the intervention in Ukraine as a template for future hybrid warfare. At first glance it appears that Russia had created an archetype, which can be replicated in any other arena of strategic competition in the world. However, there are some problems with directly transplanting Russian successes into other cases. First, the situation within Ukraine was unique. A state which has such a distinct internal dichotomy is rare. There were several divergent trends within Ukraine itself long before Russia actively intervened. Second, Ukraine is in very close proximity to Russia and already had Russian troops stationed in Crimea. Third, the confluence of different factors which culminated in the Ukrainian crisis has been very hard to predict accurately. The crisis itself was not surprising since many observers had been warning about precisely such a possibility for years. Yet the full impact and the rapid collapse of the Ukrainian government caught everyone by surprise, even Russia. A major difference between Russia and the rest of the international order in reacting to the crisis in Ukraine was the speed at which it regained composure after the fall of Yanukovych in February 2014. While NATO and the EU were still assessing the consequences of the Ukrainian crisis, Russia decided to intervene in order to protect what it perceived as its core national interests in Crimea. The greatest difference between the two sides was each's resolution. While the West was prepared to cooperate with the new Ukrainian government and perhaps offer economic aid to a country in distress, it was not prepared to intervene in order to secure Ukrainian territorial integrity. Technically, the Budapest Memorandum of 1994 required the United States, the United Kingdom and Russia to respect and uphold the neutrality and territorial integrity of Ukraine. However, the memorandum itself is very vague on how that is to be achieved and is, in any case, not legally binding. Both sides blamed the other for breaching the agreement. The West accused Russia of not respecting the territorial integrity of Ukraine while Russia argued that NATO and the EU had long before breached the Ukrainian neutrality promise. Perhaps the most significant ramification of the West's failure to respond resolutely has been the weakening of any other similar promise. Belarus and Kazakhstan were subjects of similar assurances in the Budapest Memorandum, and even NATO's eastern-most members have questioned the alliance's willingness to defend them in light of Russian aggressiveness.

The three Baltic republics are often mentioned as possible future targets for Russian hybrid warfare. Such thinking stems from the entirely erroneous perception that Russian annexation of Crimea occurred out of a desire for more territory. When coupled with the aforementioned weakening of Western resolve, questions have arisen on whether NATO would really defend the Baltic republics. In the years since 2014, NATO has put significant effort into re-assurance operations to ease the anxieties of its eastern member states. A new high-readiness task force has been created and deployed in the Baltic republics and an increased number of exercises have been conducted, designed precisely to counteract Russian aggression. To return to the question of Crimea serving as an archetype of hybrid warfare, the question must now be: How likely is such Russian activity in the near and long-term future? The answer is highly unlikely. The situation in the Baltic region, and along other borders of Russia, is fundamentally different from Ukraine. The governments of the Central Asian republics (Kazakhstan, Tajikistan, Turkmenistan and Uzbekistan) as well as Belarus, are all more or less pro-Russian and Russia already has significant influence over their domestic and foreign policies. The Caucasus, while still unstable, is already clearly divided and Russian interests are relatively secure. That only leaves the long border with China, and the Baltic republics. The relationship with China precludes Russia using hybrid warfare against it, and it would have significant trouble even attempting to do so, since the vast majority of the border is in remote Siberia, far away from significant population centres and military garrisons. Additionally, the balance of power between Russia and China is achieved through nuclear and conventional deterrence, thus limiting the utility of hybrid warfare. Similarly, the three Baltic republics are protected by the NATO collective defence provisions and Russia would most likely not want to risk a direct confrontation with NATO, particularly since Estonia, Latvia and Lithuania have little strategic value for Russia. It could be argued that they are more valuable in their current state as they can be used to divert NATO's attention towards them by simply manoeuvring a small number of troops close to their borders. While all three have ethnic Russian populations, it is highly unlikely that Moscow would want to, or be able to, use those populations as an excuse for an intervention. In the case of Ukraine, Russia did mention the protection of the Russophone people as one justification for intervention both in Crimea and in Eastern Ukraine. However, that was merely an effort to shape the public opinion of what was, fundamentally, a very pragmatic strategic calculation. Such rhetoric directed towards the Baltic republics would be precisely that – rhetoric. It would be useful as propaganda or as a form of psychological warfare, but it would not provide sufficient justification for a Ukraine-style hybrid war.

The Russian Ukraine-model hybrid warfare intervention, in short, has limited archetypal value. While it can certainly serve as an inspiration or as a theoretical model for future occurrences of hybrid warfare, the specific circumstances in which it occurred preclude it from becoming a model than can simply be transplanted into another part of the world and replicated. However, this does not diminish the value of studying the Ukraine example. The seizure of Crimea in 2014 and the continuing conflict in the Donbas region of Ukraine provide many useful lessons on how state actors can use hybrid warfare as a means of attaining goals in an environment that is politically contentious and militarily hazardous. Ukraine has been on the fault line of NATO–Russia competition ever since its independence in 1991, so both sides had to tread with caution. The absence of such caution from the West in the late 1990s and early 2000s eventually brought about the crisis of 2013–14 at which point Russia really did not have many options left. Since it was the great powers of the international order (specifically, leading NATO and EU member states) who were themselves intruding on this strategically vital part of the Russian sphere of influence, Russia could not directly challenge them without going against the system as a whole. A hybrid approach was the best of the available options. The greatest value of the whole situation is the strategic lesson of what can happen when a group of overconfident, ideologically charged states attempts to spread its policy agenda without sufficient regards for the geopolitical and strategic realities. Simply because the ideology in question was Western liberal democracy does not make such a strategic miscalculation any less grievous.

The future of hybrid warfare

There can be no definitive answer to what the future holds as predictions are always based on a number of changing variables. This is true in the world of strategy where the variables are constantly changing and the actors actively wish to challenge strategic predictions in favour of their own interests and goals. Nevertheless, in the strategic tradition of looking beyond the immediate horizon, this book will conclude with four strategic predictions concerning the future of hybrid warfare, an action hopefully legitimate at the end of such an in-depth analysis.

First, hybrid warfare is here to stay. It is a reflection of the nature of the international order. Unless the order itself undergoes any dramatic changes, hybrid warfare will continue to be a powerful tool for any revisionist challenger to the international order.

Second, the number of hybrid conflicts across the globe is likely to increase over the course of the next two decades. Since hybrid warfare exploits specific weaknesses of the international order, as well as of the guardians of that order, it will persist as long as those weaknesses can be exploited. Doctrinal change which would ameliorate these weaknesses is a slow, multi-generational process likely to last well into the middle of the century. Presuming that the change takes place at all, a hybrid approach is therefore going to be attractive to international actors until the trend of change turns against it, a process that is likely to last at least two decades. On the other hand, while the number of hybrid conflicts is likely to increase, the number is not going to rise dramatically because, as argued above, there is only a limited number of actors which can implement it. All of them will also need to be mindful of diminishing returns as a result of overuse.

Third, the costs of hybrid warfare are going to steadily increase for the actors who use it and those who are its targets. Once again, the costs need not be limited only to the monetary impact. Primarily, the costs will be strategic. As the incidence of hybrid conflicts rises, the goals are going to become more ambitious and begin moving from the periphery of strategically important areas towards their centres. To put it simply, the 'easier' goals will eventually be fulfilled and other, 'harder', aims will have to be pursued. Each additional step will carry and increased danger of escalation as it moves ever closer to the core interests of the great powers of the international order.

Fourth, hybrid warfare will continue to be an influential addition to the character of war but will not change its nature. A common mistake with proponents of the various 'new war' concepts over the decades has been the assertion that such new approaches to warfare have changed the nature of war. The nature of war has, and will, remain unchanged regardless of what methods are used to conduct it. Its purpose and aims will remain to be political and any actor that wishes to succeed in their attempts at coercion must acknowledge this reality. For those using hybrid warfare, the adherence to the political nature of war could, in fact, mean the difference between success and failure. As a fundamental feature of international relations, it is an ever present, if often wistfully ignored, staple of human interaction. The present book has provided the most precise, concise, and useful definition and overview of hybrid warfare, and there is nothing within the nature of the concept which would fundamentally change the nature of war. Hybrid warfare is not the future of war. However, the future conduct of war will, at least for the foreseeable future, be hybrid.

Notes

Introduction

1 J. Baylis and J. J. Wirtz, 'Strategy in the Contemporary World: Strategy after 9/11', in J. Baylis, J. J. Wirtz and C. S. Gray (eds.), *Strategy in the Contemporary World*, 4th ed., Oxford: Oxford University Press, 2013, pp. 13–15.

2 H. Kissinger, *World Order: Reflections on the Character of Nations and the Course of History*, London: Allen Lane, 2014, p. 9.

3 Munich Security Conference, *Munich Security Report 2015: Collapsing Order, Reluctant Guardians,* 26 January 2015, p. 35.

4 W. J. Nemeth, *Future War and Chechnya: A Case for Hybrid Warfare*, Monterey, CA: Naval Postgraduate School, 2002.

5 F. G. Hoffman, *Conflict in the 21st Century: The Rise of Hybrid Wars*, Arlington, VA: Potomac Institute for Policy Studies, December 2007.

6 C. von Clausewitz, *On War*, Oxford World's Classics, Oxford: Oxford University Press, 2008, pp. 30–1.

7 Ibid.

Chapter 1

1 E. H. Carr, *The Twenty Years' Crisis, 1919–1939*, Basingstoke: Palgrave Macmillan, 2001, p. 3.

2 C. Brown and K. Ainley, *Understanding International Relations*, 4th ed., Basingstoke: Palgrave Macmillan, 2009, p. 8.

3 Baylis and Wirtz, 'Introduction: Strategy in the Contemporary World: Strategy after 9/11', p. 5.

4 Thucydides, *The History of the Peloponnesian War*, Oxford World's Classics, Oxford: Oxford University Press, 2009, Book 1, para. 76.

5 Ibid., Book 1, para. 23.

6 G. Allison, 'Thucydides Trap Case File', *Belfer Center for Science and International Affairs*, 23 September 2015, available at: http://belfercenter.ksg.harvard.edu/publicati on/24928/thucydides_trap_case_file.html [accessed on: 26 September 2016].

7 L. Whyte, 'The Real Thucydides' Trap', *The Diplomat*, 6 May 2015, available at: http://the diplomat.com/2015/05/the-real-thucydides-trap/ [accessed on: 26 September 2016].

8 M. Howard, 'The Causes of Wars', *The Wilson Quarterly*, Volume 8, Issue 3, Summer 1984, p. 94.

9 Ibid., p. 97.

10 Ibid., p. 103.

11 According to *Encyclopaedia Britannica*, best estimates place Thucydides as living between 460 BCE and 404 BCE.

12 Howard, 'The Causes of Wars', p. 103.

13 *Oxford English Dictionary*, 'coercion', [Online], available at: http://www.oed.com/view/Entry/35725?redirectedFrom=coercion#eid [accessed on: 26 September 2016].

14 R. J. Art, 'The Fungibility of Force', in R. J. Art and K. Waltz (eds), *The Use of Force: Military Power and International Politics*, 5th ed., Oxford: Rowman & Littlefield, 1999, p. 5.

15 Quoted in Ibid., pp. 5–6.

16 Ibid., p. 6.

17 R. de Wijk, *The Art of Military Coercion*, Amsterdam: Amsterdam University Press, 2014, p. 16.

18 C. S. Gray, *The Future of Strategy*, Cambridge: Polity Press, 2016, p. 10.

19 C. S. Gray, *Modern Strategy*, Oxford: Oxford University Press, 2012, p.17.

20 L. Freedman, *Strategy: A History*, Oxford: Oxford University Press, 2013, p. xi.

21 Ibid.

Chapter 2

1 *Oxford English Dictionary*, 'hybrid' [online], available at: http://www.oed.com/view/Entry/89809?redirectedFrom=hybrid#eid [accessed on: 22 February 2016].

2 Ibid.

3 Ibid.

4 Munich Security Conference, *Munich Security Report 2015*, p. 35.

5 Ibid.

6 Department of Defense, *DOD Dictionary of Military and Associated Terms*, available at: http://www.dtic.mil/doctrine/dod_dictionary/ [accessed on: 23 February 2016].

7 *Oxford English Dictionary*, 'warfare', [online], available at: http://www.oed.com/view/Entry/225719?rskey=nhuhkZ&result=2#eid [accessed on: 22 February 2016].

8 UCDP, 'Definitions', *Uppsala Conflict Data Programme*, Department of Peace and Conflict Research, Uppsala University, 2018, available at: http://www.pcr.uu.se/research/ucdp/definitions/ [accessed on: 21 April 2018].

9 *Oxford English Dictionary*, 'war', [online], available at: http://www.oed.com/view/Entry/225589?rskey=T3lUWH&result=1#eidn [accessed on: 22 February 2016].

10 Clausewitz, *On War*, p. 13.

11 M. Sheehan and J. Wyllie, *The Economist Pocket Guide to Defence*, Oxford: Basil Blackwell Ltd, 1986, p. 258.

12 C. S. Gray, *Another Bloody Century*, London: Phoenix, 2006, p. 37.

13 Nemeth, *Future War and Chechnya: A Case for Hybrid Warfare*, p. 4.

14 Ibid., p. 29.

15 Ibid., p. 74.

16 Ibid., p. 3.

17 Hoffman, *Conflict in the 21st Century: The Rise of Hybrid Wars*, p. 14.

18 Ibid., p. 14.

19 Government Accountability Office, *National Defence: Hybrid Warfare*, GAO-10-1036R, Washington, DC: U.S. Government Accountability Office, September 2010, p. 14.

20 Ibid., p. 18.

21 Ibid., p. 15.

22 Ministry of Defence, *Security and Stabilisations: The Military Contribution*, Joint Doctrine Publication 3-40, JDP 3-40, November 2009, p. 11. Available at: https://www.gov.uk/government/uploads/system/uploads/attachment_data/file/49948/jdp3_40a4.pdf [accessed on 21 March 2016].

23 S. Jasper and S. Moreland, 'The Islamic State Is a Hybrid Threat: Why Does That Matter?', *Small Wars Journal*, available at: http://smallwarsjournal.com/jrnl/art/the-islamic-state-is-a-hybrid-threat-why-does-that-matter [accessed on: 21 April 2018].

24 Hybrid CoE, 'Hybrid Threats', *The European Centre of Excellence for Countering Hybrid Threats*, 2018, available at: https://www.hybridcoe.fi/hybrid-threats/ [accessed on: 21 April 2018].

25 Ibid.

26 US Army, *Military Operations in Low Intensity Conflict*, FM 100-20/AFP 3-20, 12 May 1990, Chapter 1, Available at: http://www.globalsecurity.org/military/library/policy/army/fm/100-20/10020ch1.htm [accessed on: 21 March 2016].

27 GAO, *National Defence: Hybrid Warfare*, p. 11.

28 US Army, *Full Spectrum Operations in Army Capstone Doctrine*, 2008 Posture Statement. Available at: http://www.army.mil/aps/08/information_papers/transform/Full_Spectrum_Operations.html [accessed on: 21 March 2016].

29 Clausewitz, *On War*, p. 223.

30 L. Hanauer, 'Crimean Adventure Will Cost Russia Dearly', *The Moscow Times*, 7 September 2014, available at: https://themoscowtimes.com/articles/crimean-adventure-will-cost-russia-dearly-39112 [accessed on: 20 April 2018].

31 S. Retson, 'Crimea Is Becoming a Russian Money Pit', *World Policy*, 24 October 2016, available at: https://worldpolicy.org/2016/10/24/crimea-is-becoming-a-russian-money-pit/ [accessed on: 20 April 2018].

32 Nemeth, *Future War and Chechnya: A Case for Hybrid Warfare*, p. 3.

33 Hoffman, *Conflict in the 21st Century: The Rise of Hybrid Wars*, p. 30.

34 Ibid., p. 19.

35 W. S. Lind, *'Understanding Fourth Generation War'*, 15 January 2004, available at: http://www.antiwar.com/lind/?articleid=1702 [accessed on: 20 March 2016].

36 A. J. Echevarria, 'Fourth-Generation War and Other Myths', *Strategic Studies Institute*, November 2005.

37 T. Huber, 'Compound Warfare: A Conceptual Framework', in T. Huber (ed.), *Compound Warfare, That Fatal Knot*, Fort Leavenworth, KS: US Army Command and General Staff College Press, 2002, p. 1.

38 R. F. Bauman, 'Conclusion', in Huber (ed.), *Compound Warfare, That Fatal Knot*, p. 307.

39 P. R. Mansoor, 'Introduction', in W. Murray and P. R. Mansoor (eds), *Hybrid Warfare: Fighting Complex Opponents from the Ancient World to the Present*, New York: Cambridge University Press, 2012, pp. 2–3.

40 R. de Wijk, 'Hybrid Conflict and the Changing Nature of Actors', in J. Lindley-French and B. Yves (eds), *The Oxford Handbook of War*, Oxford: Oxford University Press, 2014, p. 360.

41 Ibid., p. 358.

42 *Oxford English Dictionary*, 'threat', [Online], Available at: http://www.oed.com/view/Entry/201152?rskey=zLMoGh&result=1#eid [accessed on 21 March 2016].

43 Sheehan and Wyllie, *Pocket Guide to Defence*, p. 234.

Chapter 3

1 Krauthammer, C., 'The Unipolar Moment', *Foreign Affairs*, Volume 70, Issue 1, January 1991, p. 23.

2 K. N. Waltz, 'The Emerging Structure of International Politics', in K. N. Waltz (ed.), *Realism and International Politics*, Abingdon: Routledge, 2008, p. 167.

3 R. N. Haass, 'Liberal World Order, RIP', *Council on Foreign Relations*, 21 March 2018, available at: https://www.cfr.org/article/liberal-world-order-rip [accessed on: 16 April 2018].

4 Ibid.

5 G. J. Ikenberry, 'The End of Liberal International Order?', *International Affairs*, Volume 94, Issue 1, 2018, p. 8.

6 Haass, 'Liberal World Order, RIP'.

7 *The Economist*, 'The Lessons of Libya', *The Economist*, 19 May 2011, available at: https://www.economist.com/node/18709571 [accessed on: 17 April 2018].

8 R. N. Haass, 'World Order 2.0', *Foreign Affairs*, Volume 96, Issue 2, 2017, p. 2.

9   Ibid.

10 Thucydides, *The History of the Peloponnesian War*, Book 5, para. 89.

11 de Wijk, *The Art of Military Coercion*, p. 107.

12 S. Kinross, 'Clausewitz and Low Intensity Conflict', *Journal of Strategic Studies*, Volume 27, Issue 1, 2004, pp. 40–5.

13 Clausewitz, *On War*, p. 30.

14 Ibid., p. 30.

15 C. S. Gray, 'War – Continuity in Change, and Change in Continuity', *Parameters*, Issue 40, Summer 2010, p. 8.

16 M. Howard, *Clausewitz a Very Short Introduction*, Oxford: Oxford University Press, 2002, p. 14.

17 A. J. Echevarria, 'Globalization and the Clausewitzian Nature of War', *The European Legacy*, Volume 8, Issue 3, 2003, pp. 320–1.

18 Clausewitz, *On War*, p. 31.

19 Ibid., p. 30.

20 Ibid., p. 31.

21 C. Bassford, 'Primacy of Policy and Trinity in Clausewitz's Thought', in H. Strachan and A. Herberg-Rothe (eds), *Clausewitz in the Twenty-First Century*, Oxford: Oxford University Press, 2007, p. 81.

22 Clausewitz, *On War*, p. 30.

23 B. Heuser, 'Introduction', in Clausewitz, *On War*, p. xxix.

24 Clausewitz, *On War*, p. 28.

25 R. Smith, *The Utility of Force – The Art of War in the Modern World*, London: Penguin Books, 2005, p. 58.

26 B. Heuser, 'Introduction', in Clausewitz, *On War*, pp. xix–xxi.

27 In the manner of the term 'trinity', the term 'quinity' stems from the distributive Latin prefix 'quin-', referring to five of something.

28 NATO, *The North Atlantic Treaty*, Washington, DC, 4 April 1949, available at: http://www.nato.int/cps/en/natolive/official_texts_17120.htm [accessed on: 16 April 2016]

29 *Oxford English Dictionary*, 'legitimacy', [online], available at: http://www.oed.com/view/Entry/107111?redirectedFrom=legitimacy#eid [accessed on: 18 April 2016].

30 *Oxford English Dictionary*, 'legality', [online], available at: http://www.oed.com/view/Entry/107012?redirectedFrom=legality#eid [accessed on: 18 April 2016].

31 European Council, *A Secure Europe in a Better World, European Security Strategy*, Brussels, 12 December 2003, p. 9.

32 European Council, *Shared Vision, Common Action: A Stronger Europe, A Global Strategy for the European Union's Foreign and Security Policy*, Brussels, June 2016, p. 10.

33 UNSC, *Resolution 1244*, New York, United Nations, 10 June 1999, available at: https://documents-dds-ny.un.org/doc/UNDOC/GEN/N99/172/89/PDF/N9917289.pdf?OpenElement [accessed on: 16 April 2016].

34 HC, 21 March 2011, Volume 525, Column 700, available at: http://www.publicati
    ons.parliament.uk/pa/cm201011/cmhansrd/cm110321/debtext/110321-0001.ht
    m#1103219000645 [accessed on: 16 April 2016].

35 P. Perez-Seoane Garau, 'NATO's Criteria for Intervention in Crisis Response
    Operation: Legitimacy and Legality', *Royal Danish Defence College Brief*,
    Copenhagen, September 2013, p. 6.

36 Deutsche Welle, 'European Press Review: "An Act of War"', available at: http://www
    .dw.com/en/european-press-review-an-act-of-war/a-2097777 [accessed on: 16 April
    2016].

37 Clausewitz, *On War*, p. 250.

38 Ibid.

39 *Oxford English Dictionary*, 'alliance', [online], available at: http://www.oed.com/v
    iew/Entry/5290?rskey=eKLjvN&result=1&isAdvanced=false#eid [accessed on: 18
    April 2016].

40 US Department of State, *Joint Statement Issued by Partners at the Counter-ISIL
    Coalition Ministerial Meeting*, Washington, DC, 3 December 2014, available at: http:
    //www.state.gov/r/pa/prs/ps/2014/12/234627.htm [accessed on: 17 April 2016].

41 SIPRI, *Military Expenditure Database*, available at: http://www.sipri.org/research/
    armaments/milex/milex_database [accessed on: 17 April 2016].

42 IISS, 'The Future of US Syria Policy', *Strategic Comments*, Volume 23, Issue 1,
    February 2017, pp. ix–xi.

Chapter 4

1 C. S. Gray, *Strategy and Defence Planning*, Oxford: Oxford University Press, 2014, p. 2.

2 Ibid., p. 4.

3 Department of State, 'The Truman Doctrine, 1947', *Office of the Historian*, available
   at: https://history.state.gov/milestones/1945-1952/truman-doctrine [accessed on: 4
   July 2016].

4 US National Security Council, 'NSC 68: A Report to the National Security Council',
   14 April 1950, pp. 60–5, available at: https://www.trumanlibrary.org/whistlestop/stu
   dy_collections/coldwar/documents/pdf/10-1.pdf [accessed on: 4 July 2016].

5 J. L. Gaddis, *Strategies of Containment: A Critical Appraisal of Postwar American
   National Security Policy*, Oxford: Oxford University Press, 1982, p. 297.

6 G. H. W. Bush, *National Security Strategy of the United States*, Washington, DC: The
   White House, August 1991, pp. 1–2.

7 Krauthammer, 'The Unipolar Moment'.

8 SIPRI, *Military Expenditure Database*, 2018, available at: https://www.sipri.org/sites/
   default/files/Milex-share-of-GDP.pdf [accessed on: 19 April 2018].

9   W. J. Clinton, *A National Security Strategy of Engagement and Enlargement*, Washington, DC: The White House, July 1994, p. 5.

10 G. W. Bush, *The National Security Strategy of the United States of America 2002*, Washington, DC: The White House, September 2002, p. 15.

11 D. H. Rumsfeld, *Quadrennial Defense Review*, Washington, DC: Department of Defense, 30 September 2001, p. III.

12 Ibid., pp. 13–14.

13 P. Geren and G. W. Casey, *US Army 2008 Posture Statement*, 26 February 2008, p. 3.

14 R. Gates, *Quadrennial Defense Review*, Washington, DC: Department of Defense, February 2010, p. 8.

15 Ibid., p. 42.

16 Ibid.

17 SIPRI, *Military Expenditure Database*, 2018, available at: https://www.sipri.org/sites/default/files/Milex-share-of-GDP.pdf [accessed on: 19 April 2018].

18 The White House, Office of the Press Secretary, 'Statement by the President on the End of the Combat Mission in Afghanistan', Press Release, available at: https://www.whitehouse.gov/the-press-office/2014/12/28/statement-president-end-combat-mission-afghanistan [accessed on: 4 July 2016]

19 The White House, Office of the Press Secretary, 'Remarks by the President on Ending the War in Iraq', *Press Release*, available at: https://www.whitehouse.gov/the-press-office/2011/10/21/remarks-president-ending-war-iraq [accessed on: 4 July 2016]

20 C. Hagel, *Quadrennial Defense Review*, Washington, DC: Department of Defense, March 2014, p. VI.

21 B. H. Obama, *National Security Strategy 2015*, Washington, DC: The White House, February 2015, Foreword.

22 *US National Security Strategy 2015*, p. 8.

23 D. J. Trump, *National Security Strategy of the United States of America 2017*, Washington, DC: The White House, December 2017, p. 7.

24 Ibid., p. 2.

25 Ibid., p. 3.

26 J. Mattis, *Summary of the 2018 National Defense Strategy of the United States of America*, Washington, DC: Department of Defense, January 2018, p. 1.

27 Ibid.

28 Ibid.

29 Ibid., p. 2.

30 Ibid.

31 Ibid., p. 6.

32 The 1994 *Front Line First* was a list of defence cuts; the 2002 *Strategic Defence Review: A New Chapter* was a re-examination of specific policies in the light of the 9/11 attacks; 2004 *Delivering Security in a Changing World White Paper* was again,

mostly a programme of defence cuts and the 2005 *Defence Industrial Strategy* was a business-oriented policy statement outlining plans of procurement and preferential selection of materiel.

33 HC Deb 25 July 1990, volume 177, cc 468–70.

34 N. Walker and C. Mills, 'A Brief Guide to Previous British Defence Reviews', *House of Commons Library Briefing Paper*, Number 07313, November 2015, p. 14.

35 HC Deb 25 July 1990, Volume 177, c 468.

36 Ministry of Defence, *Strategic Defence Review*, July 1998, paras. 18–21, available at: http://archives.livreblancdefenseetsecurite.gouv.fr/2008/IMG/pdf/sdr1998_complet e.pdf [accessed on: 21 June 2016].

37 *UK Strategic Defence Review*, para. 27–8.

38 Ibid., para. 29.

39 *Operation Telic* was the codename given to the UK military operations in the 2003 Iraq War.

40 C. Taylor, 'The Defence White Paper', *House of Commons Library Research Paper*, 04/71, 17 September 2004, pp. 22–3.

41 Cabinet Office, *The National Security Strategy of the United Kingdom: Security in an Interdependent World*, March 2008, pp. 10–15, available at: https://www.gov .uk/government/uploads/system/uploads/attachment_data/file/228539/7291.pdf [accessed on: 21 June 2016].

42 Ibid., p. 9.

43 HM Government, *A Strong Britain in an Age of Uncertainty: The National Security Strategy*, London: The Stationary Office, October 2010, pp. 28–30.

44 Ibid., p. 13.

45 HM Government, *Securing Britain in an Age of Uncertainty: The Strategic Defence and Security Review*, London: The Stationary Office, October 2010, pp. 17–19.

46 HM Government, *National Security Strategy and Strategic Defence and Security Review 2015: A Secure and Prosperous United Kingdom*, November 2015, p. 5, available at: https://www.gov.uk/government/publications/national-security-stra tegy-and-strategic-defence-and-security-review-2015 [accessed on: 21 June 2016].

47 SIPRI Military Expenditure Database.

48 HM Government, *National Security Strategy and Strategic Defence and Security Review 2015*, pp. 11–12.

49 Ibid., p. 18.

50 Ibid., p. 28.

51 HM Government, *National Security Strategy and Strategic Defence and Security Review 2015*, p. 85.

52 M. Herzog, 'New IDF Strategy Goes Public', *The Washington Institute, Policy Analysis*, 28 August 2015, available at: http://www.washingtoninstitute.org/polic y-analysis/view/new-idf-strategy-goes-public [accessed on: 28 June 2016].

53 For the purposes of clarity, subsequent references will only list the IDF Strategy as a source, with the understanding that they refer to the English language translation provided by the Journal or Palestinian Studies, unless otherwise specified.

54 M. Matthews, 'Interview with BG (Ret.) Shimon Naveh', *Operational Leadership Experiences*, Fort Leavenworth, KS: Combat Studies Institute, 1 November 2007, p. 3. available at: smallwarsjournal.com/documents/mattmatthews.pdf [accessed on: 28 June 2015].

55 LTG Dan Halutz, Chief of the IDF General Staff signed the doctrine document in April and the 2006 Lebanon War started in July of the same year.

56 EBO had been in decline in the United States since 2008 and was removed from official US military doctrine in 2017.

57 M. N. Vego, 'A Case Against Systemic Operational Design', *Joint Forces Quarterly*, Issue 53, 2nd quarter 2009, pp. 70–1.

58 Ibid., p. 70.

59 Ibid., pp. 72–4.

60 Y. Feldman, 'Dr. Naveh, Or, How I Learned to Stop Worrying and Walk Through Walls', *HAARETZ*, 25 October 2007, available at: http://www.haaretz.com/israel-news/dr-naveh-or-how-i-learned-to-stop-worrying-and-walk-through-walls-1.23 1912 [accessed on: 30 June 2016].

61 Ibid., pp. 72–3.

62 Matthews, 'Interview with BG (Ret.) Shimon Naveh', p. 4.

63 G. Eisenkot, *IDF Strategy*, August 2015, p. 9, English translation published in: Khalidi, 'Special Document File: Original English Translation of the 2015 Gadi Eisenkot IDF Strategy', *Journal of Palestinian Studies*, Volume 14, Issue 2, Winter 2016.

64 Ibid., pp. 8–9.

65 Ibid., p. 9.

66 Herzog, 'New IDF Strategy Goes Public'.

67 Eisenkot, *IDF Strategy*, pp. 20–1.

68 Ibid., p. 9.

69 Ibid., p. 19.

70 Ibid., p. 10.

71 Ibid., p. 19.

72 Ibid., p. 10.

73 Government of Russia, *Russian National Security Blueprint*, 17 December 1997, Chapter I, available at: http://fas.org/nuke/guide/russia/doctrine/blueprint.html [accessed on: 1 July 2016].

74 Ibid., Chapter III.

75 Government of Russia, *National Security Concept of the Russian Federation*, 10 January 2000, Chapter I, available at: http://fas.org/nuke/guide/russia/doctrine/gaz eta012400.htm [accessed on: 1 July 2016].

76 Ibid., Chapter III.

77 Ibid., Chapter IV.

78 Government of Russia, *Russia's National Security Strategy to 2020*, 12 May 2009, para. 11, available at: http://rustrans.wikidot.com/russia-s-national-security-strat egy-to-2020 [accessed on: 2 July 2016].

79 Ibid., para. 47.

80 Ibid., paras. 53–60.

81 Ibid., para. 1.

82 Ibid., para. 32.

83 Ibid., para. 30.

84 Government of Russia, *Russian Federation's National Security Strategy*, 31 December 2015, para. 15, available at: http://www.ieee.es/Galerias/fichero/Otra sPublicaciones/Internacional/2016/Russian-National-Security-Strategy-31Dec2 015.pdf [accessed on: 3 July 2016].

85 Ibid., para. 17.

86 Ibid., para. 18.

87 Ibid., para. 93.

88 Government of Japan, *The Constitution of Japan*, 3 November 1946, Art. 9., available at: http://japan.kantei.go.jp/constitution_and_government_of_japan/co nstitution_e.html [accessed on: 3 July 2016].

89 Government of Japan, 'National Security Strategy', 17 December 2014, pp. 2–3. available at: http://www.cas.go.jp/jp/siryou/131217anzenhoshou/nss-e.pdf [accessed on: 3 July 2016].

90 Ibid., pp. 6–10.

91 Ibid., p. 6.

92 Ibid., pp. 20–2.

93 Ibid., p. 8.

94 Ibid., p. 11.

95 Ibid.

96 Ibid., p. 16.

97 Ibid., p. 12.

98 Ibid., pp. 12–13.

99 BAE Systems, *Destroyers*, available at: http://www.baesystems.com/en-uk/product/ destroyers [accessed on: 4 July 2016].

100 IISS, 'The NATO Capability Gap', *Strategic Survey 2012*, Volume 100, Issue 1, 1999, p. 16.

101 R. M. Gates, 'Remarks by Secretary Gates at the Security and Defense Agenda', *Department of Defense News Transcript*, Brussels, 10 June 2011, available at: http:// archive.defense.gov/Transcripts/Transcript.aspx?TranscriptID=4839 [accessed on: 20 April 2018].

102 de Wijk, *The Art of Military Coercion*, pp. 134–5.

Chapter 5

1 C. D. Freilich, 'Israel in Lebanon – Getting It Wrong: The 1982 Invasion, 2000 Withdrawal, and 2006 War', *Israel Journal of Foreign Affairs*, Volume 6, Issue 3, 2012, p. 43.

2 Ibid., p. 47.

3 Ibid.

4 UN, 'Lebanon – UNIFIL Background', 2002, available at: http://www.un.org/Depts/DPKO/Missions/unifil/unifilB.htm#background [accessed on: 25 June 2018].

5 J. Palmer Harik, *Hezbollah: The Changing Face of Terrorism*, London: I.B. Tauris & Co Ltd, 2005, p. 17.

6 Ibid., pp. 8–9.

7 Ibid., pp. 38–9.

8 Ibid., pp. 47–52.

9 As of 2017 the United States lists Hezbollah as a terrorist organization while the United Kingdom and the European Union only list the militant wing/external action wing as a terrorist organization.

10 IFES, 'The Political Affiliation of Lebanese Parliamentarians and the Composition of the Different Parliamentary Blocs', *IFES Lebanon Briefing Paper*, September 2009, available at: https://www.ifes.org/sites/default/files/lebanon_parliament_elections_200909_0.pdf [accessed on: 29 May 2017].

11 Al Jazeera, 'New Government Announced under PM Saad al-Hiri', *Al Jazeera Lebanon News*, 18 December 2016, available at: http://www.aljazeera.com/news/2016/12/lebanon-announces-government-saad-al-hariri-161218201145680.html [accessed on: 29 May 2017].

12 D. Daoud, 'Hezbollah's Latest Conquest: Lebanon's Cabinet', *Newsweek*, 12 January 2017, available at: http://www.newsweek.com/hezbollahs-latest-conquest-lebanons-cabinet-541487 [accessed on: 29 May 2017].

13 Freilich, 'Israel in Lebanon', p. 44.

14 D. I. Helmer, 'Flipside of the COIN: Israel's Lebanese Incursion Between 1982–2000', *The Long War Series Occasional Paper 21*, Fort Leavenworth, KS: Combat Studies Institute Press, 2007, p. 72.

15 Ibid.

16 Freilich, 'Israel in Lebanon', p. 48.

17 For a useful and concise timeline of the conflict, see: IDF, *The Second Lebanon War: A Timeline*, 7 July 2016, available at: https://www.idfblog.com/2016/07/07/second-lebanon-war-timeline/ [accessed on: 18 April 2017].

18 A. Exum, 'Hizballah at War: A Military Assessment', *Policy Focus*, Issue 63, December 2006, The Washington Institute for Near East Policy, p. 6, available at: http://www.washingtoninstitute.org/policy-analysis/view/hizballah-at-war-a-military-assessment [accessed on: 30 May 2017].

19 A derivate of the Iranian 'Kowsar' missile, which is itself based on a Chinese export design. There is some discrepancy as some sources mention the larger C-802 missile was used.

20 The post-2006 expanded mandate is often referred to as UNIFIL II to distinguish it from the 1978–2006 mandate, although the UN officially regards both as the same peacekeeping mission.

21 M. M. Matthews, 'Hard Lessons Learned – A Comparison of the 2006 Hezbollah-Israeli War and Operation CAST LEAD: A Historical Overview', in S. C. Farquhar (ed.), *Back to Basics: A Study of the Second Lebanon War and Operation CAST LEAD*, Fort Leavenworth, KS: Combined Studies Institute Press, 2009, p. 20.

22 *The Economist*, 'Nasrallah Wins the War', *The Economist*, 17 August 2006, available at: http://www.economist.com/node/7796790 [accessed on: 30 May 2017].

23 International recognition as a requirement is a later addition and is often disputed. It is also a violation of Article 3 of the 1933 Montevideo Convention while other criteria stem from Article 1 of the Montevideo Convention now accepted as international customary law, official text available at: https://treaties.un.org/doc/Publication/UNTS/LON/Volume%20165/v165.pdf [accessed on: 30 May 2017].

24 See Chapter 2 of this book.

25 E. Azani, 'The Hybrid Terrorist Organization: Hezbollah as a Case Study', *Studies in Conflict & Terrorism*, Volume 36, Issue 11, 2013, p. 904.

26 Ibid., pp. 904–5.

27 ITIC, 'Terrorism in Cyberspace: Hezbollah's Internet Network', *The Meir Amit Intelligence and Terrorism Information Center*, 3 April 2013, available at: http://www.terrorism-info.org.il/en/article/20488 [accessed on: 2 June 2017].

28 Exum, 'Hizballah at War', p. 5.

29 Ibid.

30 US Department of State, *Country Reports on Terrorism – 2009*, August 2010, available at: https://www.state.gov/j/ct/rls/crt/2009/ [accessed on: 5 June 2017].

31 R. Slim, 'Hezbollah and Syria: From Regime Proxy to Regime Savior', *Insight Turkey*, Volume 16, Issue 2, 2014, pp. 61, 64–6.

32 G. Aviad, 'Hezbollah's Force Buildup of 2006-2009', *Military and Strategic Affairs*, Volume 1, Issue 3, December 2009, pp. 9–10.

33 Exum, 'Hizballah at War', pp. 2–4.

34 Ibid., p. 4.

35 Ibid., pp. 10–11.

36 Matthews, 'Hard Lessons Learned', pp. 6–7.

37 R. Tira, 'Breaking the Amoeba's Bones', *INSS Strategic Assessment*, Volume 9, Issue 3, November 2006, p. 10.

38 A. Kulick, 'Hezbollah vs. the IDF: The Operational Dimension', *INSS Strategic Assessment*, Volume 9, Issue 3, November 2006, cited in: Matthews, 'Hard Lessons Learned', pp. 7–8.

39 Y. Lappin, 'In-House Hezbollah Missile Factories Could Add to Massive Arms Buildup', *The Algemeiner*, 20 March 2017, available at: https://www.algemeiner.co m/2017/03/20/in-house-hezbollah-missile-factories-could-add-to-massive-arms -buildup/ [accessed on: 7 June 2017].

40 Aviad, 'Hezbollah's Force Buildup', p. 6.

41 Exum, 'Hizballah at War', p. 6.

42 A. Rapaport, 'The IDF and the Lessons of the Second Lebanon War', *Mideast Security and Policy Studies*, Number 85, The Begin-Sadat Center for Strategic Studies, December 2010, p. 13.

43 Matthews, 'Hard Lessons Learned', pp. 19–20.

44 B. S. Lambeth, 'Learning from Lebanon: Airpower and Strategy in Israel's 2006 War Against Hezbollah', *Naval War College Review*, Volume 65, Issue 3, 2012, p. 91, available at: https://www.usnwc.edu/getattachment/e8495921-aa3f-4c7b- a626-0ceb226b0677/Learning-from-Lebanon--Airpower-and-Strategy-in-Is.aspx [accessed on: 7 June 2017].

45 The term used to describe Hezbollah network of fortified positions.

46 Exum, 'Hizballah at War', p. 5.

47 A. Kober, 'The Israel Defence Forces in the Second Lebanon War: Why the Poor Performance?', *Journal of Strategic Studies*, Volume 31, Issue 1, 2008, p. 20.

48 P. L. Mellies, 'Hamas and Hezbollah: A Comparison of Tactics', in S. C. Farquhar (ed.), *Back to Basics: A Study of the Second Lebanon War and Operation CAST LEAD*', p. 66.

49 Matthews, 'Hard Lessons Learned', p. 9.

50 Tira, 'Breaking the Amoeba's Bones', p. 2.

51 Kober, 'The Israel Defence Forces in the Second Lebanon War', pp. 27–8.

52 The last use of large-scale conventional force by the IDF was the 1973 Yom Kippur War. The later operations in 1978 and 1982 in Lebanon were much smaller. Even then, the 1982 invasion of Lebanon occurred twenty-four years prior to 2006.

53 Rapaport, 'The IDF and the Lessons of the Second Lebanon War', pp. 6–7.

54 See Chapter 4 of this book for an in-depth analysis of SOD.

55 Matthews, 'Hard Lessons Learned', pp. 11–12.

56 Ibid., p. 12.

57 Z. Schiff, 'The Foresight Saga', *Haaretz*, 11 August 2006, available at: http://www .haaretz.com/the-foresight-saga-1.195001 [accessed on: 8 June 2017].

58 Kober, 'The Israel Defence Forces in the Second Lebanon War', pp. 23–4.

59 A. Crooke and M. Perry, 'How Hezbollah Defeated Israel: Part 1 Winning the Intelligence War', *Asia Times Online*, 12 October 2006, available at: http://www.atim es.com/atimes/Middle_East/HJ12Ak01.html [accessed on: 8 June 2017].

60 Freilich, 'Israel in Lebanon', p. 49.

61 UNSC, *Resolution 1559*, 2 September 2004, available at: http://undocs.org/S/ RES/1559(2004) [accessed on: 8 June 2017].

62 Freilich, 'Israel in Lebanon', p. 49.

63 Lambeth, 'Learning from Lebanon', pp. 86–7.

64 E. N. Luttwak, 'Towards Post-Heroic Warfare', *Foreign Affairs*, Volume 74, Issue 3, 1 May 1995, pp. 121–2.

65 Kober, 'The Israel Defence Forces in the Second Lebanon War'.

66 Matthews, 'Hard Lessons Learned', pp. 17–18.

67 Ibid., p. 12.

68 Y. Katz, 'Post-battle Probe Finds Merkava Tank Misused in Lebanon', *Jerusalem Post*, 3 September 2006, available at: http://www.jpost.com/Israel/Post-battle-probe-find s-Merkava-tank-misused-in-Lebanon [accessed on: 12 June 2017].

69 Rapaport, 'The IDF and the Lessons of the Second Lebanon War', p. 25.

70 Exum, 'Hizballah at War', p. 9.

71 B. S. Lambeth, *Air Operations in Israel's War Against Hezbollah*, Santa Monica, CA: RAND Corporation, 2011, p. 71.

72 Rapaport, 'The IDF and the Lessons of the Second Lebanon War', p. 49.

73 Olmert, E., 'In Retrospect: The Second Lebanon War', *Military and Strategic Affairs*, Volume 6, Issue 1, March 2014, p. 8.

74 M. D. Snyder, 'Information Strategies Against a Hybrid Threat: What the Recent Experience of Israel Versus Hezbollah/Hamas Tell the US Army', in S. C. Farquhar (ed.), *Back to Basics: A Study of the Second Lebanon War and Operation CAST LEAD*, Fort Leavenworth, KS: Combined Studies Institute Press, 2009, p. 118.

75 Olmert, 'In Retrospect: The Second Lebanon War', p. 7.

76 Snyder, 'Information Strategies Against a Hybrid Threat', pp. 117–18.

77 Ibid., pp. 119–20.

78 UN, 'Report of the Commission of Inquiry on Lebanon Pursuant to Human Rights Council Resolution S-2/1', *UN Human Rights Council*, A/HRC/3/2, 23 November 2006, art. 11, available at: https://web.archive.org/web/20130617180405/http:// www2.ohchr.org/english/bodies/hrcouncil/docs/specialsession/A.HRC.3.2.pdf [accessed on: 12 June 2017].

79 BBC, 'Israel Accused over Lebanon', 6 September 2006, available at: http://news.bbc. co.uk/1/hi/6981557.stm [accessed on: 12 June 2017].

80 Snyder, 'Information Strategies Against a Hybrid Threat', pp. 122–3.

81 Ibid., p. 124.

82 M. Elran, 'The Civilian Front in the Second Lebanon War', in S. Brom and M. Elran (eds), *The Second Lebanon War: Strategic Perspectives*, Tel Aviv: Institute for National Security Studies, 2007, pp. 108–9.

83 Olmert, 'In Retrospect: The Second Lebanon War', pp. 4–5.

84 Lambeth, *Air Operations in Israel's War Against Hezbollah*, p. 333.

85 J. Saaman, 'The Dahya Concept and Israeli Military Posture vis-à-vis Hezbollah Since 2006', *Comparative Strategy*, Volume 32, Issue 2, 2013, pp. 146–7.

86 For a review of the latest IDF doctrine, see Chapter 4 of this book.

Chapter 6

1 This term is both a direct translation and a transliteration. The original in Russian is 'гибридная война'.

2 The state's official name.

3 M. Galeotti, *Russia's Wars in Chechnya 1994-2009*, Oxford: Osprey Publishing, 2014, p. 21.

4 D. V. Trenin, A. V. Malashenko and A. Lieven, *Russia's Restless Frontier*, Washington, DC: Carnegie Endowment for International Peace, 2004, pp. 10–11.

5 Ibid., p. 11.

6 Galeotti, *Russia's Wars in Chechnya 1994-2009*, p. 32.

7 Ibid., pp. 40–1.

8 Ibid., p. 50.

9 Trenin, Malashenko and Lieven, *Russia's Restless Frontier*, p. 111.

10 Galeotti, *Russia's Wars in Chechnya 1994-2009*, p. 54.

11 Ibid., pp. 54–5.

12 Council of Europe, 'Declaration by the Committee of Ministers on the Terrorist Assault in Beslan', 9 September 2004, available at: https://wcd.coe.int/ViewDoc.js p?p=&Ref=Decl-09.09.2004&Language=lanEnglish&Ver=original&Site=DC&Back ColorInternet=DBDCF2&BackColorIntranet=FDC864&BackColorLogged=FDC 864&direct=true [accessed on: 8 February 2017].

13 S. Cross, 'Russia's Relationship with the United States/NATO in the US-Led Global War on Terrorism', *The Journal of Slavic Military Studies*, Volume 19, Issue 2, pp. 178–80.

14 D. Fayutkin, 'Russian-Chechen Information Warfare 1994-2006', *The RUSI Journal*, Volume 151, Issue 5, October 2006, p. 53.

15 J. Arquilla and T. Karasik, 'Chechnya: A Glimpse of Future Conflict?', *Studies in Conflict & Terrorism*, Volume 22, Issue 3, 1999, p. 217.

16 R. Dannreuther and L. March, 'Chechnya: Has Moscow Won?', *Survival*, Volume 501, Issue 4, 2008, p. 101.

17 Ibid., p. 101.

18 Trenin, Malashenko and Lieven, *Russia's Restless Frontier*, pp. 10–11.

19 Ibid., pp. 114–15.

20 Arquilla and Karasik, 'Chechnya: A Glimpse of Future Conflict?', p. 217.

21 Fayutkin, 'Russian-Chechen Information Warfare 1994-2006', p. 53.

22 P. Felgenhauer, 'The Russian Army in Chechnya', *Central Asian Survey*, Volume 21, Issue 2, 2002, pp. 162–3.

23 D. Bilingsey, *Fangs of the Lone Wolf: Chechen Tactics in the Russian-Chechen Wars 1994-2009*, Solihull: Helion & Company Limited, 2013, pp. 128–30.

24 Arquilla and Karasik, 'Chechnya: A Glimpse of Future Conflict?', p. 210.

25 Ibid., p. 214.

26 Trenin, Malashenko and Lieven, *Russia's Restless Frontier*, p. 126.

27 Arquilla and Karasik, 'Chechnya: A Glimpse of Future Conflict?', p. 208.

28 Galeotti, *Russia's Wars in Chechnya 1994-2009*, pp. 45–6.

29 Bilingsey, *Fangs of the Lone Wolf*, p. 170.

30 Arquilla and Karasik, 'Chechnya: A Glimpse of Future Conflict?', p. 216.

31 Felgenhauer, 'The Russian Army in Chechnya', p. 159.

32 Dannreuther and March, 'Chechnya: Has Moscow Won?', pp. 103–4.

33 Galeotti, *Russia's Wars in Chechnya 1994-2009*, p. 84.

34 Ibid., pp. 84–5.

35 *BBC News*, 'Scars Remain Amid Chechen Revival', available at: http://news.bbc.co.u
    k/1/hi/programmes/from_our_own_correspondent/6414603.stm [accessed on: 10
    Febraury 2017].

36 Galeotti, *Russia's Wars in Chechnya 1994-2009*, pp. 83–4.

37 Russia had been involved in the Abkhazia-Georgia war in the early 1990s, and also
    backed Armenia in the Nagorno-Karabakh war with Azerbaijan.

38 D. Trenin, 'Russia in the Caucasus: Reversing the Tide', *Brown Journal of World
    Affairs*, Volume 15, Issue 2, Spring 2009, p. 147.

39 D. Lane, "Coloured Revolution' as a Political Phenomenon', *Journal of Communist
    Studies and Transitional Politics*, Volume 25, Issue 2–3, p. 115.

40 Trenin, 'Russia in the Caucasus: Reversing the Tide', p. 147.

41 NATO, 'Study on NATO Enlargement', 5 November 2008, art. 6., available at: http:
    //www.nato.int/cps/en/natohq/official_texts_24733.htm [accessed on: 13 February
    2017].

42 Ibid., p. 145.

43 UN observer/peacekeeping mission UNOMIG was present in Abkhazia from 1992 to
    2009 and was expanded in 1994 by the signing of the Agreement on a Ceasefire and
    Separation of Forces (between Abkhazia and Georgia). Peacekeepers from CIS and
    Georgia were present in South Ossetia from 1992 to 2008 based on the Agreement
    on Principles of Settlement of the Georgian–Ossetian Conflict (the Sochi agreement)
    signed by Russia and Georgia and monitored by the OSCE. The peacekeeping force
    was made up of Russian, Georgian and North Ossetian peacekeepers.

44 A. Lavrov, 'Timeline of Russian-Georgian Hostilities in August 2008', in R.
    Pukhov (ed.), *The Tanks of August*, Moscow: Centre for Analysis of Strategies and
    Technologies, 2010, pp. 42–3.

45 Ibid., p. 39.

46 M. Bowker, 'The War in Georgia and the Western Response', *Central Asian Survey*,
    Volume 30, Issue 2, 2011, p. 207.

47 Lavrov, 'Timeline of Russian-Georgian Hostilities in August 2008', pp. 48–72.
    Lavrov's chapter provides a very in-depth account of the movements and

engagements of both sides of the conflict. In this book, they are only briefly surmised as the operations themselves are not directly relevant to the debate on hybrid warfare.

48 Lavrov, 'Timeline of Russian-Georgian Hostilities in August 2008', p. 75.

49 H. B. L. Larsen, 'The Russo-Georgian War and Beyond: Towards a European Great Power Concert', *European Security*, Volume 21, Issue 1, 2012, pp. 106–7.

50 Bowker, 'The War in Georgia and the Western Response', p. 207.

51 NATO, 'Enlargement', 3 December 2015, available at: http://www.nato.int/cps/en/ natohq/topics_49212.htm? [accessed on: 1 February 2017].

52 A. P. Tsygankov and M. Tarver-Wahlquist, 'Duelling Honors: Power, Identity and the Russia-Georgia Divide', *Foreign Policy Analysis*, Volume 5, 2009, pp. 310–11.

53 K. Giles, 'Understanding the Georgia Conflict, Two Years On: Reviews and Commentaries', part 2, *NATO Research Review*, Rome: NATO Defense College, 2010, p. 6.

54 Bowker, 'The War in Georgia and the Western Response', pp. 197–8.

55 R. Sakwa, 'Conspiracy Narratives as a Mode of Engagement in International Politics: The Case of the 2008 Russo-Georgian War', *The Russian Review*, Volume 71, October 2012, p. 596.

56 Lavrov, 'Timeline of Russian-Georgian Hostilities in August 2008', pp. 45–6.

57 de Waal, 'The Still-Topical Tagliavini Report', *Carnegie Moscow Center*, 2015, available at: http://carnegie.ru/commentary/?fa=61451 [accessed on: 15 February 2017].

58 O. Vartanyan and E. Barry, 'Ex-Diplomat Says Georgia Started War with Russia', *The New York Times*, 25 November 2008, available at: http://www.nytimes.com/2008/11 /26/world/europe/26georgia.html [accessed on: 15 February 2017].

59 Lavrov, 'Timeline of Russian-Georgian Hostilities in August 2008', p. 41.

60 L. Brownlee, 'Why 'Cyberwar' Is So Hard to Define', *Forbes*, 17 July 2015, available at: https://www.forbes.com/sites/lisabrownlee/2015/07/16/why-cyberwar-is-so-har d-to-define/#1708cd4131f1 [accessed on: 4 June 2018].

61 RAND Corporation, 'Cyber Warfare', 2017, available at: http://www.rand.org/topics/ cyber-warfare.html [accessed on: 7 February 2017].

62 Department of Defense, *DOD Dictionary of Military and Associated Terms*, 2017, p. 58, available at: http://www.dtic.mil/doctrine/dod_dictionary/ [accessed on: 15 February 2017].

63 R. J. Deibert, R. Rohozinski and M. Crete-Nishihata, 'Cyclones in Cyberspace: Information Shaping and Denial in the 2008 Russia-Georgia War', *Security Dialogue*, Volume 43, Issue 1, 2012, p. 5.

64 J. Arquilla, 'From Blitzkrieg to Bitskrieg: The Military Encounter with Computers', *Communications of the ACM*, Volume 54, Issue 10, 2011, p. 63.

65 J. Robertson and M. Riley, "Mysterious' 08 Turkey Pipeline Blast Opened New Cyberwar', 10 December 2014, available at: https://www.bloomberg.com/news/

articles/2014-12-10/mysterious-08-turkey-pipeline-blast-opened-new-cyberwar [accessed on: 7 February 2017].

66 Arquilla, 'From Blitzkrieg to Bitskrieg: The Military Encounter with Computers', p. 63.

67 Lavrov, 'Timeline of Russian-Georgian Hostilities in August 2008', pp. 66, 70.

68 Both Vostok and Zapad were ethnic Chechen units within the Russian military intelligence service (GRU). Their names in Russian mean East and West, respectively, referring to the parts of Chechnya from which their fighters came.

69 A. S. Bowen, 'Coercive Diplomacy and the Donbas: Explaining Russian Strategy in Eastern Ukraine', *Journal of Strategic Studies* [online], 22 December 2017, p. 17.

70 R. Sakwa, *Frontline Ukraine: Crisis in the Borderlands*, London: I.B. Tauris & Co. Ltd., 2015, p. 8.

71 Ibid., p. 24.

72 Ibid., p. 59.

73 Ibid., pp. 58–60.

74 R. Menon and E. Rumer, *Conflict in Ukraine*, London: MIT Press, 2015, p. 22.

75 Ibid., pp. 25–6.

76 Ibid., p. 25.

77 Ibid., p. 28.

78 Ibid., pp. 28–9.

79 Ibid., pp. 30–2.

80 Ibid., p. 34.

81 The colour orange comes from the colour scheme of Yushchenko's Our Ukraine political party.

82 Menon and Rumer, *Conflict in Ukraine*, p. 39.

83 For a more nuanced explanation on the complicated history of Bandera and the different stages of Ukrainian nationalism, see Sakwa, *Frontline Ukraine*, particularly the chapter 'Countdown to Confrontation'.

84 Sakwa, *Frontline Ukraine*, pp. 19–20.

85 Ibid., pp. 10–11.

86 Menon and Rumer, *Conflict in Ukraine*, p. 44.

87 OSCE, *Ukraine, Presidential Election, 17 January and 7 February 2010: Final Report*, 2010, available at: http://www.osce.org/odihr/elections/ukraine/67844 [accessed on: 3 March 2017], particularly pp. 1–3.

88 Putin was the Russian prime minister from 2008–12 and was elected president for a third term in 2012.

89 Sakwa, *Frontline Ukraine*, p. 210.

90 Menon and Rumer, *Conflict in Ukraine*, pp. 62–4.

91 K. Holzwarth Sprehe, 'Ukraine Says 'NO' to NATO', *Pew Research Center*, 2010, available at: http://www.pewglobal.org/2010/03/29/ukraine-says-no-to-nato/ [accessed on: 3 March 2017].

92 Menon and Rumer, *Conflict in Ukraine*, p. 66.

93 Ibid., pp. 51–2.

94 Sakwa, *Frontline Ukraine*, p. 88.

95 Ibid., p. 89.

96 D. Sindelar, 'Was Yanukovich's Ouster Constitutional', *Radio Free Europe/Radio Liberty*, 2014, available at: http://www.rferl.org/a/was-yanukovychs-ouster-cons titutional/25274346.html [accessed on: 3 March 2017].

97 I. Traynor, 'Russia Denounces Ukraine 'Terrorists' and West over Yanukovich Ousting', *The Guardian,* 2014, available at: https://www.theguardian.com/world/2 014/feb/24/russia-ukraine-west-yanukovich [accessed on: 3 March 2017].

98 V. Kashin, 'Khrushchev's Gift: The Questionable Ownership of Crimea', in C. Howard and R. Pukhov (eds), *Brothers Armed: Military Aspects of the Crisis in Ukraine*, trans. I. Khokhtova, Minneapolis, MN: East View Press, 2014, p. 4.

99 Sakwa, *Frontline Ukraine*, p. 101.

100 For an excellent overview of the precise division of the Black Sea Fleet, see: D. Boltenkov, 'Home of the Black Sea Fleet: History and Disposition of Russian Forces in Crimea', in Howard and Pukhov, *Brothers Armed: Military Aspects of the Crisis in Ukraine*, pp. 136–41.

101 Sakwa, *Frontline Ukraine*, p. 71.

102 Ibid., p. 97.

103 The Sochi Winter Olympics were held between 7 and 23 February 2014.

104 Menon and Rumer, *Conflict in Ukraine*, p. 84.

105 Sakwa, *Frontline Ukraine*, p. 103.

106 J. Simpson, 'Russia's Crimea Plan Detailed, Secret and Successful', *BBC*, 2014, available at: http://www.bbc.co.uk/news/world-europe-26644082 [accessed on: 3 March 2017].

107 Nikolsky, A., 'Little, Green and Polite: The Creation of Russian Special Operations Forces', in Howard and Pukhov (eds), *Brothers Armed: Military Aspects of the Crisis in Ukraine*, pp. 124–5.

108 RT, *Crimea, Sevastopol Officially Join Russia as Putin Signs Final Decree*, 2014, available at: https://www.rt.com/news/russia-parliament-crimea-ratification-293/ [accessed on: 3 March 2017].

109 Sakwa, *Frontline Ukraine*, p. 97.

110 Ibid., p. 109.

111 K. Giles, 'Russia's New Tools for Confronting the West', *Chatham House Research Paper*, March 2016, available at: https://www.chathamhouse.org/publication/russ ias-new-tools-confronting-west [accessed on: 3 March 2017], pp. 31–2.

112 BBC, *How Far Do EU-US Sanctions on Russia Go?*, 2014, available at: http://www .bbc.co.uk/news/world-europe-28400218 [accessed on: 3 March 2017].

113 Kasapoglu, C., 'Russia's Renewed Military Thinking: Non-Linear Warfare and Reflexive Control', *Research Paper*, Number 121, Rome: NATO Defense College, November 2015, p. 3.

114 Sakwa, *Frontline Ukraine*, p. 107.

115 Menon and Rumer, *Conflict in Ukraine*, pp. 83–4.

116 Sakwa, *Frontline Ukraine*, p. 102.

117 Donbas is a name given to the region which encompasses the Donetsk and Lugansk administrative areas.

118 Sakwa, *Frontline Ukraine*, pp. 149–50.

119 Ibid., p. 150.

120 A. Lavrov and A. Nikolsky, 'Neglect and Rot: Degradation of Ukraine's Military in the Interim Period', in C. Howard and Pukhov (eds), *Brothers Armed: Military Aspects of the Crisis in Ukraine*, p. 69.

121 Ibid., p. 71.

122 Sakwa, *Frontline Ukraine*, pp. 155–6.

123 BBC, 'MH17: Four Charged with Shooting Down Plane over Ukraine', *BBC News*, 19 June 2019, available at: https://www.bbc.com/news/world-europe-48691488 [accessed on: 26 November 2019].

124 Ibid., p. 155.

125 V. Tseluyko, 'Rebuilding and Refocusing the Force: Reform and Moderinzation of the Ukrainian Armed Forces', in Howard and Pukhov (eds), *Brothers Armed: Military Aspects of the Crisis in Ukraine*, p. 188.

126 Sakwa, *Frontline Ukraine*, pp. 174–5.

127 J. Losh, 'Is Russia Killing Off Eastern Ukraine's Warlords?', *Foreign Policy*, 2016, available at: http://foreignpolicy.com/2016/10/25/who-is-killing-eastern-ukraines-warlords-motorola-russia-putin/ [accessed on: 10 February 2017].

128 E. Götz, 'It's Geopolitics, Stupid: Explaining Russia's Ukraine Policy', *Global Affairs*, Volume 1, Issue 1, 2015, p. 3.

129 Original article was published in Russian in the *Military-Industrial Kurier*. For the purposes of this research the English language translation, provided by Radio Free Europe/Radio Liberty editor Robert Coalson, will be used, as published in the *Military Review*.

130 V. Gerasimov, 'The Value of Science Is in the Foresight', *Military Review*, January–February 2016, p. 24.

131 Ibid., p. 24.

132 R. Sakwa, *Frontline Ukraine*, pp. 103–4.

133 Results from a 2001 Ukraine census, a map of which is available at: http://www.rferl.org/a/map-ukraine-percentage-who-identify-as-ethnic-russians-or-say-russian-is-their-first-language-/25323841.html [accessed on: 3 March 2017].

134 S. Jones, 'Estonia Ready to Deal with Russia's "Little Green Men"', *Financial Times*, 13 May 2015, available at: https://www.ft.com/content/03c5ebde-f95a-11e4-ae65-00144feab7de [accessed on: 3 March 2017].

Chapter 7

1 A. T. Mahan, *Influence of Sea Power Upon History*, Pantianos Classics, 2016 (originally published in 1890), p. 7.

2 Ibid., p. 18, for more information, including Mahan's explanation of all these elements, see pp. 18–40.

3 G. Till, *Seapower: A Guide for the Twenty-First Century*, Abingdon: Routledge, 2013, p. 25.

4 Ibid., p. 24.

5 I. Speller, *Understanding Naval Warfare*, Abingdon: Routledge, 2014, p. 6.

6 Till, *Seapower: A Guide for the Twenty-First Century*, p. 6.

7 Ibid., p. 37.

8 J. S. Corbett, *Principles of Maritime Strategy*, Mineola, NY: Dover Publications, 2015, p. 13.

9 Ibid., p. 14.

10 *Convention on the Law of the Sea*, Montego Bay, 12 November 1982, *United Nations Treaty Series*, Volume 1833, Issue 31363, p. 3, available at: http://www.un.org/depts/los/convention_agreements/texts/unclos/unclos_e.pdf [accessed on: 4 December 2017], Art. 29.

11 US Department of the Navy, 'The Commander's Handbook on the Law of Naval Operations', *Naval Warfare Publication*, NWP 1-14M, July 2007, available at: http://www.jag.navy.mil/documents/NWP_1-14M_Commanders_Handbook.pdf [accessed on: 4 December 2017], 2-2.

12 UK Maritime and Coastguard Agency, 'About Us', 2017, available at: https://www.gov.uk/government/organisations/maritime-and-coastguard-agency/about [accessed on: 4 December 2017].

13 R. D. Martinson, 'The Militarisation of China's Coast Guard', *The Diplomat*, 21 November 2014, available at: https://thediplomat.com/2014/11/the-militarization-of-chinas-coast-guard/ [accessed on: 4 December 2017].

14 J. Stavridis, ADM, 'Maritime Hybrid Warfare Is Coming', *Proceedings*, Volume 142, Issue 12, Annapolis: United States Naval Institute, December 2016, available at: https://www.usni.org/magazines/proceedings/2016-12-0/maritime-hybrid-warfare-coming [accessed on: 4 December 2017].

15 IMO, 'International Shipping Facts and Figures', *Maritime Knowledge Centre*, 6 March 2012, available at: http://www.imo.org/en/KnowledgeCentre/ShipsAndShippingFactsAndFigures/TheRoleandImportanceofInternationalShipping/Documents/International%20Shipping%20-%20Facts%20and%20Figures.pdf [accessed on: 4 December 2017], p. 7.

16 T. Yoshihara, 'The 1974 Paracels Sea Battle: A Campaign Appraisal', *Naval War College Review*, Volume 69, Issue 2, Spring 2016, pp. 46–51.

17 The English language translation was provided by the Foreign Broadcast Information Service, a component of the Central Intelligence Agency that translates open source foreign intelligence for distribution within the US Government. All the versions that the author has found, either printed or online, appear to use the same FBIS translation.

18 Q. Liang and W. Xiangsui, *Unrestricted Warfare*, Beijing: PLA Literature and Art Publishing, February 1999, translated by FBIS, available at: http://www.c4i.org/unrestricted.pdf [accessed on: 4 December 2017], p. 2.

19 Ibid.

20 Ibid., pp. 220–2.

21 The 'nine dash line' is a demarcation of the historical Chinese claim within the SCS, which has been one of the main points of contention between the various states involved in the territorial disputes. For further information, see the Chinese submission to the UN Division for Ocean Affairs and the Law of the Sea; Notes Verbales CML/17/2009, available at: http://www.un.org/Depts/los/clcs_new/submissions_files/mysvnm33_09/chn_2009re_mys_vnm_e.pdf [accessed on: 1 November 2017].

22 CSIS, 'Asia Maritime Transparency Initiative', available at: https://amti.csis.org/island-tracker/ [accessed on: 28 November 2017].

23 Ibid.

24 Ibid.

25 US Department of Defense, 'Annual Report to Congress: Military and Security Developments Involving the People's Republic of China 2017', *Office of the Secretary of Defense*, 15 May 2017, p. 12; the report also features useful illustrations, based on satellite imagery, of the military build-up (pp. 13–16).

26 S. Tiezzi, 'Why China Is Stopping Its South China Sea Island-Building (For Now)', *The Diplomat*, 16 June 2015, available at: https://thediplomat.com/2015/06/why-china-is-stopping-its-south-china-sea-island-building-for-now/ [accessed on: 30 November 2017].

27 J. Johnson, 'China Unveils Massive 'Magic Island-Maker' Dredging Vessel', *Japan Times*, 4 November 2017, available at: https://www.japantimes.co.jp/news/2017/11/04/asia-pacific/china-unveils-massive-island-building-vessel/ [accessed on: 30 November 2017].

28 US Department of Defense, 'Annual Report to Congress: Military and Security Developments Involving the People's Republic of China 2017', p. 12.

29 IISS, 'China's Land Reclamation in the South China Sea', *Strategic Comments*, Volume 21, Comment 20, August 2015, p. ix.

30 A. Panda, 'South China Sea: What China's First Strategic Bomber Landing on Woody Island Means', *The Diplomat*, 22 May 2018, available at: https://thediplomat.com/2018/05/south-china-sea-what-chinas-first-strategic-bomber-landing-on-woody-island-means/ [accessed on: 20 June 2018].

31 Nansha Islands is the Chinese name for the Spratly Islands group.

32 The White House, 'Remarks by President Obama and President Xi of the People's Republic of China in Joint Press Conference', *Office of the Press Secretary*, 25 September 2015, available at: https://obamawhitehouse.archives.gov/the-press-off ice/2015/09/25/remarks-president-obama-and-president-xi-peoples-republic-ch ina-joint [accessed on: 30 November 2017].

33 S. LaGrone, 'China Defends Deployment of Anti-Ship Missiles to South China Sea Island', *US Naval Institute News*, 31 March 2016, available at: https://news.usni.or g/2016/03/30/china-defends-deployment-of-anti-ship-missiles-to-south-china-sea-island [accessed on: 30 November 2017].

34 Ibid.

35 A. Macias, 'China Quietly Installed Defensive Missile Systems on Strategic Spratly Islands in Hotly Contested South China Sea', *CNBC*, 2 May 2018, available at: https ://www.cnbc.com/2018/05/02/china-added-missile-systems-on-spratly-islands-i n-south-china-sea.html [accessed on: 20 June 2018].

36 B. Westcott, R. Browne and Z. Cohen, 'White House Warns China on Growing Militarization in South China Sea', *CNN*, 4 May 2018, available at: https://ed ition.cnn.com/2018/05/03/asia/south-china-sea-missiles-spratly-intl/index.html [accessed on: 20 June 2018].

37 H. B. Harris Jr., ADM, *Spoken Remarks Delivered to the Australian Strategic Policy Institute*, 31 March 2015, available at: http://www.cpf.navy.mil/leaders/harry-harris/ speeches/2015/03/ASPI-Australia.pdf [accessed on: 30 November 2017], p. 4.

38 US Energy Information Agency, *Report on the South China Sea*, 7 February 2013, available at: https://www.eia.gov/beta/international/analysis_includes/regions_of_in terest/South_China_Sea/south_china_sea.pdf [accessed on: 1 December 2017].

39 Ibid.

40 S. L. Montgomery, 'What's at Stake in China's Claims to the South China Sea?', *The Conversation*, 14 July 2016, available at: https://theconversation.com/whats-at-sta ke-in-chinas-claims-to-the-south-china-sea-62472 [accessed on: 1 December 2017].

41 NIC, 'The Future of Indian Ocean and South China Sea Fisheries: Implications for the United States', *National Intelligence Council Report*, NICR 2013-38, 30 July 2013, available at: https://www.dni.gov/files/documents/nic/NICR%202013-38%20Fis heries%20Report%20FINAL.pdf [accessed on: 1 December 2017], p. ii.

42 U. R. Sumaila and W. W. L. Cheung, *Boom or Bust: The Future of Fish in the South China Sea*, ADM Capital Foundation, November 2015, pp. 3–4.

43 M. Tsirbas, 'Saving the South China Sea Fishery: Time to Internationalise', *Policy Options Paper*, Number 3, June 2017, National Security College, Australian National University, p. 2.

44 C. Schofield, R. Sumaila and W. Cheung, 'Fishing, Not Oil, Is at the Heart of the South China Sea Dispute', *The Conversation*, 15 August 2016, available at: http://the

conversation.com/fishing-not-oil-is-at-the-heart-of-the-south-china-sea-dispute-63580 [accessed on: 1 December 2017].

45 A. S. Erickson and C. M. Kennedy, 'China's Maritime Militia', *CNA*, 7 March 2016 available at: https://www.cna.org/cna_files/pdf/chinas-maritime-militia.pdf [accessed on: 21 November 2017], p. 5.

46 Ibid.

47 Ibid., p. 6.

48 Ibid.

49 A. S. Erickson and C. Kennedy, 'Directing China's "Little Blue Men": Uncovering the Maritime Militia Command Structure', *CSIS Asia Maritime Transparency Initiative*, 11 September 2015, available at: https://amti.csis.org/directing-chinas-little-blue-men-uncovering-the-maritime-militia-command-structure/ [accessed on: 27: November 2017].

50 Erickson and Kennedy, 'China's Maritime Militia', p. 1.

51 Erickson and Kennedy, 'Directing China's "Little Blue Men"'.

52 C. P. Cavas, 'China's Maritime Militia a Growing Concern', *Defense News*, 21 November 2016, available at: https://www.defensenews.com/naval/2016/11/22/chinas-maritime-militia-a-growing-concern/ [accessed on: 27 November 2017].

53 Erickson and Kennedy, 'China's Maritime Militia', pp. 8–9.

54 A. S. Erickson and C. M. Kennedy, 'Riding a New Wave of Professionalization and Militarization: Sansha City's Maritime Militia', *CIMSEC*, 1 September 2016, available at: http://cimsec.org/riding-new-wave-professionalization-militarization-sansha-citys-maritime-militia/27689 [accessed on: 27 November 2017].

55 Sansha City is the Southern-most city prefecture in the Chinese Hainan province and is the administrative centre of the Chinese undisputed and disputed territories in the South China Sea. It is located in the Paracels Islands group.

56 Erickson and Kennedy, 'Sansha City's Maritime Militia'.

57 Ibid.

58 Ibid.

59 C. M. Kennedy and A. S. Erickson, 'Model Maritime Militia: Tanmen's Leading Role in the April 2012 Scarborough Shoal Incident', *CIMSEC*, 21 April 2016, available at: http://cimsec.org/model-maritime-militia-tanmens-leading-role-april-2012-scarborough-shoal-incident/24573 [accessed on: 27 November 2017].

60 For more detail, including an in-depth timeline of the standoff, see: M. Green, K. Hicks, Z. Cooper, J. Schaus and J. Douglas, 'Countering Coercion in Maritime Asia; The Theory and Practice of Gray Zone Deterrence', *CSIS*, May 2017, available at: https://csis-prod.s3.amazonaws.com/s3fs-public/publication/170505_GreenM_CounteringCoercionAsia_Web.pdf?OnoJXfWb4A5gw_n6G.8azgEd8zRIM4wq [accessed on: 27 November 2017], pp. 95–123.

61 US Department of State, 'United States Oceans Policy', *Statement by the President*, 10 March 1983, available at: https://www.state.gov/documents/organization/14322 4.pdf [accessed on: 28 November 2017], pp. 383–4.

62 US Department of Defense, 'Freedom of Navigation (FON) Report for Fiscal Year (FY) 2016', 28 February 2017, available at: http://policy.defense.gov/Portals/11/FY1 6%20DOD%20FON%20Report.pdf?ver=2017-03-03-141349-943 [accessed on: 28 November 2017], p. 1.

63 T. Choi, 'Why the US Navy's First South China Sea FONOP Wasn't a FONOP', *CIMSEC*, 3 November 2015, available at: http://cimsec.org/why-the-us-navys-first -south-china-sea-fonop-wasnt-a-fonop/19681 [accessed on: 28 November 2017].

64 C. P. Cavas, 'China's "Little Blue Men" Take Navy's Place in Disputes', *Defense News*, 2 November 2015, available at: https://www.defensenews.com/naval/2015/11/03/ chinas-little-blue-men-take-navys-place-in-disputes/ [accessed on: 28 November 2017].

65 R. Pedrozo, 'Close Encounters at Sea: The *USNS Impeccable* Incident', *Naval War College Review*, Volume 62, Issue 3, Summer 2009, p. 101.

66 W. Lowther, 'US Ups Ante in South China Sea by Sending Destroyer', *Taipei Times*, 15 March 2009, available at: http://www.taipeitimes.com/News/taiwan/archives/20 09/03/15/2003438536/1 [accessed on: 28 November 2017].

67 O. S. Mastro, 'Signalling and Military Provocation in Chinese National Security Strategy: A Closer Look at the *Impeccable* Incident', *The Journal of Strategic Studies*, Volume 34, Issue 2, April 2011, pp. 220–1.

68 L. J. Morris, 'Indonesia-China Tensions in the Natuna Sea: Evidence of Naval Efficacy Over Coast Guards?', *The RAND Blog*, RAND Corporation, 5 July 2016, available at: https://www.rand.org/blog/2016/07/indonesia-china-tensions-in-the -natuna-sea-evidence.html [accessed on: 17 November 2017].

69 Ibid.

70 C. J. Dunlap, 'Lawfare Today: A Perspective', *Yale Journal of International Affairs*, Winter 2008, p. 146.

71 C. J. Dunlap, 'Lawfare Amid Warfare', *The Washington Times*, 3 August 2007, available at: https://www.washingtontimes.com/news/2007/aug/03/lawfare-ami d-warfare/ [accessed on: 5 December 2017].

72 Dunlap, 'Lawfare Today: A Perspective', pp. 148–9.

73 S. W. Tiefenbrun, 'Semiotic Definition of Lawfare', *Case Western Reserve Journal of International Law*, Volume 43, Issue 1, 2011, p. 29.

74 P. Cornish, J. Lindley-French and C. Yorke, 'Strategic Communications and National Strategy', *Chatham House Report*, September 2011, p. ix.

75 G. P. Noone, 'Lawfare or Strategic Communications?', *Case Western Reserve Journal of International Law*, Volume 43, Issue 1, 2010, pp. 83–4.

76 Cavas, 'China's Maritime Militia a Growing Concern'.

77   Stavridis, 'Maritime Hybrid Warfare Is Coming'.

78   UNCLOS, art. 60-8.

79   Ibid., art. 3.

80   Ibid., art. 121.

81   Ibid., art. 121–3.

82   Ibid., art. 13.

83   Z. Keck, 'Whit Air Defense Zone, China Is Waging Lawfare', *The Diplomat*, 30 November 2013, available at: https://thediplomat.com/2013/11/with-air-defense-z one-china-is-waging-lawfare/ [accessed on: 6 December 2017].

84   *The South China Sea Arbitration (Philippines vs China)*, The Hague: Permanent Court of Arbitration, 2016, available at: https://pca-cpa.org/wp-content/uploads/ sites/175/2016/07/PH-CN-20160712-Award.pdf [accessed on: 6 December 2017], art. 1203-A1.

85   Ibid., art. 1203-A.

86   F. Zhang, 'Assessing China's Response to the South China Sea Arbitration Ruling', *Australian Journal of International Relations*, Volume 71, Issue 4, 2017, p. 454.

87   Ibid., pp. 452–3.

88   L. Zhou, 'What Is the South China Sea Code of Conduct, and Why Does It Matter?', *South China Morning Post*, 3 August 2017, available at: http://www.scmp.com/news/ china/diplomacy-defence/article/2105190/what-south-china-sea-code-conduct-a nd-why-does-it [accessed on: 6 December 2017].

Conclusion

1   Clausewitz, *On War*, p. 15.

2   Thucydides, *The History of the Peloponnesian War*, Book 1, para. 67.

Bibliography

Al Jazeera, 'New Government Announced under PM Saad al-Hiri', *Al Jazeera Lebanon News*, 18 December 2016, available at: http://www.aljazeera.com/news/2016/12/le banon-announces-government-saad-al-hariri-161218201145680.html [accessed on: 29 May 2017].

Al Jazeera, 'Ukraine: Who Controls What', 5 February 2017, available at: https://ww w.aljazeera.com/indepth/interactive/2017/02/ukraine-map-170205081953296.html [accessed on: 22 April 2018].

Allison, G., 'Thucydides Trap Case File', *Belfer Center for Science and International Affairs*, 23 September 2015, available at: http://belfercenter.ksg.harvard.edu/publicati on/24928/thucydides_trap_case_file.html [accessed on: 26 September 2016].

Arquilla, J., 'From Blitzkrieg to Bitskrieg: The Military Encounter with Computers', *Communications of the ACM*, Volume 54, Issue 10, 2011, pp. 58–65.

Arquilla, J. and Karasik, T., 'Chechnya: A Glimpse of Future Conflict?', *Studies in Conflict & Terrorism*, Volume 22, Issue 3, 1999, pp. 207–29.

Art, R. J., 'The Fungibility of Force', in *The Use of Force: Military Power and International Politics*, edited by R. J. Art and K. Waltz, Oxford: Rowman & Littlefield, 5th ed., 1999, pp. 3–22.

Aspin, L., *Report on the Bottom-Up Review*, Washington, DC: Department of Defense, October 1993, available at: www.dtic.mil/cgi-bin/GetTRDoc?AD=ADA359953 [accessed on: 20 April 2018].

Aviad, G., 'Hezbollah's Force Buildup of 2006-2009', *Military and Strategic Affairs*, Volume 1, Issue 3, December 2009, pp. 3–22.

Azani, E., 'The Hybrid Terrorist Organization: Hezbollah as a Case Study', *Studies in Conflict & Terrorism*, Volume 36, Issue 11, 2013, pp. 899–916.

BAE Systems, *Destroyers*, available at: http://www.baesystems.com/en-uk/product/destr oyers [accessed on: 4 July 2016.]

Barnet, M., 'Social Constructivism', in *The Globalization of World Politics*, edited by J. Baylis, S. Smith and P. Owens, Oxford: Oxford University Press, 4th ed., 2008, pp. 160–73.

Bassford, C., 'Primacy of Policy and Trinity in Clausewitz's Thought', in *Clausewitz in the Twenty-First Century*, edited by H. Strachan and A. Herberg-Rothe, Oxford: Oxford University Press, 2007, pp. 74–90.

Bauman, R. F., 'Conclusion', in *Compound Warfare, That Fatal Knot*, edited by T. Huber, pp. 307–16.

Baylis, J. and Wirtz, J. J., 'Introduction: Strategy in the Contemporary World: Strategy after 9/11', in *Strategy in the Contemporary World*, edited by J. Baylis, J. J. Wirtz and C. Gray, Oxford: Oxford University Press, 4th ed., 2013, pp. 1–18.

BBC, *How Far Do EU-US Sanctions on Russia Go?*, 2014, available at: http://www.bbc.co.uk/news/world-europe-28400218 [accessed on: 3 March 2017].

BBC, 'Israel Accused Over Lebanon', 6 September 2006, available at: http://news.bbc.co.uk/1/hi/6981557.stm [accessed on: 12 June 2017].

BBC News, 'MH17: Four Charged with Shooting Down Plane over Ukraine', 19 June 2019, available at: https://www.bbc.com/news/world-europe-48691488 [accessed on: 26 November 2019].

BBC News, 'Russia Restarts Col War Patrols', 17 August 2008, available at: http://news.bbc.co.uk/1/hi/world/europe/6950986.stm [accessed on: 30 March 2018].

BBC News, 'Scars Remain Amid Chechen Revival', available at: http://news.bbc.co.uk/1/hi/programmes/from_our_own_correspondent/6414603.stm [accessed on: 10 February 2017].

Bilingsey, D., *Fangs of the Lone Wolf: Chechen Tactics in the Russian-Chechen Wars 1994-2009*, Solihull: Helion & Company Limited, 2013.

Bowen, A. S., 'Coercive Diplomacy and the Donbas: Explaining Russian Strategy in Eastern Ukraine', *Journal of Strategic Studies* [online], 22 December 2017, pp. 1–32.

Bowker, M., 'The War in Georgia and the Western Response', *Central Asian Survey*, Volume 30, Issue 2, 2011, pp. 187–211.

Brown, C. and Ainley, K., *Understanding International Relations*, Basingstoke: Palgrave Macmillan, 4th ed., 2009.

Brownlee, L., 'Why "Cyberwar" Is So Hard to Define', *Forbes*, 17 July 2015, available at: https://www.forbes.com/sites/lisabrownlee/2015/07/16/why-cyberwar-is-so-hard-to-define/#1708cd4131f1 [accessed on: 4 June 2018].

Burnham, P., Gilland Lutz, K., Grant, W. and Layton-Henry, Z., *Research Methods in Politics*, Basingstoke: Palgrave Macmillan, 2nd ed., 2008.

Bush, G. H. W., *National Security Strategy of the United States*, Washington, DC: The White House, August 1991.

Bush, G. W., *The National Security Strategy of the United States of America* 2002, Washington, DC: The White House, September 2002.

Cabinet Office, *The National Security Strategy of the United Kingdom: Security in an Interdependent World*, March 2008, available at: https://www.gov.uk/government/uploads/system/uploads/attachment_data/file/228539/7291.pdf [accessed on: 21 June 2016].

Carr, E. H., *The Twenty Years' Crisis, 1919–1939*, Basingstoke: Palgrave Macmillan, 2001.

Cavas, C. P., 'China's "Little Blue Men" Take Navy's Place in Disputes', *Defense News*, 2 November 2015, available at: https://www.defensenews.com/naval/2015/11/03/chinas-little-blue-men-take-navys-place-in-disputes/ [accessed on: 28 November 2017].

Cavas, C. P., 'China's Maritime Militia a Growing Concern', *Defense News*, 21 November 2016, available at: https://www.defensenews.com/naval/2016/11/22/chinas-maritime-militia-a-growing-concern/ [accessed on: 27 November 2017].

Choi, T., 'Why the US Navy's First South China Sea FONOP Wasn't a FONOP', *CIMSEC*, 3 November 2015, available at: http://cimsec.org/why-the-us-navys-first-south-china-sea-fonop-wasnt-a-fonop/19681 [accessed on: 28 November 2017].

Clausewitz, C. von, *On War*, Oxford World's Classics, Oxford: Oxford University Press, 2008.

Clinton, W. J., *A National Security Strategy of Engagement and Enlargement*, Washington, DC: The White House, July 1994.

Convention on the Law of the Sea, Montego Bay, 12 November 1982, *United Nations Treaty Series*, Volume 1833, Issue 31363, available at: http://www.un.org/depts/los/convention_agreements/texts/unclos/unclos_e.pdf [accessed on: 4 December 2017].

Corbett, J. S., *Principles of Maritime Strategy*, Mineola, NY: Dover Publications, 2015.

Cornish, P., Lindley-French, J. and Yorke, C., 'Strategic Communications and National Strategy', *Chatham House Report*, September 2011.

Council of Europe, 'Declaration by the Committee of Ministers on the Terrorist Assault in Beslan', 9 September 2004, available at: https://wcd.coe.int/ViewDoc.jsp?p=&Ref=Decl-09.09.2004&Language=lanEnglish&Ver=original&Site=DC&BackColorInternet=DBDCF2&BackColorIntranet=FDC864&BackColorLogged=FDC864&direct=true [accessed on: 8 February 2017].

Crooke, A. and Perry M., 'How Hezbollah Defeated Israel: Part 1 Winning the Intelligence War', *Asia Times Online*, 12 October 2006, available at: http://www.atimes.com/atimes/Middle_East/HJ12Ak01.html [accessed on: 8 June 2017].

Cross, S., 'Russia's Relationship with the United States/NATO in the US-Led Global War on Terrorism', *The Journal of Slavic Military Studies*, Volume 19, Issue 2, pp. 175–92.

CSIS, 'Asia Maritime Transparency Initiative', available at: https://amti.csis.org/island-tracker/ [accessed on: 28 November 2017].

Dannreuther, R. and March, L., 'Chechnya: Has Moscow Won?', *Survival*, Volume 50, Issue 4, 2008, pp. 97–112.

Daoud, D., 'Hezbollah's Latest Conquest: Lebanon's Cabinet', *Newsweek*, 12 January 2017, available at: http://www.newsweek.com/hezbollahs-latest-conquest-lebanons-cabinet-541487 [accessed on: 29 May 2017].

Deibert, R. J., Rohozinski, R. and Crete-Nishihata, M., 'Cyclones in Cyberspace: Information Shaping and Denial in the 2008 Russia-Georgia War', *Security Dialogue*, Volume 43, Issue 1, 2012, pp. 3–24.

Deutsche Welle, 'European Press Review: "An Act of War"', available at: http://www.dw.com/en/european-press-review-an-act-of-war/a-2097777 [accessed on: 16 April 2016].

de Waal, T., 'The Still-Topical Tagliavini Report', *Carnegie Moscow Center*, 2015, available at: http://carnegie.ru/commentary/?fa=61451 [accessed on: 15 February 2017].

de Wijk, R., 'Hybrid Conflict and the Changing Nature of Actors', in *The Oxford Handbook of War*, edited by J. Lindley-French and B. Yves, Oxford: Oxford University Press, 2014, pp. 358–72.

de Wijk, R., *The Art of Military Coercion*, Amsterdam: Amsterdam University Press, 2014.

Dunlap, C. J., 'Lawfare Amid Warfare', *The Washington Times*, 3 August 2007, available at: https://www.washingtontimes.com/news/2007/aug/03/lawfare-amid-warfare/ [accessed on: 5 December 2017].

Dunlap, C. J., 'Lawfare Today: A Perspective', *Yale Journal of International Affairs*, Winter 2008, pp. 146–54.

Dunne, T., 'Liberalism', in *The Globalization of World Politics*, edited by J. Baylis, S. Smith and P. Owens, Oxford: Oxford University Press, 4th ed., 2008, pp. 108–23.

Dunne, T. and Schmidt, B. C., 'Realism', in *The Globalization of World Politics*, edited by J. Baylis, S. Smith and P. Owens, Oxford: Oxford University Press, 4th ed., 2008, pp. 90–107.

Echevarria, A. J., 'Fourth-generation War and Other Myths', *Strategic Studies Institute*, November 2005, available at: http://ssi.armywarcollege.edu/pdffiles/pub632.pdf [accessed on: 22 April 2018].

Echevarria, A. J., 'Globalization and the Clausewitzian Nature of War', *The European Legacy*, Volume 8, Issue 3, 2003, pp. 317–32.

The Economist, 'Nasrallah Wins the War', *The Economist*, 17 August 2006, available at: http://www.economist.com/node/7796790 [accessed on: 30 May 2017].

The Economist, 'The Lessons of Libya', *The Economist*, 19 May 2011, available at: https://www.economist.com/node/18709571 [accessed on: 17 April 2018].

Eisenkot, G., 'IDF Strategy', August 2015, English translation published in: Khalidi, A. S., 'Special Document File: Original English Translation of the 2015 Gadi Eisenkot IDF Strategy', *Journal of Palestinian Studies*, Volume 14, Issue 2 (Winter 2016).

Elran, M., 'The Civilian Front in the Second Lebanon War', in *The Second Lebanon War: Strategic Perspectives*, edited by S. Brom and M. Elran, Tel Aviv: Institute for National Security Studies, 2007 pp. 103–22.

Erickson, A. S. and Kennedy, C. M., 'China's Maritime Militia', *CNA*, 7 March 2016, available at: https://www.cna.org/cna_files/pdf/chinas-maritime-militia.pdf [accessed on: 21 November 2017], p. 5.

Erickson, A. S. and Kennedy, C. M., 'Directing China's "Little Blue Men": Uncovering the Maritime Militia Command Structure', *CSIS Asia Maritime Transparency Initiative*, 11 September 2015, available at: https://amti.csis.org/directing-chinas-little-blue-men-uncovering-the-maritime-militia-command-structure/ [accessed on: 27 November 2017].

Erickson, A. S. and Kennedy, C. M., 'Riding a New Wave of Professionalization and Militarization: Sansha City's Maritime Militia', *CIMSEC*, 1 September 2016, available at: http://cimsec.org/riding-new-wave-professionalization-militarization-sansha-citys-maritime-militia/27689 [accessed on: 27 November 2017].

European Council, *A Secure Europe in a Better World, European Security Strategy*, Brussels, 12 December 2003.

European Council, *Shared Vision, Common Action: A Stronger Europe, A Global Strategy for the European Union's Foreign and Security Policy*, Brussels, June 2016.

Exum, A., 'Hizballah at War: A Military Assessment', *Policy Focus*, Issue 63, December 2006, The Washington Institute for Near East Policy, available at: http://www.wash ingtoninstitute.org/policy-analysis/view/hizballah-at-war-a-military-assessment [accessed on: 30 May 2017].

Fayutkin, D., 'Russian-Chechen Information Warfare 1994-2006', *The RUSI Journal*, Volume 151, Issue 5, October 2006, pp. 52–5.

Feldman, Y., 'Dr. Naveh, Or, How I Learned to Stop Worrying and Walk Through Walls', *HAARETZ*, 25 October 2007, available at: http://www.haaretz.com/israel-news/ dr-naveh-or-how-i-learned-to-stop-worrying-and-walk-through-walls-1.231912 [accessed on: 30 June 2016].

Felgenhauer, P., 'The Russian Army in Chechnya', *Central Asian Survey*, Volume 21, Issue 2, 2002, pp. 157–66.

Freedman, L., *Strategy: A History*, Oxford: Oxford University Press, 2013.

Freilich, C. D., 'Israel in Lebanon - Getting It Wrong: The 1982 Invasion, 2000 Withdrawal, and 2006 War', *Israel Journal of Foreign Affairs*, Volume 6, Issue 3, 2012, pp. 41–75.

Gaddis, J. L., 'A Grand Strategy of Transformation', *Foreign Policy*, Issue 133, November–December 2002, pp. 50–7.

Gaddis J. L., *Strategies of Containment: A Critical Appraisal of Postwar American National Security Policy*, Oxford: Oxford University Press, 1982.

Galeotti, M., *Russia's Wars in Chechnya 1994-2009*, Oxford: Oxford Osprey Publishing, 2014.

Garden, T. and Ramsbotham, D., 'About Face: The British Armed Forces – Which Way to Turn?', *The RUSI Journal*, Volume 149, Issue 2, 2004, pp. 10–15.

Gates, R. M., *Quadrennial Defense Review*, Washington, DC: Department of Defense, February 2010.

Gates, R. M., 'Remarks by Secretary Gates at the Security and Defense Agenda', *Department of Defense News Transcript*, Brussels, 10 June 2011, available at: http://archive.defense.gov/Transcripts/Transcript.aspx?TranscriptID=4839 [accessed on: 20 April 2018].

Gerasimov, V., 'The Value of Science Is in the Foresight', *Military Review*, January–February 2016, pp. 23–9.

Geren, P. and Casey, G. W., *US Army 2008 Posture Statement*, 26 February 2008.

Giles, K., 'Russia's New Tools for Confronting the West', *Chatham House Research Paper*, March 2016, available at: https://www.chathamhouse.org/publication/russias-new-to ols-confronting-west [accessed on: 3 May 2017], pp. 31–2.

Giles, K., 'Understanding the Georgia Conflict, Two Years On: Reviews and Commentaries', part 2, *NATO Research Review*, Rome: NATO Defense College, 2010.

Gilmore, T. J., CDR, 'Iran Owns the Gray Zone', *Proceedings Magazine*, US Naval War
    Institute, Issue 144, Issue 3, March 2018, available at: https://www.usni.org/maga
    zines/proceedings/2018-03/iran-owns-gray-zone [accessed on: 29 March 2018].
Götz, E., 'It's Geopolitics, Stupid: Explaining Russia's Ukraine Policy', *Global Affairs*,
    Volume 1, Issue 1, 2015, pp. 3–10.
Government Accountability Office, *National Defence: Hybrid Warfare*, GAO-10-1036R,
    Washington, DC: U.S. Government Accountability Office, September 2010.
Government of Japan, *National Security Strategy*, 17 December 2014, available at: http://
    www.cas.go.jp/jp/siryou/131217anzenhoshou/nss-e.pdf [accessed on: 3 July 2016].
Government of Japan, *The Constitution of Japan*, 3 November 1946, available at: http:
    //japan.kantei.go.jp/constitution_and_government_of_japan/constitution_e.html
    [accessed on: 3 July 2016].
Government of Russia, *National Security Concept of the Russian Federation*, 10 January
    2000, available at: http://fas.org/nuke/guide/russia/doctrine/gazeta012400.htm
    [accessed on: 1 July 2016].
Government of Russia, *Russian Federation's National Security Strategy*, 31 December 2015,
    available at: http://www.ieee.es/Galerias/fichero/OtrasPublicaciones/Internacional/2
    016/Russian-National-Security-Strategy-31Dec2015.pdf [accessed on: 3 July 2016].
Government of Russia, *Russia's National Security Strategy to 2020*, 12 May 2009,
    available at: http://rustrans.wikidot.com/russia-s-national-security-strategy-to-2020
    [accessed on: 2 July 2016].
Government of Russia, *Russian National Security Blueprint*, 17 December 1997,
    available at: http://fas.org/nuke/guide/russia/doctrine/blueprint.html [accessed on:
    1 July 2016]
Gray, C. S., *Another Bloody Century*, London: Phoenix, 2006.
Gray, C. S., *Modern Strategy*, Oxford: Oxford University Press, 2012.
Gray, C. S., *Strategy and Defence Planning*, Oxford: Oxford University Press, 2014.
Gray, C. S., *The Future of Strategy*, Cambridge: Polity Press, 2016.
Gray, C. S., 'War – Continuity in Change, and Change in Continuity', *Parameters*,
    Issue 40, Summer 2010, pp. 5–13.
Grieco, J. M., 'Anarchy and the Limits of Cooperation: A Realist Critique of the Newest
    Liberal Institutionalism', *International Organization*, Volume 42, Issue 3, Summer
    1988, pp. 485–507.
Haass, R. N., 'Liberal World Order, RIP', *Council on Foreign Relations*, 21 March 2018,
    available at: https://www.cfr.org/article/liberal-world-order-rip [accessed on:
    16 April 2018].
Haass, R. N., 'World Order 2.0', *Foreign Affairs*, Volume 96, Issue 2, 2017, pp. 2–9.
Hagel, C., *Quadrennial Defense Review*, Washington, DC: Department of Defense,
    March 2014.
Hanauer, L., 'Crimean Adventure Will Cost Russia Dearly', *The Moscow Times*,
    7 September 2014, available at: https://themoscowtimes.com/articles/crimean-a
    dventure-will-cost-russia-dearly-39112 [accessed on: 20 April 2018].

Harris, H. B. Jr., ADM, *Spoken Remarks Delivered to the Australian Strategic Policy Institute*, 31 March 2015, available at: http://www.cpf.navy.mil/leaders/harry-harris/ speeches/2015/03/ASPI-Australia.pdf [accessed on: 30 November 2017], p. 4.

HC Deb, 25 July 1990, volume 177, cc 468–70, available at: https://publications.parl iament.uk/pa/cm198990/cmhansrd/1990-07-25/Debate-1.html [accessed on: 23 April 2018].

HC Deb, 21 March 2011, Volume 525, Column 700, available at: http://www.publicati ons.parliament.uk/pa/cm201011/cmhansrd/cm110321/debtext/110321-0001.ht m#1103219000645 [accessed on: 16 April 2016].

Helmer, D. I., 'Flipside of the COIN: Israel's Lebanese Incursion Between 1982 – 200', *The Long War Series Occasional Paper 21*, Fort Leavenworth, KS: Combat Studies Institute Press, 2007.

Herzog, M., 'New IDF Strategy Goes Public', *The Washington Institute, Policy Analysis*, 28 August 2015, available at: http://www.washingtoninstitute.org/policy-analysis/ view/new-idf-strategy-goes-public [accessed on: 28 June 2016].

Heuser, B., 'Introduction', in , *On War*, edited by C. Clausewitz, Oxford World's Classics, Oxford: Oxford University Press, 2008, pp. vii–xxxii.

Higgins, A., 'China and Russia Hold First Joint Naval Drill in the Baltic Sea', *The New York Times*, 25 July 2017, available at: https://www.nytimes.com/2017/07/25/world/ europe/china-russia-baltic-navy-exercises.html [accessed on: 29 May 2018].

HM Government, *A Strong Britain in an Age of Uncertainty: The National Security Strategy*, London: The Stationary Office, October 2010.

HM Government, *National Security Strategy and Strategic Defence and Security Review 2015: A Secure and Prosperous United Kingdom*, November 2015, available at: https://www.gov.uk/government/publications/national-security-strategy-and-strate gic-defence-and-security-review-2015 [accessed on: 21 June 2016].

HM Government, *Securing Britain in an Age of Uncertainty: The Strategic Defence and Security Review*, London: The Stationary Office, October 2010.

Hoffman, F. G., *Conflict in the 21st Century: The Rise of Hybrid Wars*, Arlington, VA: Potomac Institute for Policy Studies, December 2007.

Holzwarth Sprehe, K., 'Ukraine Says "NO" to NATO', *Pew Research Center*, 2010, available at: http://www.pewglobal.org/2010/03/29/ukraine-says-no-to-nato/ [accessed on: 3 May 2017].

Howard, M., *Clausewitz a Very Short Introduction*, Oxford: Oxford University Press, 2002.

Howard, M., 'The Causes of Wars', *The Wilson Quarterly*, Volume 8, Issue 3, Summer 1984, pp. 90–103.

Huber, T., *Compound Warfare: A Conceptual Framework*, in *Compound Warfare, That Fatal Knot*, edited by T. Huber, Fort Leavenworth, KS: US Army Command and General Staff College Press, 2002, pp. 1–10.

Hybrid CoE, 'Hybrid Threats', *The European Centre of Excellence for Countering Hybrid Threats*, 2018, available at: https://www.hybridcoe.fi/hybrid-threats/ [accessed on: 21 April 2018].

IFES, 'The Political Affiliation of Lebanese Parliamentarians and the Composition of the Different Parliamentary Blocs', *IFES Lebanon Briefing Paper*, September 2009, available at: https://www.ifes.org/sites/default/files/lebanon_parliament_elections_200909_0.pdf [accessed on: 29 May 2017].

IISS, 'China's Land Reclamation in the South China Sea', *Strategic Comments*, Volume 21, Comment 20, August 2015, pp. ix–xi.

IISS, 'The Future of US Syria Policy', *Strategic Comments*, Volume 23, Issue 1, February 2017, pp. ix–xi.

IISS, 'The NATO Capability Gap', *Strategic Survey 2012*, Volume 100, Issue 1, 1999, pp. 15–21.

Ikenberry, G. J., 'The End of Liberal International Order?', *International Affairs*, Volume 94, Issue 1, 2018, pp. 7–23.

IMO, 'International Shipping Facts and Figures', *Maritime Knowledge Centre*, 6 March 2012, available at: http://www.imo.org/en/KnowledgeCentre/ShipsAndShipping FactsAndFigures/TheRoleandImportanceofInternationalShipping/Documents/ International%20Shipping%20-%20Facts%20and%20Figures.pdf [accessed on: 4 December 2017].

ITIC, 'Terrorism in Cyberspace: Hezbollah's Internet Network', *The Meir Amit Intelligence and Terrorism Information Center*, 3 April 2013, available at: http://www.terrorism-info.org.il/en/article/20488 [accessed on: 2 June 2017].

Jasper, S. and Moreland, S., 'The Islamic State Is a Hybrid Threat: Why Does That Matter?', *Small Wars Journal*, available at: http://smallwarsjournal.com/jrnl/art/the -islamic-state-is-a-hybrid-threat-why-does-that-matter [accessed on: 21 April 2018].

Johnson, J., 'China Unveils Massive "Magic Island-Maker" Dredging Vessel', *Japan Times*, 4 November 2017, available at: https://www.japantimes.co.jp/news/2017/1 1/04/asia-pacific/china-unveils-massive-island-building-vessel/ [accessed on: 30 November 2017].

Jones, S., 'Estonia Ready to Deal with Russia's "Little Green Men"', *Financial Times*, 13 May 2015, available at: https://www.ft.com/content/03c5ebde-f95a-11e4-ae65-0 0144feab7de [accessed on: 03 March 2017].

Kasapoglu, C., 'Russia's Renewed Military Thinking: Non-Linear Warfare and Reflexive Control', *Research Paper*, Number 121, Rome: NATO Defense College, November 2015.

Kashin, V., 'Khrushchev's Gift: The Questionable Ownership of Crimea', in *Brothers Armed: Military Aspects of the Crisis in Ukraine*, edited by C. Howard and R. Pukhov and translated by I. Khokhtova, Minneapolis, MN: East View Press, 2014, pp. 1–24.

Katz, Y., 'Post-battle Probe Finds Merkava Tank Misused in Lebanon', *Jerusalem Post*, 3 September 2006, available at: http://www.jpost.com/Israel/Post-battle-probe-find s-Merkava-tank-misused-in-Lebanon [accessed on: 12 June 2017].

Keck, Z., 'Whit Air Defense Zone, China Is Waging Lawfare', *The Diplomat*, 30 November 2013, available at: https://thediplomat.com/2013/11/with-air-defense-zone-china-is-waging-lawfare/ [accessed on: 6 December 2017]

Kennedy, C. M. and Erickson, A. S., 'Model Maritime Militia: Tanmen's Leading Role in the April 2012 Scarborough Shoal Incident', *CIMSEC*, 21 April 2016, available at: http://cimsec.org/model-maritime-militia-tanmens-leading-role-april-2012-scarborough-shoal-incident/24573 [accessed on: 27 November 2017].

Kinross, S., 'Clausewitz and Low Intensity Conflict', *Journal of Strategic Studies*, Volume 27, Issue 1, 2004, pp. 35–58.

Kissinger, H., *World Order: Reflections on the Character of Nations and the Course of History*, London: Allen Lane, 2014.

Kober, A., 'The Israel Defence Forces in the Second Lebanon War: Why the Poor Performance?', *Journal of Strategic Studies*, Volume 31, Issue 1, 2008, pp. 3–40.

Krauthammer, C., 'The Unipolar Moment', *Foreign Affairs*, Volume 70, Issue 1, January 1991, pp. 23–33.

Kulick, A., 'Hezbollah vs. the IDF: The Operational Dimension', *INSS Strategic Assessment*, Volume 9, Issue 3, November 2006, cited in: Matthews M. M., 'Hard Lessons Learned', pp. 7–8.

LaGrone, S., 'China Defends Deployment of Anti-Ship Missiles to South China Sea Island', *US Naval Institute News*, 31 March 2016, available at: https://news.usni.or g/2016/03/30/china-defends-deployment-of-anti-ship-missiles-to-south-china-sea-island [accessed on: 30 November 2017].

Lambeth, B. S., *Air Operations in Israel's War Against Hezbollah*, Santa Monica, CA: RAND Corporation, 2011.

Lambeth, B. S., 'Learning From Lebanon: Airpower and Strategy in Israel's 2006 War against Hezbollah', *Naval War College Review*, Volume 65, Issue 3, 2012, pp. 83–105, available at: https://www.usnwc.edu/getattachment/e8495921-aa3f-4c7b-a626-0ceb2 26b0677/Learning-from-Lebanon--Airpower-and-Strategy-in-Is.aspx [accessed on: 7 June 2017].

Lamont, C., *Research Methods in International Relations*, London: Sage, 2015.

Lane, D., '"Coloured Revolution" as a Political Phenomenon', *Journal of Communist Studies and Transitional Politics*, Volume 25, Issue 2–3, pp. 113–35.

Lappin, Y., 'In-House Hezbollah Missile Factories Could Add to Massive Arms Buildup', *The Algemeiner*, 20 March 2017, available at: https://www.algemeiner.com/2017/03/20/in-house-hezbollah-missile-factories-could-add-to-massive-arms-buildup/ [accessed on: 7 June 2017].

Larsen, H. B. L., 'The Russo-Georgian War and Beyond: Towards a European Great Power Concert', *European Security*, Volume 21, Issue 1, 2012, pp. 102–21.

Lavrov, A., 'Timeline of Russian-Georgian Hostilities in August 2008', in *The Tanks of August*, edited by R. Pukhov, Moscow: Centre for Analysis of Strategies and Technologies, 2010, pp. 37–76.

Lavrov, A. and Nikolsky, A., 'Neglect and Rot: Degradation of Ukraine's Military in the Interim Period', in *Brothers Armed: Military Aspects of the Crisis in Ukraine*, edited by C. Howard and R. Pukhov, Minneapolis : East View Press, 2014, pp. 57–73.

Liang, Q. and Xiangsui, W., *Unrestricted Warfare*, translated by FBIS, Beijing: PLA
    Literature and Art Publishing, February 1999, available at: http://www.c4i.org/
    unrestricted.pdf [accessed on: 4 December 2017].

Lind, W. S., "*Understanding Fourth Generation War*", 15 January 2004, available at:
    http://www.antiwar.com/lind/?articleid=1702 [accessed on: 20 March 2016].

Losh, J., 'Is Russia Killing Off Eastern Ukraine's Warlords?', *Foreign Policy*, 2016,
    available at: http://foreignpolicy.com/2016/10/25/who-is-killing-eastern-ukrain
    es-warlords-motorola-russia-putin/ [accessed on: 10 February 2017].

Lowther, W., 'US Ups Ante in South China Sea by Sending Destroyer', *Taipei Times*,
    15 March 2009, available at: http://www.taipeitimes.com/News/taiwan/archives/20
    09/03/15/2003438536/1 [accessed on: 28 November 2017].

Luttwak, E. N., 'Towards Post-Heroic Warfare', *Foreign Affairs*, Volume 74, Issue 3,
    1 May 1995, pp. 109–22.

MacAskill, E., 'British Army Creates Team of Facebook Warriors', *The Guardian*,
    31 January 2015, available at: https://www.theguardian.com/uk-news/2015/jan/31/
    british-army-facebook-warriors-77th-brigade [accessed on: 21 June 2016]

Macias, A., 'China Quietly Installed Defensive Missile Systems on Strategic Spratly
    Islands in Hotly Contested South China Sea', *CNBC*, 2 May 2018, available at:
    https://www.cnbc.com/2018/05/02/china-added-missile-systems-on-spratly-
    islands-in-south-china-sea.html [accessed on: 20 June 2018].

Mahan, A. T., *Influence of Sea Power Upon History*, Pantianos Classics, 2016 (originally
    published in 1890).

Mansoor, P. R., 'Introduction', in *Hybrid Warfare: Fighting Complex Opponents from the
    Ancient World to the Present*, edited by W. Murray and P. R. Mansoor, New York:
    Cambridge University Press, 2012, pp. 1–17.

Martinson, R. D., 'The Militarisation of China's Coast Guard', *The Diplomat*,
    21 November 2014, available at: https://thediplomat.com/2014/11/the-
    militarization-of-chinas-coast-guard/ [accessed on: 4 December 2017].

Mastro, O. S., 'Signalling and Military Provocation in Chinese National Security
    Strategy: A Closer Look at the *Impeccable* Incident', *The Journal of Strategic Studies*,
    Volume 34, Issue 2, April 2011, pp. 219–44.

Matthews, M. M., 'Hard Lessons Learned - A Comparison of the 2006 Hezbollah-
    Israeli War and Operation CAST LEAD: A Historical Overview', in *Back to
    Basics: A Study of the Second Lebanon War and Operation CAST LEAD*, edited by
    S. C. Farquhar, Fort Leavenworth, KS: Combined Studies Institute Press, 2009,
    pp. 5–44.

Matthews, M. M., 'Interview with BG (Ret.) Shimon Naveh', *Operational Leadership
    Experiences*, Fort Leavenworth, KS: Combat Studies Institute, 1 November 2007,
    available at: smallwarsjournal.com/documents/mattmatthews.pdf [accessed on:
    28 June 2015]

Mattis, J., *Summary of the 2018 National Defense Strategy of the United States of
    America*, Washington, DC: Department of Defense, January 2018.

Mearsheimer, J. J., *The Tragedy of Great Power Politics*, London: W. W. Norton & Company, 2014.

Mellies, P. L., 'Hamas and Hezbollah: A Comparison of Tactics', in *Back to Basics: A Study of the Second Lebanon War and Operation CAST LEAD*, edited by S. C. Farquhar, Fort Leavenworth, KS: Combined Studies Institute Press, 2009, pp. 45–82.

Menon, R. and Rumer, E., *Conflict in Ukraine*, London: MIT Press, 2015.

Ministry of Defence, '77th Brigade', available at: http://www.army.mod.uk/structure/39 492.aspx [accessed on: 21 June 2016]

Ministry of Defence, *Security and Stabilisations: The Military Contribution*, Joint Doctrine Publication 3–40, JDP 3–40, November 2009, available at: https://www.gov .uk/government/uploads/system/uploads/attachment_data/file/49948/jdp3_40a4. pdf [accessed on: 21 March 2016].

Ministry of Defence, *Strategic Defence Review*, July 1998, available at: http://archives.livr eblancdefenseetsecurite.gouv.fr/2008/IMG/pdf/sdr1998_complete.pdf [accessed on: 21 June 2016].

Montgomery, S. L., 'What's at Stake in China's Claims to the South China Sea?', *The Conversation*, 14 July 2016, available at: https://theconversation.com/whats-at-sta ke-in-chinas-claims-to-the-south-china-sea-62472 [accessed on: 1 December 2017].

Morgenthau, H. J., *Politics among Nations*, New York: Alfred A. Knopf, 4th ed., 1966.

Morris, L. J., 'Indonesia-China Tensions in the Natuna Sea: Evidence of Naval Efficacy over Coast Guards?', *The RAND Blog*, RAND Corporation, 5 July 2016, available at: https://www.rand.org/blog/2016/07/indonesia-china-tensions-in-the-natuna-sea-evi dence.html [accessed on: 17 November 2017].

Munich Security Conference, *Munich Security Report* 2015: *Collapsing Order, Reluctant Guardians*, 26 January 2015.

Najžer, B., 'Hybrid Defence – An Idea Worth Pursuing', *Weekly Analysis*, Norwegian Atlantic Committee, 3 June 2016, available at: http://www.atlanterhavskomiteen.no/ post/3818650/hybrid-defence-%E2%80%93-an-idea-worth-pursuing [accessed on: 29 March 2018].

NATO, *Active Engagement, Modern Defence: Strategic Concept for the Defence and Security of the Members of the North Atlantic Treaty Organization*, Lisbon: North Atlantic Council, 20 November 2010.

NATO, 'Enlargement', 3 December 2015, available at: http://www.nato.int/cps/en/nat ohq/topics_49212.htm? [accessed on: 1 February 2017].

NATO, *New Strategic Concept FAQs*, available at: http://www.nato.int/strategic-concept/ strategic-concept-faq.html [accessed on: 22 June 2016].

NATO, 'Study on NATO Enlargement', 5 November 2008, available at: http://www.nato .int/cps/en/natohq/official_texts_24733.htm [accessed on: 13 February 2017].

NATO, *The Alliance's New Strategic Concept*, London: North Atlantic Council, 8 November 1991.

NATO, *The Alliance's Strategic Concept*, Washington: North Atlantic Council, 24 April 1999.

NATO, *The North Atlantic Treaty*, Washington, DC, 4 April 1949, available at: http://www.nato.int/cps/en/natolive/official_texts_17120.htm [accessed on: 16 April 2016].

Nemeth, W. J., *Future War and Chechnya: A Case for Hybrid Warfare*, Monterey, CA: Naval Postgraduate School, 2002.

New York Times, The, 'Hezbollah's Arsenal', 18 July 2006, available at: http://graphics 8.nytimes.com/images/2006/07/18/world/0718-for-websubMIDEAST.jpg [accessed on: 22 April 2018].

NIC, 'The Future of Indian Ocean and South China Sea Fisheries: Implications for the United States', *National Intelligence Council Report*, NICR 2013-38, 30 July 2013, available at: https://www.dni.gov/files/documents/nic/NICR%202013-38%20Fisherie s%20Report%20FINAL.pdf [accessed on: 1 December 2017].

Nikolsky, A., 'Little, Green and Polite: The Creation of Russian Special Operations Forces', in *Brothers Armed: Military Aspects of the Crisis in Ukraine*, edited by C. Howard and R. Pukhov, Minneapolis : East View Press, 2014, pp. 124–34 .

No-one, G. P., 'Lawfare or Strategic Communications?', *Case Western Reserve Journal of International Law*, Volume 43, Issue 1, 2010, pp. 73–85.

Notes Verbales CML/17/2009, available at: http://www.un.org/Depts/los/clcs_new/ submissions_files/mysvnm33_09/chn_2009re_mys_vnm_e.pdf [accessed on: 1 November 2017].

Obama, B. H., *National Security Strategy 2015*, Washington, DC: The White House, February 2015, available at: https://www.whitehouse.gov/sites/default/files/docs/201 5_national_security_strategy.pdf [accessed on: 17 April 2016].

Olmert, E., 'In Retrospect: The Second Lebanon War', *Military and Strategic Affairs*, Volume 6, Issue 1, March 2014, pp. 3–18.

OSCE, *Ukraine, Presidential Election, 17 January and 7 February* 2010: *Final Report*, 2010, available at: http://www.osce.org/odihr/elections/ukraine/67844 [accessed on: 3 March 2017].

Oxford English Dictionary, 'alliance', [online], available at: http://www.oed.com/view/ Entry/5290?rskey=eKLjvN&result=1&isAdvanced=false#eid [accessed on: 18 April 2016].

Oxford English Dictionary, 'archetype', 2017, available at: http://www.oed.com/view/ Entry/10344?redirectedFrom=archetype#eid [accessed on: 2 March 2017].

Oxford English Dictionary, 'coercion', [Online], available at: http://www.oed.com/view/ Entry/35725?redirectedFrom=coercion#eid [accessed on: 26 September 2016].

Oxford English Dictionary, 'hybrid' [online], available at: http://www.oed.com/view/ Entry/89809?redirectedFrom=hybrid#eid [accessed on: 22 February 2016]

Oxford English Dictionary, 'legality', [online], available at: http://www.oed.com/view/ Entry/107012?redirectedFrom=legality#eid [accessed on: 18 April 2016].

Oxford English Dictionary, 'legitimacy', [online], available at: http://www.oed.com/v iew/Entry/107111?redirectedFrom=legitimacy#eid [accessed on: 18 April 2016].

Oxford English Dictionary, 'threat', [Online], available at: http://www.oed.com/view/ Entry/201152?rskey=zLMoGh&result=1#eid [accessed on: 21 March 2016].

Oxford English Dictionary, 'war', [online], available at: http://www.oed.com/view/ Entry/225589?rskey=T3lUWH&result=1#eidn [accessed on: 22 February 2016].

Oxford English Dictionary, 'warfare', [online], available at: http://www.oed.com/view/ Entry/225719?rskey=nhuhkZ&result=2#eid [accessed on: 22 February 2016].

Palmer Harik, J., *Hezbollah: The Changing Face of Terrorism*, London: I.B. Tauris & Co Ltd, 2005.

Panda, A., 'South China Sea: What China's First Strategic Bomber Landing on Woody Island Means', *The Diplomat*, 22 May 2018, available at: https://thediplomat.com/2 018/05/south-china-sea-what-chinas-first-strategic-bomber-landing-on-woody-island-means/ [accessed on: 20 June 2018].

Pedrozo, R., 'Close Encounters at Sea: The USNS Impeccable Incident', *Naval War College Review*, Volume 62, Issue 3, Summer 2009, pp. 101–11.

Perez-Seoane Garau, P., 'NATO's Criteria for Intervention in Crisis Response Operation: Legitimacy and Legality', *Royal Danish Defence College Brief*, Copenhagen, September 2013.

RAND Corporation, 'Cyber Warfare', 2017, available at: http://www.rand.org/topics/ cyber-warfare.html [accessed on: 7 February 2017].

Rapaport, A., 'The IDF and the Lessons of the Second Lebanon War', *Mideast Security and Policy Studies*, Number 85, The Begin-Sadat Center for Strategic Studies, December 2010.

Resor, S., 'Opposition to NATO Expansion', *Arms Control Association*, available at: http://www.armscontrol.org/act/1997_06-07/natolet [accessed on: 23 June 2016].

Retson, S., 'Crimea Is Becoming a Russian Money Pit', *World Policy*, 24 October 2016, available at: https://worldpolicy.org/2016/10/24/crimea-is-becoming-a-russian-money-pit/ [accessed on: 20 June 2018].

Reus-Smit, C., 'Constructivism', in *Theories of International Relations*, edited by S. Burchill, A. Linklater, R. Devetak, J. Donnelly, T. Nardin, M. Paterson, C. Reus-Smit, J. True., 4th ed., Basingstoke: Palgrave Macmillan, 2009, pp. 212–36.

Robertson, J. and Riley, M., 'Mysterious' 08 Turkey Pipeline Blast Opened New Cyberwar', 10 December 2014, available at: https://www.bloomberg.com/news/ articles/2014-12-10/mysterious-08-turkey-pipeline-blast-opened-new-cyberwar [accessed on: 7 February 2017].

RT, *Crimea, Sevastopol Officially Join Russia as Putin Signs Final Decree*, 2014, available at: https://www.rt.com/news/russia-parliament-crimea-ratification-293/ [accessed on: 3 March 2017].

Rumsfeld, D. H., *Quadrennial Defense Review*, Washington, DC: Department of Defense, 30 September, 2001.

Saaman, J., 'The Dahya Concept and Israeli Military Posture vis-à-vis Hezbollah Since 2006', *Comparative Strategy*, Volume 32, Issue 2, 2013, pp. 146–59.

Sakwa, R., 'Conspiracy Narratives as a Mode of Engagement in International Politics: The Case of the 2008 Russo-Georgian War', *The Russian Review*, Volume 71, October 2012, pp. 581–609.

Sakwa, R., *Frontline Ukraine: Crisis in the Borderlands*, London: I.B. Tauris & Co. Ltd, 2015.

Schiff, Z., 'The Foresight Saga', *Haaretz*, 11 August 2006, available at: http://www.haar etz.com/the-foresight-saga-1.195001 [accessed on: 8 June 2017].

Schofield, C. Sumaila, R. and Cheung, W., 'Fishing, Not Oil, Is at the Heart of the South China Sea Dispute', *The Conversation*, 15 August 2016, available at: http://theconve rsation.com/fishing-not-oil-is-at-the-heart-of-the-south-china-sea-dispute-63580 [accessed on: 1 December 2017].

Sheehan, M. and Wyllie, J., *The Economist Pocket Guide to Defence*, Oxford: Basil Blackwell Ltd, 1986.

Simpson, J., 'Russia's Crimea Plan Detailed, Secret and Successful', *BBC*, 2014, available at: http://www.bbc.co.uk/news/world-europe-26644082 [accessed on: 3 March 2017].

Sindelar, D., 'Was Yanukovich's Ouster Constitutional', *Radio Free Europe/Radio Liberty*, 2014, available at: http://www.rferl.org/a/was-yanukovychs-ouster-constitutional /25274346.html [accessed on: 3 March 2017].

SIPRI, *Military Expenditure Database*, 2018, available at: http://www.sipri.org/research/ armaments/milex/milex_database [accessed on: 17 April 2016]

SIPRI, *Military Expenditure Database*, Share of GDP 2018, available at: https://www.sip ri.org/sites/default/files/Milex-share-of-GDP.pdf [accessed on: 19 April 2018].

Slim, R., 'Hezbollah and Syria: From Regime Proxy to Regime Savior', *Insight Turkey*, Volume 16, Issue 2, 2014, pp. 61–8.

Smith, R., *The Utility of Force - The Art of War in the Modern World*, London: Penguin Books, 2005.

Snyder, J., 'One World, Rival Theories', *Foreign Policy*, Issue 145, November/December 2004, pp. 53–62.

Snyder, M. D., 'Information Strategies Against a Hybrid Threat: What the Recent Experience of Israel Versus Hezbollah/Hamas Tell the US Army', in *Back to Basics: A Study of the Second Lebanon War and Operation CAST LEAD*, edited by S. C. Farquhar, Combined Studies Institute Press: Fort Leavenworth, Kansas, 2009, pp. 103–46.

South China Sea Arbitration (Philippines vs China), The Hague: Permanent Court of Arbitration, 2016, available at: https://pca-cpa.org/wp-content/uploads/sites/175/2 016/07/PH-CN-20160712-Award.pdf [accessed on: 6 December 2017].

Speller, I., *Understanding Naval Warfare*, Abingdon: Routledge, 2014.

Stavridis, J., Adm, 'Martitime Hybrid Warfare Is Coming', *Proceedings*, Volume 142, Issue 12, Annapolis: United States Naval Institute, December 2016, available at: https://www.usni.org/magazines/proceedings/2016-12-0/maritime-hybrid-warfar e-coming [accessed on: 4 December 2017].

Sumaila, U. R. and Cheung, W. W. L., *Boom or Bust: The Future of Fish in the South China Sea*, ADM Capital Foundation, November 2015.

Taylor, C., 'The Defence White Paper', *House of Commons Library Research Paper*, 04/71, 17 September 2004.

Thucydides, *The History of the Peloponnesian War*, Oxford World's Classics, Oxford: Oxford University Press, 2009.

Tiefenbrun, S. W., 'Semiotic Definition of Lawfare', *Case Western Reserve Journal of International Law*, Volume 43, Issue 1, 2011, pp. 29–60.

Tiezzi, S., 'Why China Is Stopping Its South China Sea Island-Building (For Now)', *The Diplomat*, 16 June 2015, available at: https://thediplomat.com/2015/06/why-china-is-stopping-its-south-china-sea-island-building-for-now/ [accessed on: 30 November 2017].

Till, G., *Seapower: A Guide for the Twenty-First Century*, Abingdon: Routledge, 2013.

Tilley, C., 'Explained: Ukraine Conflict in Maps', *ABC News*, 24 October 2016, available at: http://www.abc.net.au/news/2014-02-19/ukraine-conflict-in-maps/5300900 [accessed on: 14 June 2018].

Tira, R., 'Breaking the Amoeba's Bones', *INSS Strategic Assessment*, Volume 9, Issue 3, November 2006, pp. 7–15.

Traynor, I., 'Russia Denounces Ukraine "Terrorists" and West over Yanukovich Ousting', *The Guardian*, 2014, available at: https://www.theguardian.com/world/2014/feb/24/russia-ukraine-west-yanukovich [accessed on: 3 March 2017].

Trenin, D., 'Russia in the Caucasus: Reversing the Tide', *Brown Journal of World Affairs*, Volume 15, Issue 2, Spring 2009, pp. 143–55.

Trenin, D. V., Malashenko A. V. and Lieven A., *Russia's Restless Frontier*, Washington, DC: Carnegie Endowment for International peace, 2004.

Trump, D. J., *National Security Strategy of the United States of America* 2017, Washington, DC: The White House, December 2017.

Tseluyko, V., 'Rebuilding and Refocusing the Force: Reform and Moderinzation of the Ukrainian Armed Forces', in *Brothers Armed: Military Aspects of the Crisis in Ukraine*, edited by C. Howard and R. Pukhov, Minneapolis : East View Press, 2014, pp. 187–208.

Tsirbas, M., 'Saving the South China Sea Fishery: Time to Internationalise', *Policy Options Paper*, Number 3, June 2017, National Security College, Australian National University.

Tsygankov, A. P. and Tarver-Wahlquist M., 'Duelling Honors: Power, Identity and the Russia-Georgia Divide', *Foreign Policy Analysis*, Issue 5, 2009, pp. 307–26.

UCDP, 'Definitions', *Uppsala Conflict Data Programme*, Department of Peace and Conflict Research, Uppsala University, 2018, available at: http://www.pcr.uu.se/research/ucdp/definitions/ [accessed on: 21 April 2018].

UK Maritime and Coastguard Agency, 'About Us', 2017, available at: https://www.gov.uk/government/organisations/maritime-and-coastguard-agency/about [accessed on: 4 December 2017].

UN, 'Lebanon - UNIFIL Background', 2002, available at: http://www.un.org/Depts/DPKO/Missions/unifil/unifilB.htm#background [accessed on: 25 June 2018].

UN, 'Report of the Commission of Inquiry on Lebanon Pursuant to Human Rights Council Resolution S-2/1', *UN Human Rights Council*, A/HRC/3/2, 23 November 2006, available at: https://web.archive.org/web/20130617180405/http://www2.ohchr.org/

english/bodies/hrcouncil/docs/specialsession/A.HRC.3.2.pdf [accessed on: 12 June 2017].

UNCTAD, *Handbook of Statistics* 2017, TD/STAT 42, New York: UNCTAD, 2017.

UNSC, *Resolution 1244*, New York, USA, 10 June 1999, available at: https://documents-dds-ny.un.org/doc/UNDOC/GEN/N99/172/89/PDF/N9917289.pdf?OpenElement [accessed on: 16 April 2016].

UNSC, *Resolution* 1559, 2 September 2004, available at: http://undocs.org/S/RES/1559(2004) [accessed on: 8 June 2017].

US Army, *Full Spectrum Operations in Army Capstone Doctrine*, 2008 Posture Statement, available at: http://www.army.mil/aps/08/information_papers/transform/Full_Spectrum_Operations.html [accessed on: 21 March 2016].

US Army, *Military Operations in Low Intensity Conflict*, FM 100-20/AFP 3-20, 12 May 1990, available at: http://www.globalsecurity.org/military/library/policy/army/fm/100-20/10020ch1.htm [accessed on: 21 March 2016].

US Department of Defense, 'Annual Report to Congress: Military and Security Developments Involving the People's Republic of China 2017', *Office of the Secretary of Defense*, 15 May 2017.

US Department of Defense, 'Annual Report to Congress: Military and Security Developments Involving the People's Republic of China 2017', 2017, available at: https://www.defense.gov/Portals/1/Documents/pubs/2017_China_Military_Power_Report.PDF [accessed on: 22 April 2018].

US Department of Defense, *DOD Dictionary of Military and Associated Terms*, available at: http://www.dtic.mil/doctrine/dod_dictionary/ [accessed on: 23 February 2016].

US Department of Defense, 'Freedom of Navigation (FON) Report for Fiscal Year (FY) 2016', 28 February 2017, available at: http://policy.defense.gov/Portals/11/FY1 6%20DOD%20FON%20Report.pdf?ver=2017-03-03-141349-943 [accessed on: 28 November 2017].

US Department of State, *Country Reports on Terrorism – 2009*, August 2010, available at: https://www.state.gov/j/ct/rls/crt/2009/ [accessed on: 5 July 2017].

US Department of State, *Joint Statement Issued by Partners at the Counter-ISIL Coalition Ministerial Meeting*, Washington, DC, 3 December 2014, available at: http://www.state.gov/r/pa/prs/ps/2014/12/234627.htm [accessed on: 17 April 2016]

US Department of State, 'The Truman Doctrine, 1947', *Office of the Historian*, available at: https://history.state.gov/milestones/1945-1952/truman-doctrine [accessed on: 4 July 2016].

US Department of State, 'United States Oceans Policy', *Statement by the President*, 10 March 1983, available at: https://www.state.gov/documents/organization/14322 4.pdf [accessed on: 28 November 2017].

US Department of the Navy, 'The Commander's Handbook on the Law of Naval Operations', *Naval Warfare Publication*, NWP 1-14M, July 2007, available at: http://www.jag.navy.mil/documents/NWP_1-14M_Commanders_Handbook.pdf [accessed on: 4 December 2017].

US Energy Information Agency, *Report on the South China Sea*, 7 February 2013, available at: https://www.eia.gov/beta/international/analysis_includes/regions_ of_interest/South_China_Sea/south_china_sea.pdf [accessed on: 1 December 2017].

US Joint Chiefs of Staff, *Information Operations*, Joint Publication 3-13, Joint Chiefs of Staff, Washington, DC, 13 February 2006.

US National Security Council, 'NSC 68: A Report to the National Security Council', 14 April 1950, available at: https://www.trumanlibrary.org/whistlestop/study_collect ions/coldwar/documents/pdf/10-1.pdf [accessed on: 4 July 2016].

Vartanyan, O. and Barry, E., 'Ex-Diplomat Says Georgia Starte War with Russia', *The New York Times*, 25 November 2008, available at: http://www.nytimes.com/2008/11/ 26/world/europe/26georgia.html [accessed on: 15 February 2017].

Vego, M. N., 'A Case Against Systemic Operational Design', *Joint Forces Quarterly*, Issue 53, 2nd quarter 2009, pp. 69–75.

Walker, N. and Mills, C., 'A Brief Guide to Previous British Defence Reviews', *House of Commons Library Briefing Paper*, Number 07313, November 2015.

Walt, S. M., 'International Relations: One World, Many Theories', *Foreign Policy*, Spring 1998, pp. 29–46.

Waltz, K. N., 'The Emerging Structure of International Politics', in *Realism and International Politics*, edited by K. N. Waltz, Abingdon: Routledge, 2008.

Westcott, B., Browne, R. and Cohen, Z., 'White House Warns China on Growing Militarization in South China Sea', *CNN*, 4 May 2018, available at: https://ed ition.cnn.com/2018/05/03/asia/south-china-sea-missiles-spratly-intl/index.html [accessed on: 20 June 2018].

The White House, 'Remarks by President Obama and President Xi of the People's Republic of China in Joint Press Conference', *Office of the Press Secretary*, 25 September 2015, available at: https://obamawhitehouse.archives.gov/the- press-office/2015/09/25/remarks-president-obama-and-president-xi-peoples- republic-china-joint [accessed on: 30 November 2017].

The White House, Office of the Press Secretary, 'Remarks by the President on Ending the War in Iraq', *Press Release*, available at: https://www.whitehouse.gov/the-pres s-office/2011/10/21/remarks-president-ending-war-iraq [accessed on: 4 July 2016].

The White House, Office of the Press Secretary, 'Statement by the President on the End of the Combat Mission in Afghanistan', *Press Release*, available at: https://www.whi tehouse.gov/the-press-office/2014/12/28/statement-president-end-combat-mission-a fghanistan [accessed on: 4 July 2016].

Whyte, L., 'The Real Thucydides' Trap', *The Diplomat*, 6 May 2015, available at: http://thediplomat.com/2015/05/the-real-thucydides-trap/ [accessed on: 26 October 2016].

Yoshihara, T., 'The 1974 Paracels Sea Battle: A Campaign Appraisal', *Naval War College Review*, Volume 69, Issue 2, Spring 2016, pp. 41–65.

Zhang, F., 'Assessing China's Response to the South China Sea Arbitration Ruling', *Australian Journal of International Relations*, Volume 71, Issue 4, 2017, pp. 440–59.

Zhou, L., 'What Is the South China Sea Code of Conduct, and Why Does It Matter?', *South China Morning Post*, 3 August 2017, available at: http://www.scmp.com/news/china/diplomacy-defence/article/2105190/what-south-china-sea-code-conduct-and-why-does-it [accessed on: 6 December 2017].

Index

www.ingramcontent.com/pod-product-compliance
Lightning Source LLC
Chambersburg PA
CBHW050424280326
41932CB00013BA/1981